Generation 1.5 Meets College Composition

Issues in the Teaching of Writing to U.S.-Educated Learners of ESL

Generation 1.5 Meets College Composition

Issues in the Teaching of Writing to U.S.-Educated Learners of ESL

Edited by

Linda Harklau
University of Georgia

Kay M. Losey
State University of New York, Stony Brook

Meryl Siegal
Holy Names College

LEA LAWRENCE ERLBAUM ASSOCIATES, PUBLISHERS
1999 Mahwah, New Jersey   London

Lawrence Erlbaum Associates, Inc., Publishers
10 Industrial Avenue
Mahwah, NJ 07430

Cover design by Kathryn Houghtaling Lacey

Library of Congress Cataloging-in-Publication Data

Generation 1.5 meets college composition : issues in the
teaching of writing to U.S.-educated learners of ESL /
edited by Linda Harklau, Kay Losey, Meryl Siegal.
    p. cm.
    Includes bibliographical references and index.
ISBN 0-8058-2954-7 (cloth : alk. paper) —
ISBN 0-8058-2955-5 (pbk. : alk. paper).
1. English language—Study and teaching—Foreign
speakers. 2. English language—Rhetoric—Study and
teaching—United States. 3. Report writing—Study and
teaching (Higher)—United States. I. Harklau, Linda. II.
Losey, Kay M. III. Siegal, Meryl.
PE1128.A2G434 1999
  428'.007—dc21
                                   98-53140
                                      CIP

Printed in the United States of America
10 9 8 7 6 5 4 3 2

Contents

Preface

This book is about college writing instruction and U.S. high school graduates who enter higher education while in the process of learning English. These students, primarily immigrants and students from U.S. multilingual enclaves such as Puerto Rico, are becoming an increasing presence on college campuses across the country. The title of this volume refers to Rumbaut and Ima's (1988) characterization of these students as "1.5 generation" immigrants because of traits and experiences that lie somewhere in between those associated with the first or second generation. The initiative for the book came from our realization that although nonnative language college writers educated in the United States are becoming a major constituency in college writing programs, one that draws ready recognition from most college composition and English as a Second Language (ESL) writing instructors, there has been a dearth of research or writing about the instructional issues presented by this student population. Long-term U.S. resident English learners pose a significant challenge to the conventional categories and practices governing composition instruction at the postsecondary level. With backgrounds in U.S. culture and schooling, they are distinct from international students or other newcomers who have been the subject of most ESL writing literature, while at the same time these students' status as English language learners is often treated as incidental or even misconstrued as underpreparation in writings on mainstream college composition and basic writing.

In compiling this volume, our intent is to bridge this gap and to initiate a dialogue on the linguistic, cultural, and ethical issues that attend teaching college writing to U.S. educated linguistically diverse students. The book brings together a number of experienced writing researchers and educators to identify and explore the issues. Working from an overarching perspective that casts writing and instruction as socially situated and constructed, the chapters of this book frame issues, raise questions, and provide portraits of language minority students and the classrooms and programs that serve them. From New York to midwestern land grant universities to the Pacific Rim, contributors to this volume represent a diversity of contexts, populations, programs, and perspectives. Collectively the chapters serve to characterize the shared attributes and diversity of language minority writers. Authors consider how experiences in U.S. K–12 schooling and status as nonnative language speakers and writers of English combine to create the unique linguistic and academic traits of long–term residents. They illustrate how various configurations of college writing instruction serve students and how U.S. language minority students respond in a variety of classroom settings. Together, the pieces sketch the landscape of college writing instruction for language minority students and explore the issues faced by ESL and college writing programs in providing appropriate writing instruction to second language learners arriving from U.S. high schools. The book serves not only to articulate an issue and set an agenda for further research and discussion, but also to suggest paths toward inclusive and sensitive writing instruction in college classrooms.

The book is divided into three major sections: the students, the classrooms, and the programs. In the first section, authors employ case studies and interviews to develop in-depth profiles of the backgrounds, attitudes, and college experiences of language minority students with writing. In the second section, authors address the high school and college classroom settings in which language minority students learn to write and suggest implications for improving classroom practice. Because English language learners who graduate from U.S. high schools seem to present particular difficulties in terms of program placement, authors in the third section explore the strengths and weaknesses of various configurations of writing programs for U.S.-educated second-language learners.

Because we believe that immigrant and resident students coming out of U.S. high schools span the disciplinary, programmatic, and institutional boundaries between ESL and college composition, the book addresses a diverse readership. A broad audience of ESL researchers and instructors, particularly those in Intensive English Programs and academic ESL programs, will find it of interest. The book is also relevant to college composition instructors in community college, 4-year college, and university settings. It addresses programmatic issues faced by writing center and Writing Across the Curriculum administrators educating language minority students. Finally, we expect it to be a resource for graduate courses dealing with issues of diversity and writing instruction.

ACKNOWLEDGMENTS

We have many people to thank for their assistance and encouragement during this book's development. The contributors deserve our greatest gratitude. Writing in an area where there was little existing work to serve as a blueprint, they have thoughtfully articulated previously unexplored issues in ESL and college composition. Our sincere thanks for their creativity and professionalism which have made this collection a reality. Our appreciation also goes to reviewers Ruth Spack, Tufts University, and Steven Haber, Jersey City State College, for insightful comments and suggestions which have helped to shape the book. We would also like to acknowledge Paul Matthew's careful reading of the manuscript and assistance in preparing the book for publication. Finally, we would like particularly to thank Lawrence Erlbaum Associates Acquisition Editor Naomi Silverman, Desktop Production Editor Stefany M. Jones, and Editorial Assistant Lori Hawver for their encouragement, support, and assistance throughout the publication process.

—*Linda Harklau*
—*Kay M. Losey*
—*Meryl Siegel*

REFERENCE

Rumbaut, R. G., & Ima, K. (1988) *The adaptation of Southeast Asian refugee youth: A comparative study.* (Final report to the Office of Resettlement). San Diego, CA: San Diego State University. (ERIC Document Reproduction Service No. ED 299 372).

1 Linguistically Diverse Students and College Writing: What Is Equitable and Appropriate?

Linda Harklau
University of Georgia
Meryl Siegal
Holy Names College
Kay M. Losey
State University of New York, Stony Brook

Virtually every U.S. college and university faces the challenges and opportunities entailed in adapting to an increasingly diverse student body. A growing number of students are bi- or multilingual and speak a home language other than English. Although skill in using English in academic writing is often a key criterion for gaining entry to collegiate academic studies and exiting a college degree program, these students' presence in academia has raised political and ethical dilemmas for universities regarding college writing requirements. For example, can or should students from bilingual backgrounds be held to the same writing standards as monolingual speakers of standard English, and if not, how do we establish different but equivalent and appropriate standards? What forms of writing instruction are appropriate for bilingual students? How well do nonnative language writers need to be able to function in written English in order to thrive in the academy, and when is it appropriate to impose a prerequisite threshold of proficiency to participate in college?

These dilemmas are complicated considerably by the ways in which nonnative speakers and writers of English tend to be categorized in existing literature and institutional practices, categories that may not reflect the backgrounds, experiences, and needs of linguistically diverse students in colleges today. This is particularly the case for the population that forms the focus for this volume; namely, bilingual U.S. resident students who enter U.S. colleges and universities by way of K–12 schools. On many, if not most, college campuses students who speak a language other than English at home find themselves classified first and foremost as English as a Second Language (ESL) writers. Although the research and pedagogical literature surrounding sec-

1

ond-language (L2) writing has been growing substantially in recent years, Nayar (1997) pointed out that genericized uses of ESL can mask the fact that different populations, needs, and goals are intended depending on the context. The field of college ESL in general, and academic writing in particular, focuses on a population of international students who enter postsecondary institutions in the United States after completing primary and secondary education abroad. In her overview of the field of ESL writing, for example, Reid (1993) noted specifically that she wrote about an international student population and excluded other populations from consideration. Although others may not make as explicit a statement, it is clear in many writings that international students are the population in mind. As a result, much of the pedagogical literature on academic language instruction for nonnative English speakers (NNES) at the college level remains focused on instruction for students with limited exposure to U.S. society or the English language, or teaching academic genres and conventions to academically accomplished students, often graduate students, arriving from other countries. ESL texts and curricula often contain an implicit assumption that international students are the normative population of college ESL classrooms, leading to certain suppositions concerning learners' backgrounds and skills; for example, that they have learned English through formal, metalinguistically oriented classroom instruction, that they are literate in their first language (L1), or that they have had considerable life experience abroad to be drawn on in interpreting their experience in the United States.

But growth in the international student population has not been the only source, and perhaps not even the primary source, of increasing linguistic diversity on college campuses. Since the mid-1960s, changes in immigration laws have resulted in ever-increasing immigration of entire families including school-age children and adolescents. Wars and political exigencies have also triggered waves of refugees from southeast Asia, central America, eastern Europe, Africa, and the Caribbean. At the same time, populations of indigenous language minority groups in the United States have been growing rapidly. Although in most circumstances the overwhelming presence of English in U.S. society has made these students English-dominant bilinguals by the time they enter secondary school, enclaves (e.g., Puerto Rico, Hawaii, Alaska, Los Angeles, New York) exist where students may still be English learners in high school and beyond.

As a result, there are a considerable and quickly growing number of bilingual English learners graduating from U.S. secondary schools and entering U.S. colleges and universities. Because U.S. colleges and universities collect virtually no information about U.S. residents' or citizens' native language status, we cannot say exactly how many students there are. We can, however, get some indications from the number of language minority students in U.S. high schools. Almost 15% of the limited English proficient (LEP) students in U.S. public schools are at the secondary level. More than 75,000 were high school seniors in 1993 alone (Fleischman & Hopstock, 1993). Because LEP classification represents only the most elementary level of English language proficiency, and because learning an L2 for academic purposes is a protracted process that requires up to 7 years by some accounts (Collier, 1987; Cummins & Swain, 1986), the population of English learners graduating from U.S. high schools yearly is likely to be at least double to triple that figure. The advent of open admission policies and growth of nontraditional student population since the mid-1970s, especially at community colleges, has further facilitated these students' entry into college. As a result, there has been dramatic growth in the population of linguistically diverse students who have entered college by way of an U.S. public school education. In some settings, particularly urban 2-year colleges, students from non-English language backgrounds already do or will soon form the majority of entering students (see Lay, Carro, Tien, Niemann, and Leong, chap. 10, this volume; Padron, 1994).

Postsecondary institutions in several key states are affected most dramatically by enrollment increases of U.S.-educated, U.S.-resident learners of English. With two out of every five immigrants in the United States and majority non-English language background populations in several urban areas, California is in the vanguard of this demographic shift, and it is no coincidence that many of the contributions in this volume come from that state. In fact, a 1990 California State University report contends that the unmet ESL needs of Asian Pacific American and other immigrant and refugee students "looms as a major issue confronting the state's educational system" (California State University, 1990, p. 26). As Lay, et al.(chap. 10, this volume) indicate, colleges in New York and New Jersey are also disproportionately affected by enrollment increases among U.S.-resident L2 learners. A recent *Chronicle of Higher Education* article shows the urgency of attending to the dilemmas in considering writing requirements and examinations at institutions such as the City University of New York (CUNY), where nearly half of the student body now consists of first-generation immigrants and Puerto Ricans (Ward, 1997). Also disproportionately affected are Florida, especially Miami (see Padron, 1994), Texas, and Illinois. At postsecondary institutions in these states and in major urban areas around the country, U.S.-resident language minority students are fast becoming a force with which to be reckoned, changing the entire structure and nature of writing instruction. However, as Hartman and Tarone (chap. 6, this volume) and Muchisky and Tangren (chap. 12, this volume) indicate, it is not just traditional immigration centers that are affected by increasing linguistic diversity; virtually every university is or will soon confront the same issues that institutions in these states now face.

This collection is, to our knowledge, the first devoted explicitly to articulating the issues involved in teaching college writing to English learners who reside in the United States and graduate from U.S. high schools. In the following chapters, we address three sets of intertwined questions. The first has to do with the student population—who are these students? How do their backgrounds and experiences vary, and how might they be similar? A second question has to do with programmatic issues. How are U.S.-resident English language learners placed in college writing programs? How do they fit into existing instructional categories and programs, and how do they challenge them? The third set of questions addresses classroom practices. How do established practices simultaneously serve and fail English learners who are long-term residents, and how might writing instruction be designed to help them to succeed in college?

We offer no pedagogical quick fixes, no easy definitions or solutions. The authors in this collection represent considerable diversity in their personal and institutional experiences, and they take varied stances on the education of language minority students in postsecondary settings. Rather, through the case studies and descriptions of experience collected in this volume, we illustrate significant issues commonly encountered by these students and their writing instructors and in the process, bring into question commonly employed categorizations of English language learners in higher education.

THE STUDENTS

Who are these students, and from what backgrounds do they come? The contributors to this collection offer diverse answers to this question, differing on how students are identified, what traits are considered most salient, and even on their appellation. The fact that authors differ on something so fundamental as a name for U.S.-educated English language learners shows just how difficult it is to fit these students into current ways of categorizing linguistically diverse college writers—ESL, developmental, regular (and by implication, how problematic those categories are; see Chiang & Schmida, chap. 5, this volume; Leung, Harris, & Rampton, 1997; Thesen, 1997).

Resident status and generational status is one means of distinguishing this group. Many of the multilingual students discussed in this book would fit Rumbaut and Ima's (1988) description of "1.5 generation" students—immigrants who arrive in the United States as school-age children or adolescents, and share characteristics of both first and second generation. But a generational definition fails us in considering the case of students from Puerto Rico and other parts of the United States where English is not the community language. Students from such areas may still very well be English learners at the college level.

Educational experience also tends to differentiate U.S.-resident language minority students, who graduate from U.S. secondary schools and are somewhat conversant with U.S. school and society, from international student ESL writers who are often new to the United States and have extensive academic literacy training in their home country. Here again, however, there is significant variation and exceptions. Immigrants may begin U.S. schooling in sixth grade or as a high school junior. Some complete secondary school in their native country and then attend a secondary school in the U.S. for a year or two on arrival in order to acclimate to U.S. schooling (e.g., see Lay et al., chap. 10, this volume). Students may be highly privileged and highly educated on arrival and make the transition to U.S. schooling effortlessly. On the other hand, they may have interrupted schooling histories in their home countries. Some have superlative literacy training in their native language and feel comparatively ill at ease with English language literacy practices, whereas others may only be literate in English.

As Rodby (chap. 3, this volume) and Lee (1997) illustrate, U.S.-resident English learners' college careers must often be understood within the context of social webs that surround each student. Social relationships at home, at school, and in the community and background characteristics such as race, ethnicity, class, gender, and immigrant generational status shape students' efforts as college writers (Losey, 1997). Family and community may be a significant motivation and support to immigrants in college, but performance in writing courses simultaneously may be impeded by obligations to familial networks. In particular, Lay et al. (chap. 10 this volume) and Rodby's (chap. 8, this volume) work reminds us that the financial status of immigrant families often leads students to assume heavy workloads off campus with negative effects on academic performance.

Students may self-identify as English learners. However, as Chiang and Schmida (chap. 5, this volume) point out, second-generation students may see themselves as bilingual although they have little productive command of a non-English language or designate themselves as native speakers of English when English is their second language. For students such as these, English is often the only language in which they have experienced academic preparation and literacy, and yet at the same time they often do not feel that the language is truly theirs. Chiang and Schmida emphasize that linguistic affiliations are just as much a product of sociocultural positionings as they are of technical competence. Although students have attended high school in the United States, some might feel more comfortable within the social milieus of international students in college settings (see Leki, chap. 2, this volume). Thus, students' linguistic and cultural affiliations may not always neatly parallel their generational status or the language in which they have been educated. Furthermore, as Blanton (chap. 7, this volume) indicates, even students who are still actively engaged in learning English often view language support for second language learners as stigmatized and are insulted by designation as an "ESL student." Although some students may see learner status as a distinct and negative influence on their academic experiences in college, Leki (chap. 2, this volume) illustrates that others may see their status as English language learners as a more or less peripheral issue, viewing study strategies, academic talent, and knowledge of the system as more critical to collegiate success.

In all, the picture that emerges in these chapters is of a tremendously diverse student population along continua of language proficiency, language affiliation, and academic literacy backgrounds. It is not surprising that colleges and universities have responded with a number of varying programmatic and placement options.

PROGRAMS AND PLACEMENT OPTIONS

What sorts of writing programs do U.S. colleges and universities offer for high school graduates who are English learners, and how are these students placed in such programs? Work specifically examining postsecondary institutional language programs and policies for U.S.-resident language learners is sparse (but see ESL Intersegmental Project, 1997; Gray, Rolph, & Melamid, 1996). The programmatic configurations contained in these chapters reveal a multitude of options from institutions around the country. Most of the programs described here include an ESL-specific preparatory presequence for a college-wide composition class or test requirement. Programs are housed in Intensive English Programs (IEPs), ESL departments, ESL programs that are part of other departments (e.g., English) or off-campus in university-wide extension, and academic assistance programs. Composition sequences may include adjunct or linked courses, as they do at City College of New York (CCNY; see Lay et al., chap. 10, this volume). They may also be part of a Writing Across the Curriculum (WAC) program in which students engage in intensive writing in designated discipline-area courses (see Wolfe-Quintero & Segade, chap. 11, this volume). These course sequences may be in the form of ESL and mainstream sections with parallel curricula, or they may be undifferentiated.

In which program or configuration immigrant students are placed depends on how they are classified when they arrive in college out of U.S. high schools, and the way in which bilingualism is construed in any given institutional setting appears to be quite varied, if not idiosyncratic. Although not represented by institutions discussed in this collection, one option is simply not to differentiate among entering first-year students on the basis of language background. Although that option may be the product of principled egalitarianism, it is probably more often the result of institutional reluctance to take on the issue of linguistic diversity. If colleges make an explicit effort to sensitize and train composition instructors, WAC faculty, and writing center personnel about the characteristics of nonnative language writers, this option may serve students well. However, many institutions do not appear to undertake such training efforts, pursuing a policy of not-so-benign neglect of language learners on campus (Gray et al., 1996). As a result, evidence suggests that distinct differences in the writing approaches and instructional needs of nonnative writers (Inghilleri, 1989; Schecter & Harklau, 1992; Silva, 1993) may be overlooked and superficial nonnative language textual features can be mistaken for a lack of writing expertise (Land & Whitley, 1989; Valdés, 1992; Zamel, 1995). Anecdotal evidence suggests that at such institutions, developmental writing courses may become de facto ESL writing courses, and writing centers are often overrun with nonnative language writers who have no other means of language support.

Probably the most commonplace practice is to identify and place incoming students who are English learners in an ESL presequence of courses for first-year composition. In a 1995 survey of U.S. universities, Williams found that a separate ESL course or sequence of courses exists at virtually every postsecondary institution that identifies nonnative speakers of English at admission, and at the majority of institutions ESL must be completed as a prerequisite before students can enroll in regular first-year composition courses (Williams, 1995). There are a number of logistical and equity issues in the placement of U.S. educated language minority students in ESL course presequences; among the most contentious are those of credits, tuition, and financial aid. Although Teachers of English to Speakers of Other Languages (TESOL) has long recommended that ESL coursework be accorded the same status as foreign language courses for the purpose of college credit and distribution requirements, Williams (1995) found that ESL is nevertheless treated as noncredit bearing on most campuses today. Even when such courses are credit bearing, they are seldom applicable toward any degree requirements. As Lay et al. (chap. 10, this volume) relate, immigrants often attend college on the thinnest of financial margins, and financial aid is a key factor in their persistence (or attrition) in degree programs. Noncredit-bearing status not only affects the applicability of financial aid to ESL courses, but also affects students' status as full-time students. Moreover, Lay et al. (chap. 10, this volume) and Smoke (1988) reported that CUNY research has shown that when students are kept in ESL over several semesters to the exclusion of other degree coursework, their financial resources may be depleted before they are able to complete other degree requirements. Although Lay et al. (chap. 10, this volume) indicate that such findings have led to considerable reforms in CUNY ESL policies, there is no doubt that there are other programs in which U.S. high school-educated bilingual students have similar experiences.

As Muchisky and Tangren (chap. 12, this volume) indicate, additional complications may arise when institutions make the decision to place U.S.-resident English language learners in IEPs. Because such programs are generally intended for nonresident international students, they are often self-supporting. Thus, as Muchisky and Tangren relate, U.S.-resident students in such programs may find themselves paying far more in tuition than they would in other college coursework while at the same time IEPs may find themselves in financial jeopardy for serving these students with discounted tuition.

ESL course sequences are often stigmatized as remedial and students may be reluctant or dismayed to be placed in them. ESL is also widely regarded as remedial by college administrators and policymakers, making the programs and the students they serve extremely vulnerable to the vicissitudes of institutional and state mandates. For example, ESL programs are at issue in antiremediation projects underway on U.S. college campuses. The antiremedial movement, in an appeal to higher academic standards in collegiate instruction, places the responsibility for providing courses such as ESL on institutions prior to or outside of college under the premise that once students' language is "fixed" there, they can transfer to college. It is precisely the population of U.S.-educated, U.S-resident language minority students who would be most profoundly affected by current anti-remediation efforts directed at ESL programs. Without such programs, many U.S.-educated language minority students may not gain entrance to college or founder once admitted.

It is not surprising that the equitability and appropriacy of criteria under which students enter and leave ESL programs is a particularly contentious issue in the case of U.S.-educated language minority students. In particular, it is a difficult indeed to distinguish between the population that is the subject of this book—students who are still actively engaged in the process of learning English—and those who are fully bilingual. Written text features and scores on standardized writing placement and exit measures are also commonly used to distinguish English learners from fluent bilinguals. However, as Frodesen and Starna (chap. 4, this volume) illustrate, when used in isolation such measures may not give an accurate rendering of students' linguistic development. Significant concerns are raised in this book (see Frodesen & Starna, chap. 4, this volume; Muchisky & Tangren, chap. 12, this volume; Wolfe-Quintero & Segade, chap. 11, this volume) and elsewhere (see Valdés, 1992; Ward, 1997) about bilingual college students being mistakenly defined as English learners on the basis of relatively permanent and superficial nonnative-like language features. In part, these features have been attributed to the immersion process through which learners acquire English in U.S. public schools. As Lay et al. and Reid (1997) indicated, English language learners educated in U.S. schools might be understood as "ear" learners—they have learned most of their language intuitively through exposure rather than through explicit instruction. As a result, contributors to this volume identify several ways in which they might differ from the international student archetype prevalent in college ESL curriculum. For one thing, as Ferris (chap. 8, this volume) shows, they may not be conversant with metalinguistic labels and rules for the language that they know. As Muchisky and Tangren (chap. 12, this volume) and Wolfe-Quintero and Segade (chap. 11, this volume) indicate, they may also learn English through immersion in a community speaking a nonstandard dialect of English and retain features of this dialect in their writing.

The issue of how nonnative language features are to be interpreted is crucial because such features frequently form the basis for placement in and exit from mandatory writing coursework. Inappropriate assessment measures or misinterpretation of those measures may thus result in inappropriate ESL course placements and unnecessary delays in bilingual students' progress through degree programs. Lay et al. (chap. 10, this volume) and Ward (1997), for example, noted that students at CUNY have often succeeded in the rest of their academic programs but have been unable to obtain their degrees because of their performance on writing exit tests. On a broader level, Valdés (1992) and Silva (1997) argued that the widespread expectation that adult language learners can attain completely monolingual-like command of an L2 is unrealistic and only possible in a nation that is overwhelmingly monolingual. As Ward (1997) and several of the contributors in this volume argue, in a cosmopolitan and linguistically diverse society, we may have to accept that not everyone will develop a monolingual's competence in English.

There at least two dilemmas here for college ESL and writing educators. First is the issue of differentiating true learners of English from those who are fluent in English but use some nonnative-like forms. Presumably placement and instructional assumptions and approaches would be different in each case. This issue is taken up by Frodesen and Starna (chap. 4, this volume) who argue for the use of several criteria in making such determinations. Yet, although language specialists may understand this distinction, Wolfe-Quintero and Segade (chap. 11, this volume) and Lay et al. (chap. 10, this volume) illustrate that ultimately it is students' discipline-specific professors who are most likely to penalize students for nonnative language features and who must become better educated about the nature of bilingualism. In the meantime, as Wolfe-Quintero and Segade (chap. 11, this volume) and Ferris (chap. 8, this volume) note, all bilingual students, learners and fluent bilinguals alike, need to develop strategies and resources to assist them with editing their writing throughout degree programs.

CLASSROOM ISSUES

Finally, given their backgrounds and the sorts of writing programs they are likely to experience, what forms does classroom writing instruction take and what should it look like to non-English language background students coming from U.S. schooling backgrounds? For one thing, as Lay et al. (chap. 10, this volume) and Hartman and Tarone (chap. 6, this volume) argue, U.S.-resident students' writing must be understood in terms of their literacy socialization experiences in U.S. secondary schools. Widely varying teacher philosophies and instructional practices are reported in high school classrooms and although some English learners come to college exceptionally well prepared for the linguistic and academic demands of college, many others report very little experience at all with extensive writing. Instead, in these classrooms, students engage almost exclusively in highly controlled language exercises at the sentence or paragraph level; for example, substitution drills, dictation, short answer, and writing paragraphs from models. When they do write, students and teachers note the prevalence of short writing assignments in which students are not held accountable for revising and honing prose. Writing from sources appears to be all but absent in most of the high school classrooms described here.

In part, the high school experiences with writing described in these chapters are attributable to their education in low ability classes. In many, if not most, U.S. secondary schools, language learner status is confounded with lack of perceived academic ability and even those who are avowedly college bound are placed in low track classes (Brinton & Mano, 1991; Harklau, 1994; Mehan, Hubbard, & Villaneuva, 1994; Suarez-Orozco, 1989). Students in low track classes are socialized into literacy practices that differ qualitatively from those in higher tracks, and practices that are thought to be less congruent with college level and academic demands (Oakes, 1985). As a result, U.S. educated L2 learners, like many of their native speaker peers, may need to unlearn previous literacy expectations and practices and learn new ways of approaching writing in order to be successful in college.

English language learners graduating from U.S. high schools also enter college with a wide range of experience and ability with L1 literacy and schooling. Although some students may be secondary school graduates in their native countries, other students, particularly refugees, may have experienced significant interruptions in precollegiate schooling. Moreover, the quality of schooling that students have experienced abroad can vary significantly. Long-term U.S. residents may not be literate in their native language. These differences shape students' experiences in classrooms, and shape as well the knowledge and experiences that writing instructors can assume students possess and can be built on in the classroom.

In response to these varying previous experiences with literacy and needs, Johns (chap. 9, this volume) and Blanton (chap. 7, this volume) argue that college writing courses need to emphasize a view of writing as the product of individuals in interaction with a social world. Blanton in particular argues that language minority students need to learn that the simple fact that texts exist does not make the ideas or expression contained within them authoritative or even necessarily good writing. Rather than seeing texts as being "dead on the page," Blanton argues that writing classrooms for language minority students need to engage in critical literacy, learning ways in which to bring their own perspectives to interpreting and creating texts. Arguing for a "socioliterate approach" to the teaching of writing to language minority students, Johns proposes that students and teachers engage in an examination of texts produced in their own homes and communities as well as in the popular media and educational contexts. Johns proposes that students learn to analyze how language and visual presentation in various text genres is organized to meet the writers' purposes, and in the process how they themselves can marshal the same resources to meet particular writing tasks and roles in particular social contexts.

Muchisky and Tangren (chap. 12, this volume) argue that the presence of U.S.-resident language minority students alongside international students in ESL classrooms calls for particular instructional strategies and methods. Muchisky and Tangren note that IEP teachers have tapped strategies such as cooperative learning groups in order to address widely varying listening comprehension, spoken language fluency, and metalinguistic knowledge of students in their classrooms. Such classrooms must also contend with significantly different levels of student knowledge and understanding about U.S. society between newly arrived international students and long-term residents. For example, the cultural orientation that is a frequent component of IEP course curricula may be simplistic or even insulting to U.S. residents and citizens (Harklau, in press).

Ferris notes that there has been little research on teacher feedback and effects on ESL learners in general, and virtually none on potential differences between international students and U.S.-resident L2 learners. She argues that differences in ESL student background have significant implications for teacher response and student revision in writing. For example, metalinguistically oriented writing and grammar texts typically utilized with international students in ESL writing classes may not match the needs of non-English language background students whose strengths and errors in writing are the by-product of several years of schooling in English-medium contexts, life in an immigrant community, and a rich intuitive understanding of how the language works. In her research on immigrant students enrolled in college writing courses, she finds that many cannot identify parts of speech assumed to be prior knowledge in most grammar or editing texts, but she also finds that immigrants can benefit substantially from focused instruction on formal grammatical knowledge and editing strategies. Ferris also contends that as a result of their literacy socialization experiences in U.S. classrooms, immigrants may be more conversant with the process and goals of writing response and revision cycles than many international students.

CONCLUSION

The increasing number of non-English language background high school graduates now making their way into U.S. colleges and universities adds to already considerable friction in higher education about diversity. The issues faced in providing appropriate and equitable college writing instruction for these students in many ways are emblematic of broader issues that will need to be addressed in higher education in coming years. One of these issues is how we define academic measures and standards in ways that do not unfairly penalize or stigmatize students coming from bilingual and nonstandard English backgrounds. At present, efforts of native English-speaking monolinguals to acquire a foreign language in foreign language and comparative literature departments are accorded the status of major disciplines, while at the same time bilingual students' considerably more sophisticated skills in two or more languages are often defined only in terms of perceived deficiencies in English.

Another issue is that of writing program configuration. The current division of labor among regular composition, basic or developmental composition, and ESL tends to assume discrete populations of students can be distinguished as the clientele of each. However, as Valdés (1992) and contributors to this volume have pointed out, a major reason for the variation in placement practices for U.S.-educated English language learners across institutions is that they arguably fall into all and none of these categories. Thus, these students as they are commonly configured present a fundamental challenge to program divisions. Moreover, although the contributors argue for the indispensability of ESL expertise in educating bilingual college writers, at the same time, like Zamel (1995), they point out that L2 learning is too protracted a process for it to take place entirely under the auspices of ESL or other college writing coursework. As Wolfe-Quintero and Segade (chap. 11, this volume) argue because the writing development of English learners is interdependent with their progress through coursework, there must be institution-wide willingness to accept responsibility for English learners' development as college writers. For many different reasons, including the isolation of disciplines and departments and the emphasis on "quality" (Berquist, 1995), it is indeed a difficult matter to change faculty attitudes and practices regarding writing in higher education settings.

The increasing presence of U.S.-resident language minority students in U.S. academia is also part of the impetus for recent discussions about multicultural representation in the curriculum and decanonization. Appeals to affirm the diverse perspectives represented in students' writing and in doing so to challenge existing canons for academic prose are often juxtaposed with the socializing responsibility of academia, what is seen as the obligation to impart knowledge and skills that will help students to become a functional member of academic discourse communities (Bazerman, 1992; Benesch, 1993; Bizzell, 1986; Canagarajah, 1993; Fox, 1990; Land & Whitley, 1989; Pratt, 1991; Spack, 1997). In many ways both explicit and implicit, the contributors to this volume take on the issue of how we make room for the multiple worldviews and cultural affiliations of students in the curriculum and simultaneously reconcile it with our obligation to prepare students for what awaits them outside our classroom doors.

The students we address in this collection may be too diverse, too particularistic in their backgrounds, needs, and characteristics to hold under any single label or rubric. Yet as the ranks of U.S. high school graduate English language learners continue to grow in ESL and composition programs nationwide, we feel that it is vital to raise issues that often attend their instruction. Decisions regarding writing pedagogy and policy in regard to language minority students on U.S. college campuses too often seem to be made arbitrarily and ad hoc. The intent of this volume is to articulate better exactly what is at stake in some of those decisions, and in doing so to provide a more solid foundation for such decisions.

REFERENCES

Bazerman, C. (1992). From cultural criticism to disciplinary participation: Living with powerful words. In A. Herrington & C. Moran (Eds.), *Writing, teaching, and learning in the disciplines* (pp. 61–68). New York: Modern Language Association.

Benesch, S. (1993). ESL, ideology, and the politics of pragmatism. *TESOL Quarterly, 27*(4), 705–717.

Berquist, W. H., with Arburua, C., Bergquist, J., Bergquist, K., Bishop, H., & Smith, B. L. (1995). *Quality through access, access through quality.* San Francisco: Jossey-Bass.

Bizzell, P. (1986). Foundationalism and anti-foundationalism in composition studies. *PRE/TEXT, 7*(1–2), 37–56.

Brinton, D., & Mano, S. (1991). "You have a chance also": Case histories of ESL students at the university. In F. Peitzman & G. Gadda (Eds.), *With different eyes: Insights into teaching language minority students across the disciplines* (pp. 1–25). Los Angeles: UCLA Center for Academic Interinstitutional Programs.

California State University, Long Beach, Office of the Chancellor. (1990). *Enriching California's future: Asian Pacific Americans in the CSU. Report of the Asian Pacific Ameri-*

can Education Advisory Committee (ERIC ED 348 914). Long Beach, CA: California State University.

Canagarajah, A. S. (1993). Comments on Ann Raimes's "Out of the woods: Emerging traditions in the teaching of writing": Up the garden path: Second language writing approaches, local knowledge, and pluralism. *TESOL Quarterly, 27*(2), 301–310.

Collier, V. (1987). Age and rate of acquisition of second language for academic purposes. *TESOL Quarterly, 21*(4), 617–641.

Cummins, J., & Swain, M. (1986). *Bilingualism in education: Aspects of theory, research, and practice*. New York: Longman.

ESL Intersegmental Project. (1997). *California pathways: The second language student in public high schools, colleges, and universities* . Ontario, CA: California Teachers of English to Speakers of Other Languages (CATESOL).

Fleischman, H. L., & Hopstock, P. J. (1993). *Descriptive study of services to limited English proficient students* . Arlington, VA: Development Associates, Inc.

Fox, T. (1990). Basic writing as cultural conflict. *Journal of Education, 172*(1), 65–83.

Gray, M. J., Rolph, E., & Melamid, E. (1996). *Immigration and higher education: Institutional responses to changing demographics* . Santa Monica, CA: RAND.

Harklau, L. (in press). Representing culture in the ESL writing classroom. In E. Hinkel (Ed.), *Culture in second language teaching and learning*. New York: Cambridge University Press.

Harklau, L. A. (1994). Tracking and linguistic minority students: Consequences of ability grouping for second language learners. *Linguistics and Education, 6*, 221–248.

Inghilleri, M. (1989). Learning to mean as a symbolic and social process: The story of ESL writers. *Discourse Processes, 12*, 391–411.

Land, R. E., & Whitley, C. (1989). Evaluating second language essays in regular composition classes: Towards a pluralistic U.S. rhetoric. In D. M. Johnson & D. H. Roen (Eds.), *Richness in writing: Empowering ESL students* (pp. 284–293). New York: Longman.

Lee, S. J. (1997). The road to college: Hmong American women's pursuit of higher education. *Harvard Educational Review, 67*(4), 803–827.

Leung, C., Harris, R., & Rampton, B. (1997). The idealized native speaker, reified ethnicities, and classroom realities. *TESOL Quarterly, 31*(3), 543–560.

Losey, K. M. (1997). *Listen to the silences: Mexican American interaction in the composition classroom and the community*. Norwood, NJ: Ablex Publishing Corp.

Mehan, H., Hubbard, L., & Villaneuva, I. (1994). Forming academic identities: Accommodation without assimilation among involuntary minorities. *Anthropology and Education Quarterly, 25*(2), 91–117.

Nayar, P. B. (1997). ESL/EFL dichotomy today: Language politics or pragmatics? *TESOL Quarterly, 31*(1), 9–37.

Oakes, J. (1985). *Keeping track: How schools structure inequality*. New Haven, CT: Yale University Press.

Padron, E. J. (1994). Hispanics and community colleges. In G. A. Baker (Ed.), *A handbook on the community college in America: Its history, mission, and management* (pp. 82–93). Westport, CT: Greenwood Press.

Pratt, M. L. (1991). Arts of the contact zone. *Profession 91*, 33–40.

Reid, J. M. (1993). *Teaching ESL writing*. Englewood Cliffs, NJ: Prentice-Hall.

Reid, J. M. (1997). Which non-native speaker? Differences between international students and U.S. resident (language minority) students. *New Directions for Teaching and Learning, 70,* 17–27.

Rumbaut, R. G., & Ima, K. (1988). *The adaptation of Southeast Asian refugee youth: A comparative study. Final report to the Office of Resettlement.* (ERIC ED 299 372). San Diego, CA: San Diego State University.

Schecter, S. R., & Harklau, L. A. (1992). *Writing in a non-native language: What we know, what we need to know.* Berkeley, CA: National Center for the Study of Writing and Literacy (ERIC document reproduction service no. ED 353 825).

Silva, T. (1993). Towards an understanding of the distinct nature of L2 writing: The ESL research and its implications. *TESOL Quarterly, 27,* 657–678.

Silva, T. (1997). On the ethical treatment of ESL writers. *TESOL Quarterly, 31*(2), 359–363.

Smoke, T. (1988). Using feedback from ESL students to enhance their success in college. In S. Benesch (Ed.), *Ending remediation: Linking ESL and content in higher education* (pp. 7–19). Washington DC: Teachers of English to Speakers of Other Languages.

Spack, R. (1997). The rhetorical construction of multilingual students. *TESOL Quarterly, 31*(4), 765–774.

Suarez-Orozco, M. M. (1989). *Central American refugees and United States high schools: A psychosocial study of motivation and achievement.* Stanford, CA: Stanford University Press.

Thesen, L. (1997). Voices, discourse, and transition: In search of new categories in EAP. *TESOL Quarterly, 31*(3), 487–512.

Valdés, G. (1992). Bilingual minorities and language issues in writing. *Written Communication, 9*(1), 85–136.

Ward, M. (1997, September 26). Myths about college English as a Second Language. *Chronicle of Higher Education, 44*(5), B8.

Williams, J. (1995). ESL composition program administration in the United States. *Journal of Second Language Writing, 4*(2), 157–177.

Zamel, V. (1995). Strangers in academia: The experiences of faculty and ESL students across the curriculum. *College Composition and Communication, 46*(4), 506–521.

I

THE STUDENTS

2 "Pretty Much I Screwed Up": Ill-Served Needs of a Permanent Resident

Ilona Leki
University of Tennessee

Once during a trip to the Grand Canyon we participated in an outing to Anasazi ruins led by a park ranger. In trying to get us to understand what it's like to try to imagine how the Anasazi lived, he picked up from the ground a stray, discarded pop top from some previous visitor's can of Coke®. He told us to imagine not knowing anything about 20th-century U.S., finding this little circular light metal item, and trying to reconstruct the life in this culture from this artifact. Perhaps a sacred item? A piece of body ornamentation? Currency? Junk? How can you know?

Qualitative research, which also tries to (re)construct or (re)present a culture in order to understand it, labors under a similar, if less dramatic, handicap. The task is to create a picture that is comprehensible and takes into account the evidence in some logical way, but since the task is undertaken in a postmodern context, the researcher cannot help but be aware of the arrogance of the enterprise and of the impossibility of "telling the truth." You can only tell a story, not the truth. All experience with reality is interpreted. From a postmodern perspective, then, no empirical reality exists outside interpretation that would warrant the truth, the faithfulness of the reproduction of reality. Because the goal of research reporting cannot, therefore, be to reproduce a reality that exists independent of the reproduction, the goal of research reporting becomes to narrate an experience (Newkirk, 1992). Now the question must be "what to tell and how to tell it" (Brodkey, 1987, p. 38).

In some ways, writing up qualitative research is like writing a novel, with the basic elements—actors and setting—given to the writer beforehand as if in some novel writing contest, and then also writing the literary analysis of that novel—researcher as novelist and literary critic in the same piece of writing. And like literature and literary criticism, qualitative research is successful to the degree that it helps us to understand ourselves and our actions. As Brodkey (1987) said,

One studies stories not because they are true or even because they are false, but for the same reason that people tell and listen to them, in order to learn about the terms on which others make sense of their lives: what they take into account and what they do not; what they consider worth contemplating and what they do not; what they are and are not willing to raise and discuss as problematic and unresolved in life. (p. 47)

We try to understand the human condition by watching what humans do and trying to make sense of it. For this reason, I make no apology for the single case focus of this chapter, no caveats about this case not being generalizable to a broader sample of a population. As Stake (1995) maintained, "The real business of case study is particularization, not generalization" (p. 8). Case study research does not gain its strength from generalizability but from an experience that is unique, as all experience is, but that may also give us insights and help us understand.

Still, even if we admit that research constructs rather than reproduces reality and that case study research does not have generalizability as its goal, the researcher's position in a postmodern intellectual context is full of irony and discomfort. In the study reported here, I am acutely aware that what appears in my research notes is incomplete; I cannot be everywhere, see everything. Some of what I note contradicts what my research participant says; his interpretation is different from mine. Much of what he says at one time contradicts what he says at another. I am also aware that in order to tell this story, a story that cannot be the truth, I have had to select from all those events and comments the ones that plausibly fit an interpretation. These are inescapable dilemmas of qualitative research.

To further complicate matters is the question, "By what right do I speak for my participant?" To answer this question, I have been guided by Sullivan's argument for qualitative research as advocacy; my words speak for my participant, but "speak for" not in the sense of speaking "instead of" but in the sense of speaking in support of. To do otherwise, as Sullivan (1996) argued, puts us at risk of falling "prey to the temptation ever before us as academics to view research as an end in itself and the knowledge we produce as its own justification" (p. 112).

The research reported here, which is part of a larger exploration of nonnative English-speaking (NNES) students' experiences in higher education in the United States is intended to add to the small but slowly growing number of in-depth investigations of the academic lives of both native English speaking and NNES students in high school and in undergraduate higher education (Adamson, 1993; Anderson et al., 1990; Chiseri-Strater, 1991; Currie, 1993; Fu, 1995; Haas, 1994; Harklau, 1994; Herrington, 1985; Leki, 1995; Leki & Carson, 1997; McCarthy, 1987; McKay & Wong, 1996; Spack, 1997; Walvoord & McCarthy, 1990).

METHODS

Data for this study consisted primarily of biweekly interviews with the participant, Jan (a pseudonym), including special anticipatory and summative interviews at the beginning and end of each term. The interviews typically lasted about 1 hour each and were conducted variously by research assistants or by me. I have also collected Jan's class notes, course work, and course handouts including syllabuses; done interviews with the professors or teaching assistants in all his courses which included even short writing assignments or essay exams; inspected course textbooks; and observed as many of his classes as my research assistants and I could attend, focusing particularly on courses with writing components of some kind. Depending on the semester, we visited at least one of his classes each week, often several classes in a week, where we were able to observe not only his participation but his interactions before and after class with classmates. In addition, for perhaps a year, Jan kept a journal for this research study, but we eventually abandoned that source of information because he felt it created too great a time burden for him.

Data was and continues to be analyzed through reiterative readings of the interview transcripts, field notes made from the class observations, course materials, and other data sources. In other words, analysis is ongoing, such that comments made or issues raised in the past are used to try to understand current circumstances. Categories that emerge as important are noted and kept in mind in subsequent rereadings. Because data analysis has been ongoing, the core interview guide (see appendix) has often included new questions based on Jan's previous comments, enabling me to check my understandings of those previous statements against Jan's intentions in making them.

The central research question is as follows: "What are the experiences, particularly literacy experiences, of NNES students at a U.S. university?" Although this chapter includes information on the research participant's literacy experiences, it also reflects the fact that literacy as conceived by English and English as a second language (ESL) departments is not always a central feature of students' academic lives. Rather literacy and literacy issues are embedded in a network of social, academic, psychological, and emotional experiences and responses to those experiences that may dwarf literacy's importance, despite our sense as English/ESL/writing teachers of its centrality.

An added complication with this participant is the question of the reliability of his statements, which sometimes contradicted each other. This is not to say that he tried to fool me or give patently false information. I am convinced that he lived his contradictions, as do all people to some degree and certainly adolescents, at one moment saying he believes one way and saying the very opposite a moment later. I take both assertions to be true at the same time. Furthermore, although with Jan the contradictions are often obvious, there is a threat to reliability in all self-reports, and yet the value of such self-reports, however contradictory, is that they are also too revealing and suggestive to dismiss as a research tool. Ultimately, I have had to trust the statements that he repeated to different interviewers and over time intervals. Even if they were to prove somehow false, presumably if Jan was repeating them, he had probably come to believe them, and so their status in reality becomes irrelevant as well as indeterminate. The effect of such beliefs on him was the same as if these statements were facts. At times in the interviews Jan's comments seem naive or his ideas about, for example, some aspect of U.S. or university life clearly mistaken. But they do reveal the perspective from which he operates and through which he filters his experiences.

BACKGROUND

Jan immigrated from Poland in 1992 when he was 17. Tall, thin, and pleasant looking, he is very sociable, with an animated manner and ironic, dry wit that he calls into play readily and almost off-handedly. He has great personal charm, which works to soften his sometimes disturbing opinions and observations on his experiences. He repeatedly asserts his pleasure at being with people and often engages in friendly and joking chatting with classmates, mostly international students, before and after classes. His oral skills in English and his command of idiomatic language and teenage slang were clearly not well reflected in his relatively low 527 TOEFL score, only 2 points above minimum for admission to the university when we met him. The prosody of his accent is very nearly native and although individual phonemes may be somewhat nonnative sounding, overall his pronunciation matches his fluency and never blurs understanding of what he says, although he often speaks very rapidly and repeats segments of phrases.

He is also a survivor. Such a generalization about a person can constitute flattery or criticism, and Jan's survival has been closely entwined with both admirable resilience and less commendable practices and defensive postures. But our interest here is not primarily biographical. It is rather an attempt to understand the positive and negative forces around this individual that have impeded and enhanced his educational and personal experience. Jan is our telescope and microscope into a context that we as members of the educational community have shaped, or reproduced, just as surely as it has shaped us. We too are subject to the very forces that we create for him to live with, ones that form him.

THE STORY: LITERACY BACKGROUND

In interviews with Jan he consistently depicted himself as completely uninterested in reading or writing anything academic in English or Polish. Jan reported that in high school in Poland one day a week of Polish class consisted of learning the complexities of correct Polish grammar, which he said he was not good at, describing himself as not speaking or writing good Polish.[1] The rest of the days of class were devoted to reading, discussing, and writing about books. He remembered having regular 10-page (he says!) writing assignments in those courses on topics he described as being "about life and philosophy stuff." He remembered well, and considered rather outrageous, for example, the assigned topic of one paper, sex symbols in the bible. However, it is not clear what he learned from these intensive writing assignments because, as he explained,

> My mom was pretty much helping. Teacher said grade is probably not for you; it's for your mom, because she [the teacher] already knew I was not doing this [writing]. My mom helping me and my mom's sitting every day, cause we had essay every day to write, lots of essays, so my mom was pretty much sitting every day after work and doing essays with me. [For the sex symbols in the bible assignment] my mom was like, let's see the bible, where is sex symbols? My mom was thinking long, long time.

No matter how hard his mother worked, however, Jan did not get better than Bs on these papers. Despite his depiction of his mother as doing all the work, in talking about these papers he also seemed to claim them for himself.

> Teachers always find something wrong, … if she didn't like my ideas I could get lower grade. … My essay was always like two pages and her [the teacher's] ideas were for the next three pages in red, what she thinks what I should change.

Later in college in the United States, Jan referred to himself as "a numbers guy"; he used his computer to search Web sites and to read an electronically delivered Polish newspaper. Other than these, his reading in Polish consisted of Polish joke books; his reading in English was limited to the minimum: just enough so he could still take exams and do course-required assignments. Yet he described his mother's house as crammed with books she brought from Poland; his stepfather kept his college philosophy books, which Jan actually found useful in completing a college course assignment. But Jan had no use for fictional readings and found most humanities reading to be "b.s.ing around."

As for writing in college in the United States, aside from short e-mail messages, Jan wrote only in relation to his course work. Except for his English classes, he had only three courses in his first 3 years of college that required any writing beyond a sentence or two, an international business course, which required short reports and valued primarily neatness and grammatical correctness, a music history course in which students wrote two weekly 100-word journal entries in response to a question (these were not read or

[1]This comment should not necessarily be interpreted to refer to language attrition. Proud of their language and literary traditions, many native speakers of Polish of my acquaintance refer to each other's good or bad Polish, but in doing so, they refer to their linguistic elegance and facility at maneuvering around the complexities of Polish, with its elaborate declension systems, not their basic proficiency as native speakers.

evaluated by the teacher), and a course on religions of the world, which required seven short out-of-class papers in response to an open-ended question on the readings. In these courses Jan cut literacy corners as much as possible, doing only as much of the course reading as needed to find the information required for the papers. One of the papers in the religions course, for example, called for students to use the class information on Buddhism to discuss the significance of Buddhism in Maxine Hong Kingston's *Woman Warrior*, one of the four assigned novels in the course. Jan read only one chapter of the book and wrote his paper based on this limited perspective.

The books in Jan's parents' home, his comment that his mother is "always reading something," and her willingness to help him with writing assignments in Poland all point to a solid foundation of respect for learning and literacy in his family. Jan's educational experience in Poland, including his high school teacher's three-page commentaries on his papers, would appear to contribute to such a foundation as well. And yet perhaps somewhat paradoxically, Jan's first 3 years at the university seem to have contributed little to a sense that reading and writing are valuable either for personal intellectual growth or as tools for learning specific material in an academic setting. Rather Jan's postimmigration experiences, including both the anti-intellectual climate of U.S. adolescent culture and the demands of the educational institutions he experienced, supported the ferment of other kinds of values.

HIGH SCHOOL IN THE UNITED STATES

When Jan immigrated to the United States with his mother, stepfather, and baby sister, he had had no training in English at all. He flew directly from Poznan, in Poland, to his new U.S. home in a medium-sized town and 3 days later started as a junior in high school. The school enrolls enough NNES students to be able to run several levels of ESL classes, which Jan attended, quickly skipping from the lower levels to higher ones, while he simultaneously took junior-level high school classes, including junior and, later, senior English. In January 1993, while still in high school, he got a full-time job at Burger King, where he worked from January 1993 to September 1994, and where, he said pointedly, he learned English.

Jan's experiences in high school could not help but be formative. He described the classes in his U.S. high school as being behind where he had been in his Polish high school. In Poland he had been among the bottom 20% of students academically; in the United States despite, as he said, not knowing English, he was making As in his courses, relying partly on his academic background from Poland and partly on the low level of intellectual demands made on him in this high school. Whatever the teachers expected students to learn was spelled out in detail on the blackboard; then students were quizzed using multiple choice questions that were so obvious that, he claimed, he could guess the correct answers without studying the material or with only a

5-minute glance through it just before the quiz. When asked if he understood
the material in his senior level English class, for example, he replied:

> Not really. For quizzes you got four choices and the answer was so stupid you
> can pretty much figure out what's the best answer. So that was pretty easy....
> In high school I was sleeping pretty much all day. I just look what [the quiz] was
> asking, what was today on chapter, I just look over pretty fast between classes
> or 5 minutes before the class.... High school was easy pretty much.... I got A av-
> erage without speaking English.... I was doing high school and a full time job
> [working at] McDonald's and Burger King, then Service Merchandise.

The value for him of his ESL classes, where, he said, the material was
"baby stuff," was in the friendliness of the other "foreign people." Although
he appeared to have dismissed them as potential friends (possibly because
they were younger than he, possibly because they were from very different
cultural backgrounds, mostly Asian), their friendliness to him was in sharp
contrast to the attitudes of the U.S. students in the school, who he repeatedly described as uninterested in anyone who did not speak perfect English.
In his experience it was not being a "foreigner" that precluded friendship
from these Americans but lack of English proficiency. In answer to questions about how he learned English, Jan said:

> It's really hard; people are very unfriendly if you don't speak pretty good Eng-
> lish. I don't have any friends because [they say] you are foreign, you're on the
> side, you know.... [They say] Oh, your English sucks, OK, bye, go away.

> My cousin he speaks perfect English, so nobody cares he is Polish, so pretty
> much you can know only from his name that he's Polish because he's got a per-
> fect accent. And [a] second [cousin], he's got a Polish accent but he's got a bigger
> vocabulary than average American person.... So it's pretty hard to learn English
> because people don't want to talk to someone who has an accent.

Jan clearly envied his cousins' social success, although Jan's interpretation
that these high schoolers were friendly to his cousin because they were impressed with his vast vocabulary would seem implausible to many. But how
else could this engaging, sociable young person explain to himself his cousins'
social success and his own failure?

Although Jan appeared to appreciate his ESL classmates' willingness to
overlook his limited English, he found other circumstances in those courses
repugnant.

Jan: I hate the class.

Interviewer: Did you like the students in there?

Jan: They got on my nerves. Ass-kissing. Oh professor!
                [imitating an ingratiating tone]. Shut up, just sit
                down and shut up. And the professor was just so
                sweet—just shut up, oh hell, I HATE this. They're

> like, I LOVE this country, I love you all. I was like, just
> shut up and teach. I just hate like people just being so
> sweet in class. So I was like, ech, I was just shaking
> [shudders]. I hate you being so sweet, you know.

His vehemence in venting his rage several years after the fact signals the frustration he must have experienced both in the overly Mr. Roberts-like ESL class and in his failure to attract the interest of his U.S. high school classmates.[2]

It was also in high school that Jan formed or confirmed ideas about U.S. competitiveness and unwillingness to cooperate. As he later wrote in an essay for a college-level English class,

> When I came to the United States, I was very surprised about the way people compete. I was never in touch with competition to this degree before.
>
> The first time I observed competition was when I was in high school. When I came from Poland I did not speak any English and nobody besides foreign students was willing to help me. Most American students did not want to help me because they were afraid that some way I may get a better grade. I thought that in some degree the lack of cooperation was not their fault. I thought that it was the teachers' fault. Teachers say all the time: Do not let anybody copy your homework, do your own work, you will make better grades doing your own work, etc. In Poland the situation was different. Over there I was in the lowest twenty percent of students in content of the grade point average. I had alots of problems in passing some of my classes, but as soon as my classmates found out that I was not doing so well, they offered me help right away. Most Polish students did not care if someone got a better grade than he or she did. Everybody wants to make the best grades they can, but nobody cares if more people make A's. Because of cooperation with my classmates I passed all my classes and made a few good friends.

Making those few good friends did not happen in his U.S. high school.

Although Jan was able to have many of his credits from his school work in Poland transferred to his U.S. high school, he was required to take several courses in order to get a U.S. high school diploma. He mentioned in particular English, history, and economics, in addition to ESL. His English requirements appear particularly odd and inexplicable. He took junior and senior English (while simultaneously taking ESL courses), which he did well in, and then in summer school, in order to graduate, he was required to take sophomore level English. That course was devoted to Shakespeare and, from Jan's description, focused more or less exclusively on plot. Jan's classmates struggled with the Elizabethan language, which would have surely been fairly incomprehensible to Jan, but he had no difficulty. "It was pretty easy. We read Shakespeare stuff

---

[2]Jan is not alone in his sense of ESL classes as friendly but not challenging. We find similar depictions in Harklau (1994), Leki (1995), and Leki and Carson (1997).

all the time. I have done Shakespeare in my country so pretty much I had higher grades than American students." He had studied Shakespeare in Poland, remembered the plots, and was able to do perfectly well in the sophomore class, which, of course, he was required to take even though he had already successfully completed the senior English class.

The sequence of English courses he took, if not also the content, was not particularly logical. Instead, it fulfilled a bureaucratic requirement. Anyone who has dealt with the Immigration and Naturalization Service (INS), as Jan's family had, cannot be surprised by bureaucratic requirements. Still it might be hoped that educational systems function somewhat less bureaucratically. For Jan, this clearly did not prove to be the case. As he explained, "I was taking summer school in high school because they put me in the 9th grade and they try to make me take all the high school over. So I had to make up more credits in one year." Jan ended up being required to take a jumble of English courses in an illogical sequence to earn credits for material he already knew before taking the courses. But he wanted to go to college.

In fact, Jan says that he had always wanted to go to medical school to become a doctor or dentist ("I was always just thinking about medical school"). When asked how he thought he could have been accepted at medical school in Poland, having been, as he claimed in the lowest 20% of his class, he said: "I don't know if I would get in even to the college because only the top 20% is going to college. It's really hard to get in, you gotta be really good to get it. I don't think I would get in anywhere [in Poland]."

The worry about being accepted in college may have informed Jan's decision not to apply to Yale and Cornell, where his socially successful cousins were also doing brilliantly academically, but rather to set his sights no higher than the major state university and two regional universities, to which he applied for admission. Nevertheless his easy academic success in high school may have convinced him that medical school might still be within reach because he declared microbiology as his major in his freshman year in college and registered for the difficult chemistry and math courses required of premed majors.

The salient themes, then, that come out of Jan's brief high school experience are:

- His U.S. classmates are uninterested in foreigners.
- The work in U.S. schools is easy and requires little effort.
- The U.S. school system is bureaucratic, requiring jumping through hoops in order to get what you want.

These themes thread their way through his first 2 years at the university and appear to dramatically color his outlook and behaviors.

THE UNIVERSITY: THE FIRST YEAR

Unfortunately, his first semester at the university was a disaster, preceded by a series of unhappy accidents. Although he had applied for admission to his three selected institutions well in advance, January 1994, he heard nothing back from any of them. Finally, shortly before classes were scheduled to begin in August, he called his first choice, the state university, only to learn that they had put his application on hold because they had inexplicably not received his SAT and TOEFL scores. The panic this state of affairs generated was apparent in Jan's recounting this situation even months later:

> I was late [starting at the institution], like three days before the semester start. They put me on hold on the computer and they didn't send me the letters, nothing. And when I called, [they said] we didn't get any score from your SAT and TOEFL and anything so I had to make rush, give them my copy because SAT they didn't send any copies or nothing. They lost all my files. And three days before!

Again inexplicably, he never heard at all from the two regional institutions. Because he was so late in being admitted, he did not participate in the careful orientation the office for international students conducts for new visa and permanent resident students. This meant he met none of the new international students who might have become friends or at least served as sources of information. It meant that he was not assigned to a dorm that housed many of the new international students and he found himself in a dorm with freshman U.S. students with whom he ended up having no relationship. And it also meant that he came too late to be advised about the courses he hoped to take in fall. He was essentially operating blind, alone, fairly cocky about his academic strengths, based on his experience in high school, and somewhat wary, if not hostile, about relationships with Americans.

In his first semester, he took chemistry, math, English, psychology, a two-credit pass–fail study skills course (17 hours), and held a full-time job! Because he had been admitted so late, there was no one to advise him of the folly of such a heavy first semester load. Furthermore, having had no orientation to the school and not being aware of school policies, he did not realize he could drop courses once he started them. To exacerbate the situation are his mistaken notions about the difficulty of university study.

Jan: It was pretty hard, problems understanding the lecture all that stuff. Also the material, chemistry stuff, and I took too many classes. I took 17 [hours] and it was too much.... Big difference between college and high school because of my language. Problems with my language, I should have taken 12 maximum.... The material, stuff to memorize, and I let it go for the first month. I went easy and after that it was pretty hard to catch up.

Interviewer: How come you went easy?

Jan: I didn't know it was gonna be that big difference. Like chemistry, I remember this stuff from high school [so I thought I studied enough, but] it was kind of different learning this in Polish and in English.... Like in high school they put all the stuff on the board and just get it from the board. And over here the teacher is talking and you gotta make the notes and I can't make the notes. Like you know he's talking and I can make half the sentences, I'm losing some. I leave spaces. After, I don't understand the notes. When I try to study something after in my dorm and I don't know what I wrote because it's like I can't find it, the word in the dictionary....

Interviewer: Did you get nervous when you realized you were having trouble understanding the lectures?

Jan: Yeah.

Interviewer: What did you do then?

Jan: There was nothing much to do. I didn't know that I can withdraw. No one told me I can withdraw and get a W just. And I got D in most of my classes, so I took them over in spring.

One avenue of aid that might have saved him did not open up to him, connections to peers. Because he had missed the international orientation, he knew no international students. In his all-American dorm, he did not meet any other internationals. He had no U.S. peers to turn to because he came to this university having made no U.S. friends in high school. Perhaps the impressions he had gotten in high school stood in the way of more friendly relations with his U.S. peers. When asked if he ever had group work to do in his classes, he replied:

Pretty much I do all my job by myself. Because nobody wants to [work] with me pretty much. I would, but like, you know, only like if I find some foreign people. The foreign people keep together and so if I find like any foreign people, probably I gonna make group but I didn't see any [foreign people in this class, so] probably I gonna work with myself.

Although his ability to communicate informally in English by now was excellent, it was not enough to deal with the demands of university study. The lectures went too fast for him to take notes and did not repeat the material in the book, so he could not turn to the book to make up for what he did not get in the lecture. As he said,

Jan: And the exams ... short essays now, like you've got a few sentences, you gotta express something. You know what's asked for, but you can't express. You get it like on the end of your tongue but you can't say it. On the essays I was spending like hours doing essays,

> and like on exams I didn't finish even because of time.... I know the stuff but people don't understand what I mean and this always lower my grades pretty much.
>
> Interviewer: Can you think of anything you wrote in English that you were frustrated with because you thought you could do better but the English was getting in the way?
>
> Jan: Every time.... My paper is always red. Everywhere.

Jan's predicament seemed poignantly summed up in some prewriting work that he did for an English class. For the prewriting assignment, students were instructed to think of some object, activity, or concept that they were very familiar with, that other students in the class would probably not be familiar with, and that they would then explain to the other students in a paper. At the top of his note page he wrote "computer," under that "Excel," a program he was learning in his statistics class. He brainstormed a list of a few other phrases and then organized the list into the branching hierarchy; shown in Fig. 2.1.

Because he had trouble writing in English, in his first semester at the university Jan was required to take a prefreshman composition reading/writing/grammar course. But in this ESL class, which he failed, there appeared to be little room for recognizing his oral skills, his excellent ability to comprehend, and his Basic Interpersonal Communication Skills (BICS; Cummins,

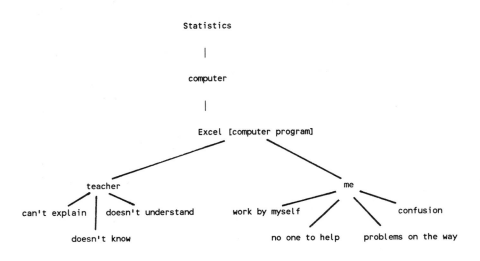

FIG. 2.1.

1979). He described the class as made up primarily of Asian graduate students with strong skills in grammar. In Jan's perception, the class focused on grammar; as a result, they did well, but he did not. The abilities he had developed were not valued; the teacher told him his English was only slang and street language.

Jan returned the disdain. He considered his teachers' calls for development of ideas in his papers to be requirements to "b.s.," which he repeatedly said he hated and which he increasingly came to see as the perfect expression to sum up everything required of him in college. It was all a game. He played, the professors played, the institution played.

Jan eventually moved beyond this course to ESL sections of freshman composition. Here he found echoes of his experiences in high school ESL classes and reacted with similar disgust.

Interviewer: What about the English class?

Jan: It sucks. Boring, boring, boring.

Interviewer: Boring? Why is it boring?

Jan: I don't know. Mostly people are so, like involved in discussing topics ... discussing stupid topics, like abortion or something. Who cares?... Discuss women in military. Who cares?... They love to discuss ... you know, talking, comparing the story to [their] own experiences in U.S., and blah, blah, blah. ... People sit for like 45 minutes discussing how interesting it is, you know. People are kind of boring in this class.

Jan's alienation from his classmates, signaled in his defensive contempt for their class discussions in his interview comments, remained hidden from both those students and his teachers. He played the required game. He sat with his group and behaved in class as if he were participating in the group's discussions; he made a point, not of actually reading the assigned texts, but of finding out, quickly before class from a classmate, about their contents so that he would be minimally prepared. Still his scorn of these students was apparently reflected back to him as well. By his own account, the "foreign people" in his classes found him too Americanized, too quick to think of everything as b.s. At the same time the U.S. students in his other classes and his dorm continued to show no interest in him—as he told the story—because he was foreign and did not speak perfect English. He regularly described his social life as being his computer ("I socialize with computer") or his TV, where he watched *Baywatch*, *Heidi*, or *Robocop*, anything that appeared.

By the end of his first semester at the university Jan's GPA was .65. This sad beginning was to haunt him for at least the next 2 years and perhaps partially accounts for his relentless focus on the GPA and on grades, scores, and the percentage that any given class activity was worth in calculating final course evaluations. Numerous interview exchanges on his grades give the impression that you might awake him from a deep sleep in the middle of the night, and he would be able to instantly recalculate not only his current GPA but also what it would be if he got this or that grade on some assignment in any of his courses.

Jan's subsequent experiences at the university did little to discourage his focus on grades. After his calamitous first semester, and having sought out statistics on how many students graduating from his campus were admitted to medical school in a given year, Jan decided that he must switch majors. His first switch was to international business, which required proficiency in a foreign language and a 3.0 GPA. Discussions of his course work at this point would often be characterized by panicky sounding repetitions and verbal calculations, as in this example in which he discussed changing majors to business:

> I gotta make the 3.0 GPA so to let me major, I gotta make 3.0 GPA, to sign up for the major. In order to major in International Business [with Russian as the required foreign language], I gotta have 3.0 GPA and I can't make lower grades than B in the Russian classes.

As it turned out, Jan despised the introductory course in this major and decided then to switch to business, which required a 2.75 GPA. In each semester after the first he managed to surpass or at least come very close to meeting that minimum but the initial .65 was not overcome despite his struggles until the end of fall 1996, when he brought his average up to 2.75 and was finally admitted to the College of Business.

By this time, however, clear patterns had been established. Any interest in learning that might have inspired Jan before was silenced, buried beneath the war to beat the system. Education became viewed as a bureaucracy and Jan's prime directive was to get around the system toward his goal, which became to get a degree so that he would be able to get a job where he could sit at a desk and "dress nice, wear a tie."

BEATING THE SYSTEM

The attempts to beat the system were numerous and inventive. For example, despite his relatively low overall GPA, in his second year in school, he applied for admission to a prestigious private university because, as he explained, the very same degree from that prestigious school would add $10,000 to his yearly income for the next 30 to 40 years. He cheerfully calculated that he had less than a 1% chance of being admitted but his ace in the hole was that one of his famous cousins at Yale had agreed to write the admissions essay for him. Jan's attitude during his accounts of this whole episode varied between smug confidence and a kind of sunny realism that he would never be admitted. He was not.

Many of his other schemes also failed. In his geography labs Jan organized an elaborate (and illegal) work exchange system whereby each student (all NNES students) in the conspiracy did only one page of the lab work and then they all copied each other's pages. This system backfired when questions about the lab turned up on an exam and Jan was unable to answer them, not having done any more than his one page of the lab work.

In the library he, amazingly, uncovered a copy of the teacher's manual for the accounting course text, complete with elaborate answers to all the exercises and even commentary written to the teacher about how the exercise might best be used and what kinds of difficulties students might be expected to encounter. When the professor called on students in class to give answers to the exercises, Jan was always the first to volunteer and his answers were always correct. He shared those answers with a group of students that sat near him in class, and yet these students ranked his contribution lowest of the group in a required project they did together.

But Jan thought of himself as lucky, and he succeeded in many of his evasions of real work. In the introductory international business course that he hated so much it inspired him to change out of that major, students were expected to do a "corporate shadow." The assignment directed students to learn about the daily work life of a corporate executive by visiting the person's office and observing his or her activities for an entire day. In place of the time and intensive work this assignment required, Jan substituted a 10-minute visit with the manager of a blood bank and a conversation with his roommate, who worked there. His grade was an A.

The same approach was used to complete an accounting course requirement of an interview with a business leader. Jan acquired the business card of a friend of his mother's, stapled it to his "interview report," and made up nearly all the information in the report except the name of the company. He got full credit.

In another accounting class he knew the accounting teacher checked only that the students did the homework problems assigned but did not check the actual homework; he turned in the very same assignment over and over.

In his study of Russian, because he had previous high school course work in Russian and a native command of Polish, another Slavic language, he was placed out of Russian 101. But after completing his second year in Russian with As in every semester, he decided he needed to assure himself of one more A to bolster his GPA and he enrolled in Russian 101. The teacher said she did not care one way or the other. He made an A.

In his greatest coup, however, he used three papers that he was required to write for his international business course for three essays due in his English composition course. He did not even attempt to adjust the papers to accommodate the differing page number requirements, simply figuring that one teacher would be willing to take a little less and the other would be impressed with a little more. They were.

CREATING MASKS

During the time he used smoke and mirrors to create a public image of himself to his teachers as a serious, hard-working student, he was also busy constructing another persona—the wily, street-smart manipulator he displayed during interviews. Here he actively, even pointedly, embraced positions he knew others would find reprehensible perhaps as a way of protecting himself against imagined accusations or even self-recriminations about his own failures or incompetence. In his account of his use of the university's writing center, for example, he described how he managed to pervert one of the few institutionally created support systems available to him. He told us frequently in interviews that the university's writing center was an enormously useful resource for him. Referring to it as the place where he could "make [his] paper perfect," he clearly saw its role as one of correcting his grammar. He seemed to be reliving his experience at the dining table in Poland with his mother working on his Polish essays after work. He talked about signing up for hours of appointments at the writing center, a month in advance so as to be sure that other students did not take up his potential slots. Jan had discovered its usefulness while taking one of the required English courses. His course instructor, Jane, was also one of the writing center's tutors. Although he thought another tutor, Marti, was a much better tutor and that he learned much more from her about writing, he made all of his appointments with Jane as long as he was in her class because, he reasoned, to get a good grade on his papers in her class he would have to write what she wanted. If he went only to her at the writing center, she would let him know how to revise the paper to suit what she wanted. Besides, if he kept coming to her for help, she would also see how hard he was trying. "She gonna have to give me A."

Jan had become stubbornly convinced that the whole educational enterprise was a game, or at least that is the understanding he repeatedly articulated as shown in these sample interview questions and responses taken over a 3-year period and treating a wide variety of courses he took.

Interviewer: What is the purpose of this assignment?

Jan: To keep us busy.

Interviewer: What are you doing to deal with your problem in this class?

Jan: Guess the best I can.

Even if he did not know why he was doing an assignment, he knew its value for his grade and he admitted only the grade as pertinent or worth his attention.

Interviewer: What are you doing in labs?

Jan: I don't know.

Interviewer: What are you getting on your labs?

Jan: 4 or 5 [points] out of 5, 80%–90% for final grade.

Interviewer: What are you expected to get out of the assignment?

Jan: 10% of grade.

~~~

Interviewer: How was the economics exam?

Jan: It sucked.

Interviewer: What sucked?

Jan: My grade.

Teachers and TAs were viewed as participating in these charades as well.

Interviewer: Why were you asked to do this assignment?

Jan: To give TAs something to do.

~~~

Interviewer: Why do you think the geography teacher is showing the class movies?

Jan: It's more easy for her, probably, than to lecture. She's tired of them [lectures].

Often when asked what he thought the purpose of a particular assignment was, Jan would answer "to make up 10% of the grade in the course" or "to have something to grade us on." And, in fact, several of the professors interviewed said much the same thing; they had to evaluate the students somehow and so instituted assignment requirements that would allow evaluation. But these explanations Jan gave were generally not laments; they were simple facts without implications for the "real" Jan because these tests, grades, and GPAs were no more than hoops to jump through, which he did uncomplainingly, in order eventually to collect his college degree.

Jan's need to survive at the university and the unfortunate assumptions he made about university work created the need to develop both the personas of the good, hard-working student and the wily manipulator of the system. Image construction and preservation appeared to be primary concerns in the interviews and in his relations to his teachers and classmates. His need to survive and to preserve his image in his own eyes also required that he view his failures as beyond his control. If he was having a hard time in math, it was because the teacher was not a native speaker of English. In fact, every TA who was a NNES of English was described simply: "He's not speaking English" and so could not be of help. Time after time when reporting on how he figured out how to do particular course work or on how well he did on an exam, he claimed he was just "guessing," or he had "no clue" what the professor was talking about, no idea how to go about doing his work. Even when he did well, magic or luck or accident was the cause:

Interviewer: What are the quizzes like?

Jan: Guessing, pretty much.... I got maximum points on each of them. I don't know how I did it. I didn't have any idea what he is asking for. I was like guessing, totally guessing ... correctly somehow.

But difficult homework exercises were never difficult for just Jan; rather, "no one had any idea how to do this," "no one knows what she's [the professor's] talking about," "even the TA said she didn't understand, no one can understand," "no one finished." When he did not do well on an exam, which was fairly often, Jan frequently claimed to have been tricked in some way: "There were definitions on the math exam; I didn't think there was going to be definitions on math exam." The teacher became the most important factor in his success or failure in a course. If he did not do well, Jan did not have to blame himself; it was the teacher's fault; she could not explain, none of the students understood; even the course TA could not get it. He would cram for an exam for 2 days straight, then toss his fate to the wind. Would the teacher happen to ask what he had studied or would he be surprised and lose points? Luck and magic.

But in a back-handed way Jan blamed himself, not for failing to study enough, not for failing to understanding, not for being unable to do well, but for employing the wrong strategies. His refrain of "pretty much I screwed up" was in one sense a way of letting himself off the hook but was also directed primarily at his miscalculations. His mistake was that he studied the lecture notes instead of the readings; or he did not go back over the lab reports that the exam tested; or he did not study because he did not understand any of the material; or he did not study because "there's no way to study" this material. About studying for an exam in his management class, he said,

> It's just like give you random phone numbers. You have the numbers; there's no way you gonna remember them. You remember five of them but 95% of them you're not gonna remember.

UNDERGRADUATE EDUCATION

Anyone who has ever gone back into the undergraduate classroom as an observer cannot help but sympathize with the task facing undergraduates (and their teachers). Many introductory courses enroll hundreds of students who sit sleepily or indifferently taking notes in what seems like interminable lectures often focusing on the minutiae of the discipline. Several faculty described this focus on minutia as an attempt to lay the groundwork for later courses that actually deal with interesting issues. Jan's course notes were filled with definitions, for example, as were many of his exams. He referred frequently to the importance of getting the vocabulary of the discipline. After he failed his first chemistry course in his first semester, he repeated the course and was able to make a C, he said, because he had the vocabulary from the first course. He knew the definitions. Even the math course he took required definitions on the exam.

This focus on disciplinary vocabulary and ground-zero concepts encouraged Jan's odd study habits. Typically, Jan only kept up with course material that was to appear on quizzes or to be turned in for homework. In courses in which readings were not regularly tested until the two or three major exams, Jan's system was, like that of many other students, to ignore the material, making time for the more immediate demands of courses that required overt signs of keeping up. Then at the time of the exam he would spend 2 or 3 days "studying" 7 or 8 or more hours each day in order to "learn" the material, which he then claimed to forget within 12 hours of the exam. Ordinary cramming. But the cramming took an odd form. Jan's goal was to memorize material, and he did this by recopying it on different sheets of paper over and over by hand until it had become etched on his memory. Furthermore, this memorizing had no particular implications for understanding the material:

> I saw this in my notes; I think this is the right answer. I don't understand what it is, but I think it was in my notes, so I think that's the right answer. It's kind of guessing, guessing game. I have no idea what I'm doing, just guessing.

Jan didn't study to understand, only to memorize, which was why his system of copying notes over and over worked. Nearly all the tests he took in his first 3 years of university were multiple choice. At first multiple-choice exams were his second favorite type of exam, after true–false, where he figured he had a 50% chance of guessing right each time. Multiple choice gave him a 20% to 25% chance, that is, except in courses, which miffed Jan, in which the choices were too numerous, "abcdefgh," as he said. In a characteristic contradiction, he also occasionally expressed a preference for essay exams in which he could, as he often said, either b.s., write in garble so that the professor might give him the benefit of the doubt (particularly when he would open by announcing himself as a NNES and express the sincere hope that he would be understood), or simply write illegibly ("You can write so bad some professor can't read your writing, and if it's close enough they give you credit for it. It works. It works").

In his first 2 years at the university he persisted in his preference for multiple-choice exams, with his 25% chance of guessing the correct answer. In the second half of his junior year, however, the professor in his marketing class gave students the individual option of continuing with multiple-choice exams or doing an essay exam over the same material. Jan seriously considered taking the essay option because he had finally come to material (in the second half of his junior year!) that required more than memorizing. About the first exam in the course, he said for the first time that although he knew the material he could not answer the multiple-choice questions; they were asking for more than definitions; they were asking for sophisticated understanding and reasoning. He had asserted earlier that, for example, in high school, any answers to multiple choice questions that could not simply be memorized could be reasoned through logically by anyone who was not "stupid." It took until his junior year in college to experience a counterexample.

Rarely was Jan able to see beyond the test. In the geography course he took, however, the professor had described one of the goals of this general education requirement as being to enable students to use the information in the course to help them understand the world they inhabited in a very real everyday sense, how weather works, for example. And in fact this was the one course that, when pressed, Jan described (though flippantly) as useful to him beyond the test and beyond laying the vocabulary groundwork for future courses.

Interviewer: Is there anything in this class that strikes you as being important for your education?

Jan: Oh yeah! Weather Channel. I understand whatever, everything they say, high fronts, low fronts, why it's cold, and all this stuff. I can understand when I watch the Weather Channel. I see those maps moving, all this stuff; I understand that stuff. When I watch the Weather Channel, I know exactly what's going on.... When I look at the stream, I know why [the water moves in the opposite] direction on the other side, and I know what's on the middle. You know, I know why the sand is moving. I can impress someone, walking on the beach with my girlfriend, I can impress her: "See? The sand is moving; know why?" [grinning]

This impressive knowledge, however, was not enough to seduce Jan into pursuing any further what seemed to be the only discipline in which he had expressed any intellectual interest. When asked what geographers do, he said:

Something to South America, making big holes all around the ground. I mean he [the professor] was showing us picture all the time, you know, of this geographer going to South America, digging holes, and taking samples. I think this is what they do, and yeah, be professor, teaching, you know, students, or just go to South America, digging holes.... On those slides he's showing us in class. "There's Harry," you know, digging holes, catching snakes, and stuff like that. I was like, "Okay, whatever."

This last valley girl comment was followed up by his final remark about whether he had learned anything interesting in this class: "Not really. I mean, like, we've got a science requirement, so you try to get it over as soon as you can." He consistently trivialized the field and anything he had learned in the courses.

IS THERE A STUDENT BEHIND THE MASK?

His pragmatism framed in an interest in making money and wearing a nice suit and tie to work short circuited a brief admission that it might be interesting to major in geography. Despite the system of cooperative labor he had worked out in the geography lab, which might suggest lack of ability, he consistently did well in the labs, although he denigrated his own efforts by saying that he always took the easiest sections of the lab work to make his own contribution. And yet, at least three times in the year of geography lab work, he pointed out to the TA errors in the lab manual, errors the TA agreed were there. Twice he pointed out errors in class material in the management course, a class he hated. Incidents like these clearly show that Jan is not only clever but also intelligent, and that his description of his study habits, mindlessly, mechanically copying incomprehensible notes to memorize, belie the actual efforts he made and the depth with which he in fact engaged the material.

Furthermore, he rarely missed class, even in courses that really would be described by outside observers as far less than stimulating. When asked about why he never missed class, Jan usually referred to having nothing else to do or to wanting to impress his teacher by always showing his face. And in some cases, clearly this is what was going on. But Jan often surprised me by citing some moment or comment made in a course, showing that not only was he listening and paying attention but that he seemed to remember without effort, often meaningless details mentioned in class like what edition of the textbook the class was using or exactly where and when each of three different review sessions would be held.

From one point of view he worked hard. He did look like the good student. He nearly always did exactly what was asked of him in classes, often doing work earlier than required. "If a paper is due in two weeks, I want to get it done now." He always came to class on time, handed work in on time, sat near the front of the class, went to see his teachers in their offices with questions. In his geography lab he constantly called the TA over to his station to answer his questions. He wrote several heartfelt-seeming papers where he talked about what life has been like for him; when he talked about these papers in interviews it was impossible to tell if he was snowing us or snowing the teachers that read his paper. Probably both and neither.

Desperation to stay in school caused him to fixate on grades and on requirements for grades. At the same time in his interviews, he consistently highlighted his shrewdness and cleverness over his efforts and his academic abilities. An institutional focus on GPA fed into his insecurity about his ability to knock out each obstacle in his way toward making a good living. In a single revealing comment, Jan once regretted that universities had grades, saying that he thought he would actually learn something if it were not for the need to make good grades. In commenting on the course on world religions which he was taking, he also remarked that educated people should know something about world religions.

Interviewer: What are you getting from these assignments?

Jan: I understand more religions kind of, getting my own point of view, something to talk about if someone ask me a question. I'm not gonna [say], duhh. I'm gonna have my point of view.... Like if somebody ask you about Buddhism, you say duhh, Buddha, he was a fat guy, or stuff like that. You can talk about, making conversation. It's gonna be useful.

And even Jan's stubborn focus on his interest in making money was undermined during the summer between his sophomore and junior years when he worked at a car dealership. He was extremely successful selling cars, so much so that after only one week the dealership took him off salary, put him on commission, and asked him to come back to work for them the following year. He made enough money so that for the first time since he came to the United States he did not have to take yet another 40-hour-a-week job in the fall after that summer. Despite the money and the nice clothes he could wear, despite his success at the job, he did not look forward to working there again, finding the other salesmen "stupid," crude, and racist.

WHERE THE SYSTEM FAILED

The wisdom that comes from going from 18- to 20-years-old certainly played a role in allowing Jan to begin to portray himself less as a wheeler-dealer and more as someone with broader interests than just tricking the system. But the institution bears some responsibility for repressing the more committed, intellectual part of his character, the part that prefers no grades and wants to be able to express a point of view on religion. The system went wrong for Jan in a number of places. He had no orientation to the university because, through no fault of his own, he was admitted late; he was not advised that he could drop courses; he was not advised to work fewer hours; he had no international friends to rely on for support; he was unable to engage the interest of potential U.S. friends. In addition, most of his courses enrolled more than 50 students, many with hundreds of students in the large auditorium lecture-style classrooms that administrators favor for their economic value but that prevent students like Jan from being able to ask questions or to indicate their confusion or inability to keep up with the lecturer's delivery speed. Impersonal rules and regulations to assure quality control went alongside the institution's focus on exams, grades, and GPAs.

Finally, Jan's case should serve to blunt U.S./Western smugness about how U.S. or Western educational institutions work to develop critical thinking skills. The critical thinking that Jan was encouraged to develop both in high school and in his first 3 years at the university ran along the lines of figuring out how to use trickery to succeed and how best to memorize for multiple-choice exams. He experienced very few writing assignments, and none of those required any sustained writing; his first multiple-choice exam that required more than memorization came in his third year. Although it could be argued that the reason Jan did not do much better in his work is that he conceived of it as memorizing and trickery, nevertheless, his educational experience did little to discourage that view. U.S./Western education has little to congratulate itself about here.

In response to his own failures, Jan developed adaptive but not particularly commendable attitudes and study habits. In some ways his attempts to outsmart the system mimic those of "frat boys." But the obvious, huge missing ingredient was a community of peers that might help him slip past the system. Jan had none.

DISPOSSESSION AND ADAPTATION

This portrait is one of a young man who was in a sense tricked into making certain assumptions about what his college experience would be, and when he found he was drowning in the actual college experience, there was no real place to turn. So he frantically developed means of surviving, cutting corners where necessary, tabulating his GPA every hour. He was not an outstanding student before moving to the United States, but it must have been a heady experience to be getting good grades in an English-speaking high school where no one was his friend but where he could rely on previously learned material to do well. Suddenly he was a star, and then just as suddenly he almost flunked out. Jan is a very clever fellow but that cleverness had no reward or outlet in legitimate college endeavors.

In certain ways, in Jan's accounts of his academic life, he sounds very much like Miller's five U.S. students who published their field notes on their undergraduate courses in *College Composition and Communication* (Anderson et al., 1990). Some of them too felt exam questions were mysterious and arbitrary and claimed the only possible response was not to work harder but to throw their hands up and guess; some registered for courses mainly because they thought these courses were easy ones they could get good grades in; they too were not "planning schedules around ... intellectual interests, but cooperating with the institution's provision of paths toward degrees" (p. 16). It is difficult to say whether or not, in sharing these responses, Jan was reflecting attitudes he had absorbed in his U.S. high school.

His account did differ from theirs, however; its tone was more subdued, more self-reflective. Miller's students seemed to display no critical distance on their own behavior, no sense of awareness of their own complicity in the educational encounters they describe. Their descriptions of their teachers seemed to cast the teachers in the role of hired help, these students' employees, whose performances the students had the right to sit back and judge, remaining uncontaminated themselves. Miller's students were privileged honors students headed for law school or foreign missionary work. Their voices signal their own sense of ownership and of their right to complain or be disgusted by their experiences. Jan's more acquiescent and ironic voice, a voice more conscious of and coerced by the rules of the game, was more likely to acknowledge his complicity and awareness that he was navigating through bureaucracy, and so was everyone else, including the professors. It is possible that he felt that being an immigrant precluded both whining and a sense of self-righteousness. Instead, to survive, what was needed was to develop a scrambling, scrapping, self-reliant resourcefulness, to confront whatever the system threw his way. In this sense, it is a system that he accepted, one that was not protestable, not resistible, only occasionally cheatable. He did not want to be a loser.

I would argue, although on somewhat speculative grounds, that Jan's status as a immigrant and as a learner of English also contributed heavily to his anti-intellectual behavior at the university. Evidence, although admittedly circumstantial, from Jan's literacy background, the occasional glimmers of respect for being an educated person and developing his own considered point of view (e.g., on world religions), and his probably mistaken idea that it was his cousin's large vocabulary that won him friends despite his Polish accent, all of these suggest the possibility that Jan's struggle to survive educationally, socially, and economically in a new culture and language preempted any potential inclination toward a richer intellectual life. Jan's behavior is adaptive. He is proficient at suppressing his own inclinations in order to fit in, as demonstrated by his cooperative actions in his college ESL writing class despite his very negative feelings about that class and his classmates. If he perceived the teen culture around him as condoning a stance of anti-intellectualism, he was quite capable of adopting that approved stance, at the expense of one more committed to education, possibly in hopes of fitting in better with his classmates. The illogical sequences of requirements for graduating from high school may have helped to reinforce the idea that what is important is not education but fulfilling requirements. In many ways the central problem for a newcomer to any culture is precisely to determine which cultural regulations one can ignore in favor of asserting one's own preferences without incurring too harsh a social retribution. In Jan's terms, could he afford to be interested in anything besides surviving the gauntlet of academic bureaucracy?

But more than the story of a language minority student or an immigrant student, perhaps Jan's is primarily a story of late adolescence, an adolescence cut off from its natural allies, other adolescents. Perhaps Jan's defiant insistence on scorning the bourgeois virtues of real work and pious study is the defensiveness of bruised youth.

In any case, Jan's story does not fit well into our construction of the language minority student; he does not fit the image of the "toiling masses," the nearly saint-like immigrant. He does not appear to have the genuine desire to learn we assign to and approve of in immigrant students. His struggle is not a story of the dramatic and very apparent difficulties of poverty or specific ethnic and racial prejudices. He will in fact perhaps appear to readers as not worthy of much sympathy. But Jan's is not a story we can be especially proud of, either, neither for ourselves nor for him. It is the story of Jan's adaptation to a not particularly praiseworthy educational environment that we daily and presumably unwittingly help create. Neither is his story one that points to clear advice about how to make possible a better experience for someone like Jan, an experience that might let him make use of his resourcefulness in ways that might enhance his personal life and contribute more constructively to a broader social life. But we can see where the system we have created perhaps did little to dissuade Jan from predispositions he had coming into higher education, where it abandoned him to his own resources and us to trying to figure out how to deal with students like him.

Although I have attempted to present some of the complexity of Jan's situation, it is never possible to represent even a brief portion of a life adequately, in its web of conscious and unconscious motivations. Furthermore, Jan, as represented here, has been forcibly squeezed into the limitations of my own intellectual and literary abilities. Perhaps the story he would have told would have been dramatically different, making himself more sympathetic. Perhaps in my effort to be on his side, and imagining that I know something of the tastes and inclinations of the probable readers of this volume, I have portrayed him in a more flattering light than he would have, had he been writing. In either case, qualitative research of the type reported here confers a special kind of obligation on researchers and on readers of the research. We must "recognize the vulnerability of those [we] study" (Newkirk, 1996, p. 5). Students and teachers who allow us into their worlds lay themselves open to easy criticism. At the same time, examination of any human context would be pointless if it were forbidden, as Newkirk said, to uncover "bad news." Research of the type presented here is, as Stake (1995) described it, not a "fixation on failure" (p. 16); rather it reflects "a belief that the nature of people and systems becomes more transparent during their struggles" (p. 16) and has as a primary aim "stimulation of further reflection" (p. 42).

APPENDIX: BASIC INTERVIEW QUESTIONS AND GUIDE[3]

1. How are your classes going generally?
2. How did you do this assignment? (Probe: Did you do it at one sitting, revise a lot, get help? Goal is also to find out if they had trouble and if so, how they dealt with it.)
3. What is/was your goal in this assignment? (Probe: What are you trying to do/show? What's your job here? Get them to be as specific as possible. If they say: To get a good grade, ask how, what they tried to do to deserve a good grade on the assignment.)
4. Why did your teacher give you this assignment to do? (Probe: What is the professor's purpose in assigning it? What are you supposed to learn from it or get out of it? What are you supposed to show your professor?)
5. Is this assignment similar to or different from (name some other assignment they've done). In what way?
6. How are you reading the material for this course? What are you supposed to learn from the reading you're doing? How well do you have to learn it?
7. Why did your teacher assign this reading for you to do? How does it fit with other parts of the course?

---

[3]This group of questions represents the core issues to be addressed in the interviews. What was actually discussed at any given interview varied depending on the concerns of the moment.

8. Were any papers returned to you since the last interview? (Discuss any returned work, including teachers' written comments.)

9. Did any of your profs say anything about any of your writing assignments or essay exams since the last interview? What?

10. What do you think will be the hardest thing about the next piece of work or about any of your upcoming writing/reading this term? How will you handle those problems?

11. What is interesting to you in this course? What isn't? Why?

Interview questions for exams

12. What were you being tested on? (i.e., what did you have to learn for this test or show on this test?) How did you study for this test?

REFERENCES

Adamson, H. D. (1993). *Academic competence*. New York: Longman.

Anderson, W., Best, C., Black, A., Hirst, J., Miller, B., & Miller, S. (1990). Cross-curricular underlife: A collaborative report on ways with academic words. *College Composition and Communication, 41*, 11–36.

Brodkey, L. (1987). Writing ethnographic narratives. *Written Communication, 4*, 25–40.

Chiseri-Strater, E. (1991). *Academic literacies*. Portsmouth, NH: Boynton/Cook.

Cummins, J. (1979). Linguistic interdependence and the educational development of bilingual children. *Review of Education Research, 49*, 222–251.

Currie, P. (1993). Entering a disciplinary community: Conceptual activities required to write for one introductory university course. *Journal of Second Language Writing, 2*, 101–117.

Fu, D. (1995). *My trouble is my English*. Portsmouth, NH: Boynton/Cook.

Haas, C. (1994). Learning to read biology: One student's rhetorical development in college. *Written Communication, 11*, 43–84.

Harklau, L. (1994). ESL versus mainstream classes: Contrasting L2 learning environments. *TESOL Quarterly, 28*, 241–272.

Herrington, A. (1985). Writing in academic settings: A study of the contexts for writing in two college chemistry engineering courses. *Research in the Teaching of English, 19*, 331–359.

Leki, I. (1995). Coping strategies of ESL students in writing tasks across the curriculum. *TESOL Quarterly, 29*, 235–260.

Leki, I., & Carson, J. (1997). "Completely different worlds": EAP and the writing experiences of ESL students in university courses. *TESOL Quarterly, 31*(1), 39–69.

McCarthy, L. (1987). A stranger in strange lands: A college student's writing across the curriculum. *Research in the Teaching of English, 21*, 223–265.

McKay, S., & Wong, S. L. (1996). Multiple discourses, multiple identities: Investment and agency in L2 learning among Chinese adolescent immigrant students. *Harvard Educational Review, 66*, 577–608.

Newkirk, T. (1996). Seduction and betrayal in qualitative research. In P. Mortensen & G. Kirsch (Eds.), *Ethics and representation in qualitative studies of literacy* (pp. 3–16). Urbana, IL: National Council of Teachers of English.

Newkirk, T. (1992). The narrative roots of case study. In G. Kirsch & P. Sullivan (Eds.), *Methods and methodology in composition research* (pp. 130–152). Carbondale: Southern Illinois University Press.

Spack, R. (1997). The acquisition of academic literacy in a second language. *Written Communication, 14*, 3–62.

Stake, R. (1995). *The art of case study research*. Thousand Oaks, CA: Sage.

Sullivan, P. (1996). Ethnography and the problem of the "other." In P. Mortensen & G. Kirsch (Eds.), *Ethics and representation in qualitative studies of literacy* (pp. 97–114). Urbana, IL: National Council of Teachers of English.

Walvoord, B., & McCarthy, L. (1990). *Thinking and writing in college*. Urbana, IL: National Council of Teachers of English.

3 Contingent Literacy: The Social Construction of Writing for Nonnative English-Speaking College Freshman

Judith Rodby
California State University, Chico

In their own words, they are "still learning English," "struggling with writing and reading," and "having deficiencies in language." They call themselves Hmong, Mien, Cambodian, Lao, Vietnamese, Chicano, Latino, and Hispanic although their professors may describe them simply as "ESL students." Many of these students were born in the United States or arrived here when they were small children. Many have grown up in the small towns and agricultural land surrounding the university where I work, and a smaller number come from the large metropolitan areas of the San Francisco Bay and Los Angeles. Mostly they speak a language other than English at home with their parents and extended family, and many continue to speak their first language with their roommates on or off campus. Some appear nearly native in their English language proficiency. In elementary or high school, they were tracked into English as a Second Language (ESL) classes, and for the most part they do not want to take ESL at the university.

These nonnative English speakers (NNES) were both a force for change and a concern when we restructured our freshman composition program to eliminate all remedial writing courses. These students and some of the faculty at large had differed in their views of the remedial curriculum. The students claimed that they did not require language or writing courses with either an ESL or a "basic" curriculum. Instead they wanted support to do the difficult academic reading and writing tasks of the freshman composition course. They did not want to prepare for freshman composition, but rather they needed to do the thing itself, and to be guided in doing it. Some faculty and advisors, however, raised concerns that these students needed remedial courses as a safety net, giving students time to adjust and work on their English before attempting to cope with the demands of the required writing course. As we contemplated restructuring the writing program, we heard both students' voices asking for change, a way out of the remedial holding tank, and faculty caveats against putting these students at risk.

Now, nearly 4 years since the writing program restructuring, we know that most (89%) NNES resident students pass freshman composition without taking remedial courses first. Although this success rate is gratifying, we have been confounded by the patterns of failure and success. For example, there appears to be no statistically significant correlation between students' entering test scores and their pass–fail rates in this class. Some students with low test scores do quite well, whereas others with higher scores struggle and even drop the course. Faced with these conundrums, we wanted to know more about how the context of freshman composition contributed to students' writing development.

THE STUDY

To study the relation of classroom context to writing development, my research partners, Cindy Cannoy and Jackie Howland, and I became participant observers in three freshman composition classes for a semester.[1] Two of us taught freshman composition. Two of us also taught adjunct workshops that supported the freshman course. My own freshman composition class was observed and logged by a graduate student assistant, Gretchen Smolka, and I kept a journal of observations for this freshman composition course as well. I observed all 20 adjunct workshops at least once. My research partners and I interviewed 25 students, many faculty members, and all of the adjunct workshop leaders, and collected course evaluations and student writing.

As is typical in participant observer research, we moved iteratively between the data and its analysis. While collecting information, we refined our research questions and the categories through which to code and interpret data. We had begun with a very general question—how was the classroom context involved in student writing development, which we were assessing by the grades students received in the course. As we observed classes and talked with faculty and students, we became interested in the more specific issue of what determines success and failure among the NNES students who describe themselves as having "difficulty in English" and low placement test scores. What did students do in this course to succeed? What produced failure? Placement test scores had not been shown to correlate (significantly) with these students' successes and failures in freshman composition. Their years in residency did not correlate with passing rates for students who had been in the United States 5 years or more (as most had). The question then became how was it that the course affected student learning and student writing development?

---

[1]Both Cindy Cannoy and Jackie Howland were graduate student researchers in this project.

In the process of gathering data we selected representative students for case studies based on gender, native language, and their grades on papers in freshman composition. The case study students had received a range of grades (from A to F) on papers in freshman composition, were 50% male and 50% female, and 50% Spanish speakers and 50% South East Asians. This chapter reports on four of the case studies of resident NNES who were enrolled in freshman composition and adjunct workshops. All of them had low entering test scores that in prior years would have placed them in remedial courses.

Once we had selected the students for the case studies, the context of the freshman writing course helped us to refine our research questions and categories for analysis. In this course all instructors expected their students to revise and to learn to write well through revision. As students revised, they created a series of "approximations" of academic discourse. In successive revisions, they had learned to "take on our [academic] … ways of reading, writing, speaking and thinking," to quote Bartholomae (1985, p. 276). The faculty expected that with each revision students would develop a better understanding of the assignment they had been given, so that they would gradually appropriate the craft of the academic argument, its ways of using evidence, sentences, and words. Because revision based on feedback was seen as the key to student success, we counted the number of revisions each student finished and looked for correspondences between the number of revisions and final grades.

Because revision was such a salient feature of the curriculum, it was not a surprise that when students passed the course, they had repeatedly revised their essays based on feedback from their instructor and the adjunct workshop. Those who did not pass generally did not persist in revising more than once. Why did some students do multiple revisions and others not? Narrowing our original question, we asked which aspects of the classroom context contributed to students' persistence in revising. Which physical and material things, which assignments, readings, roles, activities and social interactions would be salient to these students' development? What motivated some students to revise so that they could successfully approximate academic argument? Did students enter with the motivation, did the course itself motivate them, or did they find or discover motivation to work on their writing elsewhere?

MOTIVATION AS ECOLOGICAL SYSTEM

As we worked with our observation and interview notes, the construct of *motivation* became a kind of black box that we used to account for the differences we saw among the students' abilities to revise recurrently. As we reexamined our data, however, the construct of motivation accrued details and explanatory power. Based on our observations, we theorized that motivation was located in the context rather than inside students' heads. Students were motivated by elements of the environment in which they were studying. As their environs changed so did their writing, their persistence in revising, and hence their writing skill.

We were not alone in understanding motivation to be dependent on context. In a landmark article, "The Ethnography of Literacy," Szwed (1981) argued that motivation for literacy emerges through the "nexus at which reader, or writer, context, function and text join" (p. 15). Farr (1994) was even more emphatic about the interdependence of context and motivation. There is always, she argued, a "combination of factors that yields motivation." Furthermore, "Motivation may be something an individual feels, but it clearly is not a quality that a particular person either has or does not have across various settings. Instead *it emerges out of the setting* ... " (italics added, p. 27). She used this insight to explain how the Chicago Mexicanos she studied were "highly motivated to learn literacy skills" although they had "virtually no formal schooling." The fact that they "were working in a foreign country without much competence (initially) in the dominant language and ... had left an extended network of very close relatives and friends 'back home'" produced a strong motivation to learn to read and write so as to communicate and maintain their connection with their families and friends in Mexico (p. 27).

In considering the motivation for the NNES students to revise, the important theoretical points are twofold: first, motivation is not located in the individual, per se. Motivation results from a combination of factors often beyond the individual's control. It is produced by a confluence of relationships, ideologies, institutions, and activities with and in which the individual is engaged. Second, as these factors change from one context to another, either synchronously or chronologically, so does motivation. As Szwed pointed out, when the nexus of motivation changes, so may the actual skill with which the individual reads and writes. Although Farr and Szwed point us to the nexus of context, text, function and writer as determining motivation for literacy, it was not at all obvious why one student continued to revise and another did not. Initially we were not able to detect patterns that would explain how this confluence of factors worked.

To move beyond this impasse and understand more about when and how a combination of writer, text, context, and function would result in student motivation to revise, and thus writing skill, we turned to the work of Bronfenbrenner (1979). Bronfenbrenner developed a framework for thinking about how skill develops as a result of the interplay between an individual and the "ecological environment" (p. 3). Bronfenbrenner maintained that all development, but literacy in particular, is enhanced when connections or affiliations exist among the settings where students engage in learning. He argued that "A child's ability to learn to read in the primary grades may depend no less on how he is taught than on the existence and nature of ties between the school and the home" (p. 5).

One of our case studies, Luciana, became a test for the relevance of Bronfenbrenner's ideas to our work. Luciana was an 18-year-old freshman from the industrial outskirts of a large urban area. She had been born in El Salvador and had come to the United States at age 7. She was exceedingly motivated in freshman composition, doing multiple revisions of each essay, making use of her instructor, the writing center and the adjunct workshop. The diagram entitled *Social Ecology of Writing Development* (see Fig 3.1) illustrates how Bronfenbrenner's framework can be used to analyze the ecological environment of students' writing development.

Bronfenbrenner's framework led us to see that Luciana's writing development would be affected by the contexts of her life—her freshman composition class, her adjunct workshop, her work-study job in retention services, the Movimiento Estudio Chicano de Aztlan (MECHA) club, the apartment where she lived with her brother and his wife—which are all labeled as *micro-*

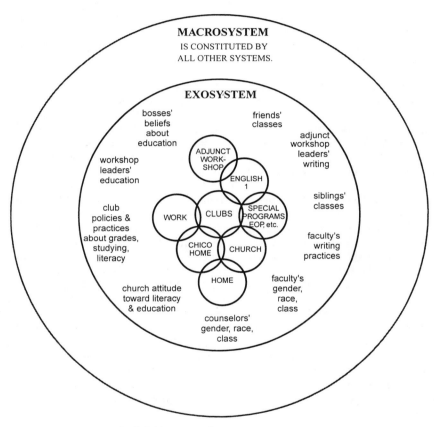

- *Small circles represent microsystems.*

- *Intersections among small circles represent mesosystems.*

FIG. 3.1.   This diagram represents interconnecting contexts actively shaping development in freshman composition. (Terms from *Ecology of Human Development*, Uri Bronfenbrenner)

systems (see Fig. 3.1). The microsystem is more than a physical and material setting. It is also comprised of the perceived interconnections between people in each setting as they engage in common, complementary, or even relatively independent activities (Bronfenbrenner, 1974). Most research in literacy development examines only the effects of the microsystem context. Bronfenbrenner's theory, however, recognizes that context includes more than the immediate setting (the composition class or the apartment); context includes events and conditions outside the immediate setting that have a profound influence on behavior within that setting.

The microsystem circles overlap and the intersections among these microsystems are what Bronfenbrenner calls the *mesosystem*. The intersections represent consistencies among the people, ideas, belief systems, activities, and roles from one microsystem setting to another. If a student has friends from home and work in her freshman composition class, the connections she perceives form a mesosystem. Bronfenbrenner hypothesized that a densely interconnected mesosystem would motivate student learning.

Luciana had an extraordinarily rich mesosystem. She had begun her university work in a summer program in which she had lived on campus with students with whom she had also taken classes. In fall many of those students had scheduled their classes together so that they were in the same sections of freshman composition and the adjunct workshop. They were together in mandatory group tutoring sessions for other classes as well. The subject matter of her courses was interrelated; Chicano Studies employed language and knowledge from Spanish and U.S. history courses; in both her speech and freshman composition courses faculty used rhetorical terminology. She worked in the retention services office where she saw not only her sister-in-law, who had gotten her the job, but many of her friends and counselors from the summer program. There were many other ties between Luciana's school and home life. Her sister-in-law/godmother was particularly important in Luciana's forming and maintaining social connections between home and the university. Luciana said her sister-in-law was like an advisor. "She knew the people that [she] should talk to and get in contact with." When she had trouble in freshman composition her sister-in-law "made her" find the office hours, call the instructor, and go to ask questions seven times over the course of one semester. The mesosystem functioned like glue holding Luciana's world together, so that when she moved from school to home, or from one class to another, she inhabited a single, nearly seamless universe of meaning. She did not encounter conflicts of values or even much cultural diversity among her relationships.

The diagrammatic circle labeled *exosystem* refers to events, activities, and people that did not directly involve Luciana herself but affected her nonetheless. For example, if her adjunct workshop leader held beliefs about family and school that were similar to Luciana's beliefs, and if the workshop leader herself succeeded in school, this would constitute an exosystem connection. Because Luciana's brother had graduated from the university and his wife worked in retention services, Luciana had very stable exosystem that was primarily built out of connections established by her brother and sister-in-law. Luciana's sister-in-law took a Spanish class at the local junior college. Because Luciana and her sister-in-law were both taking Spanish, this course became an exosystem connection. Luciana had considered joining a Hispanic sorority and living on campus, but was worried about doing this because she said her main goal was to get and keep a high GPA. She recognized the value of her exosystem to her educational goals. She said that her brother's presence kept her focused even when "we say nothing about school."

Finally for Luciana all the consistencies in ideologies, beliefs, roles, activities, and structures among the social systems of her life resulted in a densely woven *macrosystem,* which might be pictured as a web linking all the other contexts. A macrosystem is dialectically related to the other systems of connections in a social ecology; it is constituted out of the connections among other systems and yet in some sense it constitutes the systems themselves. For example, Luciana's belief that good grades in writing classes would ensure economic success after graduation was part of her home life, part of her classmates' beliefs, part of the atmosphere at her work-study job at retention services, and part of the clubs such as Latino Leadership that she had belonged to in high school. These shared beliefs and ideologies were part of what constituted the mesosystems and exosystems that were aggregated as a macrosystem.

Luciana was conscious of consistencies in her own history. Woven in and among the primary events, situations, and places in her everyday life was an ideological thread that told her that if she worked hard, financial and social success would follow. She said her family told her to "put education first. Educate more yourself so you won't be in a factory for your life with no low-paying job." Her brother was "an inspiration" to her as were her parents who had worked "really really hard," her mother in a sewing factory and her father as a body shop mechanic. She repeatedly said that she "needed to be someone," and she was aware that years before college she had begun making connections with others who shared this value. In high school she had been La Raza leadership president and had "mostly hung out with Latino friends who had also wanted to go to college." She had gone to a Latino leadership conference in San Francisco where the speakers had told that students that "getting to know each other" in college was a "key to success."

For Luciana motivation resulted from ties that accumulated among the nested social systems. The connections among these systems could be thought of as valences that motivated students to do "successive approximations" of the assignments. This sense of motivation is drawn from Lewin (1931) who wrote that motivational forces "[emanate] not from within the person but from the environment itself. Objects, activities, and especially other people send out lines of force, valences, and vectors that attract and repel, thereby steering behavior and development" (p. 23). Luciana was guided by these vectors to the degree that she had practically no choice but to revise until her writing was "successful."

Bronfenbrenner's schema was also useful for our thinking about students who failed in freshman composition. Vu, for example, struggled with the course and the requirement to revise, in large part because he had no mesosystem, exosystem, or macrosystem to motivate him to success. Vu lived approximately 30 miles from campus. No one among his family or friends had gone or was going to college. He told me he was "like a lone guy" on campus. He had not made friends at the summer program because "the other Asians involved were Hmong girls who [he] had to stay away from." He had not lived on campus for this program but had commuted and tried to maintain his work schedule in his home town. Symbolic of his tenuous connection to anything at the university was Vu's old and unreliable car. Daily, Vu was uncertain whether he would make it to campus or not because his car was his only way to commute to the university from the rural community where he lived. Furthermore, strong were the pulls on Vu to stay home and drive his mother and brother around for errands and work.

Vu had few connections with the university and many with his home community. Perhaps Vu was trying to bridge this gap between home and the university when he wrote his first essay in freshman composition about how Asian youth in his hometown are frequently assumed to be in gangs even when they have no gang affiliations. As a link between two worlds, and as a freshman composition paper, the draft was inadequate, very short, and incohesive at the level of the paragraphs. He was told he would need to revise it, probably several times to expand the ideas in each sentence and to connect them to each other, but he did not. His attendance became sporadic, and he turned in no other work. When the instructor told him in conference that he could not possibly pass the class, he said he had not understood the expectations of the instructor. When she explained to him the paper requirements, as detailed on the syllabus, he became very quiet and said "yeah, this isn't like high school" as if he understood something about what he was being asked to do for the very first time. He had tried to interpret the university through his experiences in high school and to forge mesosystem connections by connecting his high school and university classes. This strategy was a dead end, however, because the connections he imagined between high school and the university were not expanded on by his instructor. Instead, she lectured him for half an hour about the ways in which college was not like high school. She recommended an instructor for the following semester and told him to pre-register for the class.

Vu began spring semester knowing that his instructor from fall had given his work to his new instructor. The instructors' connections to each other formed an exosystem, and the paper itself was a nascent mesosystem connecting his struggles from home and high school to the university and his work from one semester to another. His freshman composition instructor advised him to start her course by revising the Asian gang paper from the previous fall. This was useful for the growing connectedness he felt among faculty, university writing assignments, and his home and history. That spring he visited the instructor's office at least once a week, he said, because his fall instructor had told him to do this and his Educational Opportunity Program (EOP) counselor had concurred that Vu "should stay in close contact with his teachers." Providing more evidence that he was beginning to form mesosystem and exosystem connections at the university, Vu said he was embarrassed that he had failed freshman composition while "the [Hmong] girls had passed." He said he was going to "watch what they do." Whereas he had said that he needed to stay away from them, he now felt connected to them and motivated by their successes.

CASE STUDIES OF REVISION

As we examined the work, grades, test scores, interviews and our observation notes, we used Bronfenbrenner's ecological framework to interpret the interdependence among students' literacy development and their social roles and contexts. This network of interdependent contexts seemed everywhere, invisible and all-consuming, both obvious and oblique. Rich mesosystems, exosystems, and macrosystems motivated students to get feedback and to revise their texts. We wanted to know more about this revision process, so we chose to look carefully not only at the motivational valences but their relationships to actual revisions done by two students, Horatio and Kaying.

Horatio

Horatio had had a history of success in school, although his achievements were not strictly academic. He had been president of the student body at a large south central Los Angeles high school. He had also scored in the lowest quartile on the placement test and he attributed his writing problems to his "English." In early drafts his papers exhibited problems at all levels; organization, development, and sentence structure, but he revised his early papers five or six times, with feedback on each draft. In each revision, he would work on a few sentences or the organization of one or two paragraphs. Although his writing processes were not at all remarkable, his tenacity as he continued to revise was compelling.

As we looked at his writing, actions, and attitudes in adjunct workshops and classes and thought about his life in this small university town, we saw that connections between the microsystems, mesosystems, macrosystems, and exosystems were what enabled them to seek out feedback on their drafts and use it to revise. Horatio had strong mesosystem connections in that many people overlapped in or shared the contexts of his everyday life at the university. He had begun his studies in a summer program, and during the academic year, he had lived in a dorm with two friends from that program. Moreover, he was pledging an academic Hispanic fraternity. Many of his fraternity brothers were taking English 1 and adjunct workshops and most had been in the Summer Bridge program at one time or another.[2]

There was a remarkable coherence in Horatio's world, the consistency of people, activities, and beliefs that Bronfenbrenner refers to as the macro-

---

[2]Summer Bridge is a program, typical of many in the country, which brings socioeconomically disadvantaged students to campus for study and orientation the summer before their freshman year.

system; his friends were his classmates, and they were his fraternity brothers, and they were his roommates. These young men surrounded each other with a shared system of values and beliefs. For example, so strong was their belief that if they worked on their writing, they would get ahead, that one of Horatio's roommates took an adjunct workshop although he did not get into a section of English 1 because he had registered too late. He was applauded for doing so by his friends. He was viewed as bold and strong.

The ideological environment was thick with these notions: that university education was important; that these young Hispanic men rightfully, even "righteously," belonged in college; and (cannily) that they needed to stick together to succeed. The academic successes of Horatio's fraternity brothers, one of whom was student body president, were more than scenery for Horatio's work; all of these social and ideological connections to English were crucial to Horatio's ability to revise. Horatio reported that he read his papers aloud to his roommates who gave him feedback on his "street language." He said they would tell him " you can't say it like that, man. That's too street." Then they would help him to reformulate his sentences. Horatio reported that the adjunct workshop was useful most of the time but his roommates were most helpful to him in his revisions. "They are slave drivers," he said, adding that he "[made] them work too."

We were interested in what motivated these dormitory room revision sessions. Bronfenbrenner's terms show that the revision process may be induced by mesosystem interrelations that are developed, in turn, by the exosystem and macrosystem. Connections among contexts become salient to participants through ideological coherence. Horatio and his roommates may not have been aware of their shared participation in English 1, if they had not had the belief that writing well would enable them to succeed, and they might not have held this belief had it not been nearly part of the creed of their fraternity of which the student body president was a member. These mesosystem, macrosystem, and exostystem connections accumulate to form a vector-like force that pushed Horatio on to revise his papers.

However, Horatio seemed to lose interest in his composition course in the middle of the semester, missing 2 weeks of class. When the instructor asked him about the absences, he said he had been preoccupied with campaigning against Proposition 187 which would be on the California November ballet. In spite of his interest in this topic, his first draft of the fourth paper—a long research paper about illegal immigration in California—was a collage of quotations and statistics, unfocused and disorganized. It seemed to reflect a lack of understanding of the assignment itself. The instructor began to wonder whether he would pass English 1 because he still had to revise several of his early papers as well as finish the final research essay. Even after the instructor talked with him about his progress, he missed two more classes. The instructor felt he might be "lost," so she sent word to him, through another student who was his friend from Summer Bridge, that his research paper draft needed enormous revision.

Not just any distraction could have threatened Horatio's progress in the English 1 class; although he often joked about and compared notes with other students on parties and dorm soccer games, he always did his work. Rather, the very content of Proposition 187, which would deprive undocumented immigrants of many government services, threatened the macrosystem, the coherence of Horatio's ideological world. This ideology and Horatio's relationships and activities at the university were dialectically intertwined. When he had believed he belonged at the university and that he was entitled to this education, he participated in the class, he was a leader in small group work although his first drafts were extremely difficult to understand. With the specter of 187, Horatio disappeared even when he did come to class. He slouched often and slept when possible. The effect of Horatio's work with Proposition 187 made apparent just how tenuous was his sanguine belief that he belonged in college.

His paper on 187 contributed to his problems in the class. It did not motivate him to succeed in the course. In fact while writing it, he had unraveled his exosystem and macrosystem connections to the university itself. In the first draft the paper nervously jumped from one topic to another. Horatio began his critique of 187 by separating himself from "the immigrants." "Sure," he wrote "the immigrants are illegal but, who are we to turn a wounded person in hospital or an child of the education just because of there skin or ending surname?"

In the next paragraph he took an historical approach by writing "What happen or will happen with Proposition 187 is similar to the 1950s. Minorities has been consistently oppress. For instance,'Operation Wetback,' by which the INS formed in the 1950s." He concluded this section by writing "In my opinion, the U.S. uses minorities for there cheap labor and now there is a crisis, immigrants are scapegoats for government policy. History has proven this for itself." As the paper accumulated this historical evidence of discrimination and as Horatio connected that history to the present day context of Proposition 187, he also began to establish his affiliations with the "immigrants." He expressed his fears and vulnerability, "Being suspicious is having brown skin, dark hair, slanted eyes and an accent. To my knowledge if this initiative passes I will be a suspect and deported," and later in the same paragraph he added a parenthetical "(Take a look at me, I'd be the number one suspect)."

Horatio's instructor recognized that he had lost interest in being part of the class. Without membership in the class, it was unlikely that he would revise the paper, and without revision he would fail the course. She talked with him and persuaded him to revise. In the second draft Horatio only added three pages about the effects of Proposition 187 on children and the elderly who would be deprived of education and health care, respectively. He wrote, "This proposition doesn't make sense because for one they picking on the elderly. In my culture always I am to respest the elderly, I guess the American way does not have the same value and moral like me and my people." With these words, Horatio separated himself from U.S. culture, severed his affiliations with Americans and by implication with the university, its courses, and its uses of language.

His instructor again talked to Horatio about the draft asking him what he wanted to accomplish with this paper and who he thought he could or should influence and educate about Proposition 187. Once Horatio started to conceive of the paper as persuading an audience of college students, he was interested in revising once again. He began draft three with the phrase "College students who's voted for 187 do not understand its purposes and history." He reorganized it and added to the history section. In describing the present day situation of Mexican immigrants in the United States, he acknowledged the problems of illegal immigration. He wrote "It affects the United Farm Workers because their can't be a strong union if their are people who will work for less money" and then built an argument that Proposition 187 was not a reasonable solution to illegal immigration. In this third and final draft he ended with "I am totally against this proposition because the government is trying to do away with my people and I know that my people don't have a voice because they are immigrates. But my voice and many like me can be heard and when something is done we must join together." Revising this text was possible for Horatio because while he was writing he was renewing his affiliations both with "his people" and with the freshman composition course in which he was enrolled.

In the end his final research paper contained a whole argument that was well organized. Unfortunately he was only able to finish three drafts, and he did not have time to revise this paper the fourth and fifth times he would have needed to find and focus on the problems with mechanics and language conventions errors. His early papers were more polished than the final research essay, but in the final paper he had managed to sustain a cogent argument over eight pages. He passed the course with a C+.

Kaying

Kaying, an 18-year-old Hmong woman, began freshman composition with a very young baby. She lived with her husband near his family about 20 miles away from campus. Her husband was a student and thus provided her with a nascent mesosystem. Through the adjunct workshop for freshman composition and the other required tutoring groups for the EOP, she did have mesosystem connections but they were not salient for her. Unlike Luciana or Horatio she was not conscious of these affiliations as important to her education. She said "I talk to nobody." She went to school by bus, went to class, to the library to study and there she waited for her husband; then they went home.

Much like Luciana, Kaying had densely woven exosystems and macrosystems based in her family. Two of her five brothers had graduated from college. Although she did not see her brothers daily, she said she always felt their presence. She said that because of them she "understood what college was like." They helped her with study habits and "obstacles." Her parents wanted her to continue her education; they had worried about her "wildness" in high school so were pleased that she had married and was in college. Her mother-in-law took care of the baby so Kaying could go to school.

She talked very directly about her motivation as coming from her relationships and environment. "Sometimes I feel like I never want college" she said, but because her brothers "support her" she tried to do her work before it was due. She mentioned that she had just finished a paper for her history class 3 weeks before the due date. She expressed her reasons for working hard in school by saying "I study because I have to study" as if she had no choice or agency in her study habits. Because of the force of her mesosystems, exosystems, and macrosystems, Kaying studied, whether she wanted to or not.

Her motivation depended on her family and an ever present ideology about what would be good for her son, her culture, and her "people." She often judged her activities and actions by saying that they would be good or bad for "Hmong culture." Kaying wanted to become a teacher because this would "be good for [her] people." When she worried that she "doesn't have right stuff to be a teacher," she claimed her brothers, and Hmong culture, and Hmong people motivated her.

She deeply believed that because of schooling in a democracy with "a free market" she would achieve her most cherished goal: "most of all I do not want be poor" she told me over and over. This goal and the idea that financial security can be achieved through hard work in the United States was one she had been saturated with since she was 10 and her family came to the United States. Her parents moved several times in the United States to find work, especially the ever-elusive "good jobs." At the time of these interviews her father and mother were living in the East with relatives who had told them tales of extraordinary employment opportunities.

Kaying's motivation and literacy development were dialectically intertwined as she worked on her essays and revisions in her semester in freshman composition. The first assignment of the semester asked her to explore Edward Said's ideas about the Western media's representation and interpretation of the "Orient." The students were asked to think about a group they affiliated with and how this group was represented in the media. They were also asked to discuss and evaluate Said's explanation as to why misrepresentation occurs. Kaying's first try at the essay began with the statement "I don't think our belief will never change." She continued on, writing about cultural differences between Hmong and U.S. girls:

> Like the Hmong girls teach to be mature at a young age, responsible and help around the house. They suppose know how to be mother already. Now if you compare to American culture, there will be a lot of bias. And by this I tell you my past experience with this girl in high school. In high school, a lot of discrimination between Americans and Asians. She say Asians should go back to their own county ... That pissed me and I want to tell her. We have no choice to come here! I wanted to tell her alot. but I wasn't brave enough back then. If I told her, we fight. She get her friends after me and I not really interest in fight. Even if I

told her off, she's too ignorant. I just wish I could find her now and tell her everything I write here.

The draft went on to reiterate that there was much "bias in between U.S. culture and Hmong" because American girls do not do housework. "Now, the Hmongs would say Americans are lazy and that would be their bias. And the Americans would say that the Hmong doesn't let girls be teen at all. They will definitely different toward one another." In this same paragraph, however, she goes on to assert that she herself did not have to do "everything around the house" and she would not make her daughter "to cook and clean so soon. (If I had daughter.)"

Although Kaying did not appear to respond very directly to the assignment in her first draft, she did use literacy to assert the difference between the Hmong and U.S. cultures. She also wanted to communicate to Americans (the girls from high school) what they do not understand about Hmong people and culture. She never directly engaged with Said's ideas or the notion of representation, but she did understand his point to be that cultural differences create misunderstandings. The word bias seemed to contain many meanings for her—both racism and cultural difference, for example.

By asserting this cultural difference and using literacy to explain her people and her culture, she found a purpose for writing that would also strengthen her macrosystem and by implication the subsystems of which it was made. The draft connected her to the university (if only because it was written for a class) while it maintained her difference. She could use literacy to explain that difference, and in so doing reproduce and reinforce it. Importantly, the specific difference discussed here is that the Hmong people are hard working, expecting much from their teenagers, while the U.S. girls are lazy. Although Kaying uses this ideology of hard work to reproduce difference, in actuality it can and will become a macrosystem connection for her to the world of the university where many narratives emphasize the value of hard work.

The teacher recognized the potential in this draft and asked her to revise by using Said to explain why the U.S. girl does not understand the Hmong culture; Kaying was also asked to consider what she does not understand about U.S. culture and why. The instructor wrote in an end note to Kaying "use this paper to tell that girl what it is she needs to know." In the second draft, Kaying used Said to explain that our "bias" is created from "the way we were raised or the environment we were in." She wrote that Americans do not understand "why Hmong people are here because they help the Americans in the war." She eliminated any hint of her own emotional response to the U.S. girl. Gone was the specter of Kaying and the U.S. girl fighting. Instead she wrote that the girl should look to "history"; she should do research and find out "who really is on welfare."

In a revision, Kaying included several paragraphs about the history of the Hmong in the United States and wove in her own story about how her parents have migrated from place to place to find work. In effect, she revised her essay to approximate the academic tradition of using multiple sources to make an argument, while she retained the purposes she had established in the first draft—to communicate and reproduce her difference from Americans while she corrected cultural misunderstandings.

On the second draft, the teacher commented that she would like to see Kaying discuss an apparent contradiction that obfuscated her argument: that is, Kaying claimed "we will always believe what we believe" yet as she tells it, neither she nor her parents have adhered to the Hmong custom of making young girls do most of the housework. Instead of working with the contradiction—explaining it further, expanding on its implications and including them in her argument—Kaying simply eliminated the contradiction. She deleted the information about her family's attitude toward Hmong customs and added more examples of cultural "bias," not from her own life but from an article in the newspaper entitled "Racism in Redding." The article detailed an incident in which a Redding resident shouted racial slurs at some Southeast Asian children about being on welfare. Kaying said that when her teacher had asked her to "explain the part about her family," she had realized that her family was different from most Hmong in their attitude toward housework, and she did not want to talk about "difference in Hmong" because this would "not be good for Hmong people."

She included the article on Redding in this draft because she had realized "the draft needed to be longer and about the media" and she wanted to show that the "racism here was bad, all over" not only "in [her] own experience." She also paraphrased what Edward Said had written about how to overcome ethnocentricity and xenophobia. She did not agree with him and wrote again that although "the world would be a better place if we could change our believes, we will always believe what we believe. We can not change it." Again, Kaying insists on using her writing to reproduce her ties to the Hmong community. This is crucial if she is to stay motivated to work in school. By her fourth draft many (but certainly not all) of the grammatical errors had been worked out. In the adjunct workshop, and during a Writing Center appointment Kaying had also worked with the conventions of introducing Said's text and ideas (Said argues ...), and citation. She got assistance in editing her language for plural morphemes and verb endings.

Her final text (fourth or fifth draft) was a coherent argument about the sources and content of cultural misunderstandings between the Hmong and the Americans. She had used multiple sources, made a claim, and supported it with evidence. She had understood Said's argument and both agreed and disagreed with it. Her essay was still rough; her (lack of academic) vocabulary made it difficult for her to write elegantly, or in some cases very precisely, but the draft was "definitely passing" according to the instructor. Remarkably she was able to sustain her work on this paper through what seemed endless drafts, with her teacher unremittingly calling Kaying's attention to the same points—lack of clarity, contradictions, and lack of coherence. In this case the growing coherence in the paper topic and the purposes she had found for writing built her microsystems, exosystems, and macrosystems that in turn motivated her to write.

Implications of this Research

All the students in these case studies had strong macrosystems that instructed them that education, literacy, and good grades would guarantee good jobs and a good future. At one level, this macrosystem ideology pushed these students to revise their writing repeatedly.

Not to be forgotten, however, is the fact that macrosystems are comprised of material, physical, and social networks and connections at other levels in students' lives. The very structure of education through programs like Summer Bridge, learning communities, linked or blocked courses, service learning components, and adjunct workshops or tutoring, especially if and when the connections are salient for the students themselves, creates mesosystems. Additionally, the structure of activities can contribute to mesosystems, exosystems, and macrosystems. Through group work and collaborative assignments of various sorts, students connect. More subtly and perhaps more importantly is curriculum and the work it can do to motivate students through a nexus of context and textual function. For these students, for example, literacy development was contingent on the relationships among social and material networks and the topics, purposes and audiences of their texts. Horatio and Kaying worked on assignments through which they came to construct the history, present, and future of their relationship to the university and the United States. Finally it is Kaying who understood best what had happened to her writing. In our last interview, she said that "freshman writing had helped [her] a lot" because now she understood that everything she read and wrote affected her relationship to Americans and to her own culture. Knowing this, she said, made her reading and writing "not so hard to do."

REFERENCES

Bartholomae, D. (1985). *Inventing the university*. In E. Kintgen, B. Kroll, & M. Rose (Eds.), Perspectives on literacy (pp. 273–285). Carbondale: Southern Illinois University Press.

Bronfenbrenner, U. (1979). *The ecology of human development*. Cambridge, MA: Harvard University Press.

Farr, M. (1994). *En los does idiomas: Literacy practices among Chicano Mexicanos*. In B. Moss (Ed.), Literacy across communitites (pp. 1–9). Cresskill, NJ: Hampton Press.

Lewin, K. (1931). *Environmental forces in child behavior and development*. In C. Murchison (Ed.), A handbook of child psychology (pp. 15–17). Worcester, MA: Clark University Press.

Szwed, J. (1981). The ethnography of literacy. In E. Kintgen, B. Kroll, & M. Rose (Eds.), *Perspectives on literacy* (pp. 303–311) Carbondale: Southern Illinois University Press.

4 Distinguishing Incipient and Functional Bilingual Writers: Assessment and Instructional Insights Gained Through Second-Language Writer Profiles

Jan Frodesen
Norinne Starna
University of California, Santa Barbara

Problems with the validity of the single, holistically scored essay exam for assessing writing ability have been widely discussed in the literature on writing assessment (e.g., Hamp-Lyons, 1991; Huot, 1996; White, 1990; White, Lutz & Kamusikiri,1996), and alternative methods such as portfolios have been implemented increasingly, especially for ongoing assessment within institutions. Nevertheless, due to both time and funding constraints, many colleges and universities still rely almost exclusively on a single essay exam to assess the writing of entering students.

The University of California (UC) is no exception. Each year at testing centers throughout California, close to 20,000 graduating high school students who have been accepted into one of the nine UC campuses take the "Subject A," UC's version of the one-time assessment exam. In this 2-hour exam, students read a passage of 700 to 1,000 words concerning an issue considered accessible to freshmen and at a level of difficulty representative of readings required in beginning university courses. They then write an essay responding to a single topic about the passage. Most of the Subject A examinations are read in a single holistic scoring session at the Berkeley campus by composition and English as a Second Language (ESL) teachers from the UC campuses; raters also include instructors from the state's high schools and community colleges. Although the holistic scores do not determine placement into courses on the various campuses, a nonpassing score by two raters does require the student to take at least one preparatory writing course before freshman composition. In

addition, those nonpassing essays with significant nonnative English errors
are designated ESL, with confirmation by at least one ESL specialist. In the
first university-wide administration of the Subject A examination, held in
1987, almost two thirds (63.7%) of those who identified themselves as nonnative English speakers (NNES) did not pass the exam, as compared with less
than half (44.2%) of the native speakers (Frodesen, 1991). The essays of
many, although not all, of these NNES students were designated ESL.

Sent to the campuses where students have indicated intentions to enroll,
the nonpassing essays are reviewed and the writers placed into various preparatory courses. For campuses with an ESL program separate from the composition program, such as UC–Santa Barbara, where we teach, the ESL-designated nonpassing essays are reread, and available biodata about students are
considered by ESL and writing program instructors to determine whether a
student needs ESL instruction or should be placed into a mainstream writing
course.[1] Thus, some ESL-designated students will begin their university writing instruction in one of three levels of ESL; others, considered more advanced
in their second-language (L2) writing, will be placed into a mainstream preparatory writing course. As a last "check" on appropriateness of placements,
students in both ESL and mainstream courses write a first-day diagnostic essay to be compared with the Subject A exam performance, and changes are
made where warranted. Only in exceptional cases, however, are students
placed into mainstream courses asked to re-enroll in an ESL course, and even
in these cases, the student has a choice of remaining in that course or volun-
tarily switching to an ESL course.

Although administrators and instructors in both ESL and writing programs at our university take great care to ensure appropriate placements for
NNES, nagging doubts remain each quarter given the complexity of the immigrant ESL students' linguistic, educational, and cultural histories. In California, as in other states with large immigrant populations such as Texas,
Florida, and New York, university ESL and composition programs are encountering increasing numbers of students who are not easily characterized
as ESL students. Having immigrated to the United States in early adolescence
or even earlier, these students have spent years in mainstream classes in the
public schools. When they arrive at the university, two sources of discontent
may arise. On the one hand, students are dismayed to discover they have been
placed into ESL after having been mainstreamed in secondary school; some
even find themselves unable to exit university ESL courses and make the transition to mainstream composition. On the other hand, some composition instructors may also register dismay when encountering NNES with obvious
L2 writing characteristics among the native speakers in their writing courses.
In a few cases these instructors may, as Braine (1996) discussed in his study of
ESL students in mainstream classes, lament or resent the fact that ESL writers

---

[1]By *mainstream*, we mean preparatory (or developmental) writing courses for native speakers
as well as regular (freshman composition) writing courses. Some researchers, such as Braine
(1996) distinguish regular classes as mainstreaming in contrast to developmental
(nonmainstream).

demand a disproportionate amount of their time outside of class. Braine cited the rather chilling comment of one mainstream teacher on the first day of class, reported by two ESL students in interviews, that ESL students "soaked up" all her office hours (p. 99). From our experience, however, such reactions are quite rare. Typically, mainstream instructors are troubled by the uncertainty of how best to assist these L2 students in developing writing proficiency. Because mainstream instructors often lack knowledge of L2 acquisition processes and of linguistic features characterizing various stages of L2 writing proficiency, assessment and placement problems, unfortunately, but not surprisingly, are ongoing.

Mainstream composition instructors at our university were asked in an ESL program questionnaire to discuss their concerns regarding the nonnative students enrolled in their classes. Their responses confirmed that assessment and placement were significant areas of concern. Instructors were often not sure what level of linguistic control they should expect from NNES students.

These concerns are addressed by Valdés (1992) in "Bilingual Minorities and Language Issues in Writing." Citing writing research on bilingual students, she criticized the lack of proficiency assessment of non-English background students. Most studies she reviewed failed to measure the language competencies or proficiencies of the groups investigated. Valdés argued that it is crucial for educational institutions to establish criteria that will distinguish students who have not yet acquired fluency in English and need ESL instruction from those who may have some problems with standard English, but are beyond the realm of ESL. She referred to these two nonnative English groups as "incipient bilinguals" and "functional bilinguals," respectively.

Valdés (p. 104) characterized incipient bilingual students as those whose writing shows many grammatical "errors." These students, Valdés concluded, are still learners of English and should be placed into ESL courses, where they will receive specialized instruction. In contrast, functional bilingual students produce systematic "errors" that are ongoing and persistent. These errors, or nonnative-like forms that persist in speech or in writing long after a learner has acquired advanced proficiency, are often referred to as "fossilized elements" or "fossilizations." Some of these forms, such as past tense verbs or past participles with missing -ed endings, or present tense verbs lacking agreement with third-person singular subjects (including missing -s endings and use of "have" rather than "has"), are similar to those made by monolingual speakers of contact varieties of English. Valdés recommended that functional bilingual students should be treated as mainstream. In their mainstream composition courses, these students should receive instruction in identifying their fossilized forms and be given practice in editing.

Making these distinctions may, at times be a challenge for ESL instructors, especially with the long-term immigrant students who are entering universities in increasing numbers. But as Valdés reminds us, evaluating proficiency levels is even more difficult for inexperienced mainstream writing instructors who are constantly called on to make placement decisions. Current research on L2 writing assessment supports the notion that appropriate evaluation is critical and that measures intended for native English writers are often problematic for L2 writers. Hamp-Lyons (1996) contended that it is imperative for educators involved with NNES students to "find assessment methods and measures whose fairness to language minority test takers can be shown" (p. 226). As a placement tool, holistic scores of a single essay exam cannot make the kinds of distinctions about language errors to which Valdés referred. Still, the reality is that in many universities, this is the starting place for assessment. So the question is raised: Where do administrators and writing instructors go from there?

Huot (1996) stated that we need to explore alternatives to the traditional models of writing assessment, with their emphasis on generalizability. The assessment procedures he advocated would be "content rich and rely upon raters knowing as much as possible about the papers, the students, the purpose of the evaluation [and] the consequences of their decisions" (p. 563).

Although the alternative procedures Huot discussed are intended to replace large-scale assessment schemes, his proposals may also be applied to placement procedures following holistic scoring (e.g., rereadings of essays to identify specific language and rhetorical features) and to ongoing assessment of writers in composition courses. His recommendation that we know as much as possible about contexts and students seems especially relevant for NNES based on our experience and in light of Valdés' call for the need to characterize different types of bilingual writers and to investigate educational, linguistic, cultural, and social influences on bilingual learners' writing development. For the NNES immigrant students who enter mainstream composition classrooms, instructors need to find out as much as they can, within the constraints of their teaching contexts, about the students' first language (L1) as well as L2; literacy experience; the kinds of L2 education they received in their native countries and in U.S. schools, as well as their reactions to these experiences (including, of course, their experiences in university ESL programs prior to entering mainstream classrooms); the nature and extent of their L1 and L2 use, both written and spoken, outside of the writing classroom; their attitudes about themselves as L2 speakers and writers; and the investment they have in acquiring various types of writing proficiency for their academic and career goals. As Valdés noted, assumptions about learners' L2 proficiency cannot be based on just a few factors such as the language spoken at home or age of arrival in the United States.

Initially, we may need to make placement decisions based primarily on careful rereadings of essay exams and limited information about educational background, as well as other testing data such as SAT verbal scores. However, even in these contexts, mainstream composition instructors can develop greater awareness of language features that indicate learners who are still actively acquiring many of the features of academic written English in contrast to writing that reflects advanced levels of L2 proficiency.

In the following sections, we present profiles of two nonnative English writers, both of whom we have worked with in writing classrooms or tutorial courses over a number of terms and whom we have now known for almost their entire undergraduate careers. These students spent at least part of their high school years in the United States. We consider the educational, cultural, and social experiences our students shared with us through writing conferences, interviews, and their written texts. We also describe their experiences as they worked with us in ESL and mainstream courses. Through these profiles, we hope to provide insights into the linguistic criteria that may distinguish nonnative English writers at various stages in the acquisition of L2 proficiency and into the complex variables that may affect the level of proficiency at which some writers seem to fossilize.

For the two students, Alex and Min, the data consist of Subject A examination essays, drafts and papers from composition coursework, and interviews. Writing data for Alex covers 4 years, including a preuniversity summer enrichment program, three mainstream composition courses, and a letter he wrote after completion of his university composition requirements. Oral data consist of interviews with Alex and with the tutor who worked with him during his freshman year. The writing data for Min cover 7 years, including papers from 3 years of high school English and ESL with written comments and corrections by his teachers; drafts, final papers and final writing exams from two university ESL courses and two mainstream composition courses; and papers written for content courses from freshman through senior year. Oral data include two interviews with Min, which were audiotaped and transcribed and audiotapes of 20 tutorial sessions.

ALEX: A FUNCTIONAL BILINGUAL

Entering Profile

Alex's background resembles that of many first-generation Mexican American students whose families move back and forth between the United States and Mexico. Like his older brother and sister, Alex was born in Los Angeles and lived there with his immediate family and relatives—including his maternal grandmother—until he was 5 years old. At that time, his father and mother, who had emigrated to the United States from Mexico 8 years earlier for economic reasons, found themselves, once again, in a similar situation. No longer able to support a family of five in Los Angeles, Alex's father moved his wife back to Mexico along with their three U.S.-born children, while he continued to live and work in Los Angeles. As often as possible, he would visit his family, staying for extended periods to share the responsibility of raising five children—two additional younger daughters were born in Mexico. Although the separation lasted for almost 12 years and often created difficulties, Alex's memories of this time are generally positive.

At the age of 6, Alex enrolled in a private Catholic school, which he attended from Grades 1 to 6. There he learned to read and write in his native language. At the same time, knowing that it was important for his children to acquire fluency in English for future educational opportunities, Alex's father sent him to academic school, the equivalent of a private school in the United

States, three afternoons a week during Grades 4 and 5, to learn English. Alex recalls that he resented having to attend these classes, but in retrospect, he understands their significance in his ongoing L2 development. Having become more fluent in English while living in the United States, Alex's father, when he visited Mexico, would reinforce the English his children were learning in school. Spanish, of course, remained Alex's primary language in and outside of school. Alex explained that although his father encouraged him to learn English, he also stressed the importance of maintaining his Mexican identity through his language and culture.

After completing elementary school and transferring to public secondary school for Grades 7 through 9, Alex enrolled in classes that had been designed to teach English to native speakers. In reflecting on these classes, Alex describes them as "too easy," because from them, he learned only how to speak and write basic vocabulary, phrases, and simple sentences. By this time, Alex was on his way to becoming a highly motivated student who wanted to excel in all his courses—not just in math and science. By the end of Grade 10, his first year of preparatory school, Alex had decided that he wanted to attend college. Knowing that educational opportunities beyond preparatory school were financially prohibitive and highly competitive in Mexico, Alex moved back to Los Angeles at the age of 16 to live with his father and attend school.

After an initial assessment, Alex was enrolled in public school at the 10th-grade level and, given his limited practice with English at all levels, was assigned to ESL classes, which he continued to take until the end of 11th grade. He recalls these classes with enthusiasm and appreciation. As he stated in an interview, "I desperately wanted to understand [English] and apply it." With the primary goal of becoming a fluent speaker, reader, and writer of English, he did not resist studying and learning correct pronunciation, grammar, and vocabulary. He said that he loved his ESL classes, and described reading and writing about short stories as one of his favorite assignments. In addition, he praised his teachers, explaining that they not only challenged him to do well but also supported him when he became discouraged. Throughout his first year of ESL classes, Alex usually spoke Spanish outside of class when socializing with his Latino friends who were also enrolled in ESL classes. As they all became more proficient L2 speakers, however, English became their primary language at school in and outside the classroom. At home, he communicated with his family in Spanish. He also read Spanish newspapers and books, listened to Spanish music, and watched Spanish television. He recalls moving very comfortably between Spanish and English. Earning a 3.5 GPA, Alex graduated from high school with honors.

Initially, Alex's college plans were limited to attending either a junior college or 4-year state school in the Los Angeles area. He explained that in his senior year of high school he felt socially and financially unprepared to leave his family and community. However, with the encouragement of his English teacher along with the availability of openings for qualified minority students through UC's recruitment program, Alex applied to the UC system. He was not only accepted into UC, Santa Barbara (UCSB) but was awarded a

4-year academic scholarship, entering UCSB as a biology major with plans to attend medical school.

Entering Writing Assessment

Alex's freshman year got underway a few weeks before the term officially began when he enrolled in the Summer Transition Enrichment Program (STEP) at UCSB. Funded and administered by the Equal Opportunity Program (EOP) for minority students, STEP is designed to help freshman make the transition from high school to the university with greater ease. Along with taking classes in English, science, and math, students also attend seminars to prepare them for their first term at the university.

Placement in writing courses for STEP is based on the Subject A examination. Alex received a nonpassing score and was placed in a mainstream preparatory writing course, Writing 1. An analysis of Alex's exam supports the appropriateness of the initial writing assessment in STEP and subsequent placement in Writing 1.

For the Subject A examination, Alex responded to a passage by Stephen Jay Gould on the credibility of perception and memory. His writing shows a general understanding of Gould's argument and the ability to respond to the two-part prompt, which asked students to summarize Gould's thesis and to evaluate it. A five-paragraph essay supported with examples from personal experience, Alex's writing reveals his familiarity with the conventions of the academic essay. In addition to these rhetorical strengths, however, the exam includes problems that are common among developing writers who are native English speakers: an unfocused introduction, a lack of coherence within and between paragraphs, limited paragraph development, and illogical reasoning.

Alex's writing also reveals language problems at the word and sentence level that suggest L2 difficulties. These problems include errors in verb tense and form, word forms, idiomatic usage, and function words. The following sentences illustrate verb form and lexical errors:

> The brain can be looked at as a microcomputer that can stored millions of memories....

> Every memory goes to a vary specific bank of information in which it could be storage.

> So, I can say that some pictures can be storage in everyone's mind....

The two error types shown—a past tense (or past participle) ending on a verb following a modal auxiliary ("stored" after modal "can") and the word form error of using the noun *storage* as a verb—are, in our experience, common errors among advanced L2 writers. These word-level errors do not necessarily reflect a low level of overall proficiency in written English.

Some of the most common errors that occur in Alex's writing involve nonidiomatic phrasing, including incorrect prepositions and nonidiomatic forms. Frequently misusing "in" and "on," a common problem for native speakers of Spanish, in one example he writes: "I saw something like a man standing in the way and carrying two buckets on each hand." In another sentence he substitutes "in" for "on" in the compound preposition "depending on." Evidence of problems with idioms include the phrase "All at suddenly" instead of "all of a sudden," and "it came up to my mind" instead of "it came to my mind."

Although Alex received a nonpassing score on his Subject A exam, he was not given an ESL designation. His errors on the exam are consistent with those Valdés identified as features of functional bilingual writers: systematic, few in number, and often involving problems with idiomaticity. In addition to these characteristics, Alex's prose demonstrated a fluency often lacking in the writing of L2 writers who have not yet mastered a variety of complex sentence structures.

As we expected, the informal writing Alex completed in STEP reflected the level of syntactic control required of writers in a mainstream writing course. The excerpt below from an in-class writing illustrates his writing competency:

How many high school graduates go to college and find themselves completely lost in the new environment? Obviously, the number is huge. Is there any way we can help them so they can make adjustments before classes begin? Yes, there is a program called the Summer Transition Enrichment Program (STEP) created by the EOP office to help students in this transition.

University Writing Development and Ongoing Assessment

In the fall, Alex enrolled in Starna's preparatory writing class (Writing I), which was offered through the Program of Intensive English (PIE), a component of the writing program. PIE's three-course writing sequence provides continuity and consistency in writing instruction. Its structure gives students the choice of staying with the same instructor, tutor, and classmates as they move through the sequence.

In PIE Writing I, students completed an assignment sequence from *Ways of Reading* by Bartholomae and Petrosky (1990). The first assignment involved writing a draft about a personal experience they find puzzling and would like to understand better or differently. This draft was the only paper for the course, but one that students continued to reflect on through rereading and rewriting. They also read essays about the reading and writing processes they enacted. For example, after reading about Adrienne Rich's "Writing as Re-Vision," students applied some of the revision strategies she outlines to revise their own narratives.

Between the first draft of the course and the final narrative, Alex's writing demonstrated significant changes in organization, paragraph development, and coherence. Changes also occurred in language accuracy at the sentence level. In the early weeks of the course, Alex's informal writing—drafts, reading logs and in-class writing—revealed distinct patterns of error such as subject–verb agreement. In a response to John Berger's "Ways of Seeing," he writes: "Seeing is a factor that *help* us to understand" and "I think the teacher should use certain techniques which help the students *memorizes* the material...." Once Alex became aware of his patterns of errors, he met weekly with his tutor or scheduled conferences with his instructor to discuss and practice editing strategies to identify and correct his errors. His peer editing groups, which included both native and nonnative speakers, provided a third source of instruction. As a careful reader of other students' writing, Alex learned to transfer this skill to identify problems in his own writing.

At the end of Writing 1, although fewer errors appeared in Alex's writing, they had not disappeared completely; this can be seen in an excerpt from his retrospective on his reading and writing development:

> Finally, I will examine what brought about these changes on my writing. The most important factor that motivate me to improve my skills were the self analysis. The self-analysis helped me expose my topic more openly.

Continued problems with idiomatic usage, such as "on my writing" instead of "in my writing," and verb tense (the base form "motivate" rather than a past or present perfect form) reflect persistent patterns of errors typical of functional bilinguals. Starna read beyond the errors to evaluate his writing for its strengths and progress; she also spent conference time helping Alex develop editing skills. Rhetorically and syntactically, his writing at the end of the course compared favorably to the writing of native speakers in the class. That term, he received a B+ in both his writing class and a Chicano Studies course that required a number of writing assignments.

To satisfy his university writing requirement, Alex completed Starna's Writing 2 and Writing 3 courses; he earned an A- in both. A review of his writing in these courses revealed the progress made between them, which can be attributed at least in part to Alex's decision to remain with Starna and his tutor. Already familiar with abilities, they could provide him with consistent, uninterrupted instruction. Although he excelled in these courses, Alex's writing continued to have nonnative features after he completed the sequences. In a letter to Starna at the end of his sophomore year requesting a recommendation for a year-abroad program to which he was applying, he wrote: "I feel that without your wisely advice and concerns on my academic studies, I wouldn't be able to accomplish my goals." However, these apparently fossilized forms did not prevent Alex from successfully completing writing-intensive courses in his major or from participating in a competitive summer internship program in biology that required students to write an upper level research report.

As Alex's writing profile reveals, a variety of factors contributed to his development as a writer: His linguistic, cultural, and educational backgrounds along with the appropriate assessment, placement, and instruction in his writing courses are among them. However, Alex's personal commitment, beginning with his early L2 experiences, to become more proficient in both spoken and written English, is certainly one of the most notable factors.

MIN: MAKING THE TRANSITION

Entering Profile

Emigrating from the People's Republic of China with his mother and older sister in 1987 at the age of 13, Min arrived in Los Angeles speaking almost no English; in his native country he had learned the English alphabet and a few words. Although his sister knew a little English, his mother, like Min, spoke only Chinese. Min's father, who was in ill health at the time, remained in China. Although Min is a native speaker of Taisan, a dialect that he describes as similar to Cantonese, he also learned to speak Mandarin fluently between the ages of 5 and 10.

In Los Angeles, the family settled into a Chinese community with relatives, including Min's grandparents, who had been in the United States for about 10 years. During his first year in their new environment, Min did not attend school because, according to him, he had arrived too late to start the new school year; he did, however, accompany his uncle, a college student, to a local community college on numerous occasions; there he often wandered around the library.

Unlike Alex's experience, Min's first years in a U.S school, as he recalls them, seem at odds with the engaged scholar he had become by the time he entered the university. Enrolled in public school at the eighth-grade level, Min was put into an ESL track where he would remain for the next 3 years. Learning English during his first year of school was not a positive experience. He does not recall it as being too difficult; he "just didn't like it." Nor, later on, did he enjoy reading most of the assigned books in his ESL courses. The culture was strange to him; he "got lost." Although he excelled (at least by the school's standards) in this strange new environment, receiving As in his ESL courses, Min had little interest in developing English skills. His primary interest in junior high school was playing basketball with his Chinese friends, the only ones at school with whom he could communicate well.

Min's attitude toward learning English changed when, in 10th grade, he discovered he was unable to get into a biology course because his English proficiency was too low. In high school, Min made more of an effort to improve his English, actually enjoyed some of his literature courses, and took considerable pride in the papers he had written. He still has many of his high school papers that he brought with him to the university. His grades on these papers range from Cs to As, with comments such as "Good insights!" and "Good use of quotes." However, as Min recalls, neither he nor his teachers paid much attention to his grammatical problems. Although his high school papers do show some evidence of corrections and a few grammar notes (e.g., "unclear verb tense"), the teachers in his mainstream classes, according to Min, "just give points on ideas; they don't correct grammar." As for social interactions during high school, Min had a few friends who were native English speakers but continued to associate mostly with Chinese speakers and to speak mainly Chinese outside the classroom.

At the end of Min's senior year of high school, certain aspects of his educational and social profile resemble those of many NNES who are placed into ESL rather than mainstream composition at our university. First of all, he had received all of his secondary education in the United States, starting out in ESL but progressing to mainstream English during his last few years. Second, most of his social contacts were with those who spoke his native language; thus, English was for him primarily an academic language, the language that formed his student identity. Third, although he was an excellent high school student, his SAT verbal score of 300 placed him among those considered "at risk" for academic success in a research university. Finally, his Subject A examination had received an ESL designation from raters along with a nonpassing score. Two factors—length of U.S. residency and SAT verbal score—along with a close rereading of his placement essay on campus by two ESL composition specialists resulted in a placement into the highest level ESL course rather than in a mainstream basic writing course.

Entering Writing Assessment

Min's Subject A exam, a response to a passage by Wendell Barry about the satisfaction gained through hard work, revealed a writer who had some understanding of the passage's main points and was able to draw on background knowledge to support his agreement with it. Min's essay also showed his ability to respond more or less appropriately to a prompt, in this case, a two-part question asking writers to state how Barry defined satisfaction and to give their view on the topic. His introduction, although only a few sentences, directly addresses both questions. Not strictly speaking a five-paragraph essay (two short paragraphs rather than one comprise his conclusion), it nevertheless has that genre's structure, including three examples drawn from his personal experience.

Min's essay does, however, also fit Valdés' category of having many errors, especially when we consider its brevity (412 words).[2] By "many," we refer not only to numbers but the varieties of language errors in his essay, which include word forms, verb forms and tense, subject–verb agreement, article usage, noun number, word choice and sentence structure. Some errors are repeated a number of times, suggesting they are not "careless mistakes"; for example, the noncount nouns *food* and *work* are repeatedly expressed as plural forms: *foods* and *works*.

---

[2]In Frodesen's (1991) study of 60 nonpassing ESL essays written by native speakers of Chinese, Korean, and English, the average number of words was 534.6. The 20 Chinese writers did, however, have the lowest average mean of all groups, nonnative and native alike, in the 100-essay database.

The two types of errors that provide the strongest evidence that Min would benefit from ESL instruction are the word choice and sentence structure problems. Consider the following excerpts. The first opens the essay; the other begins a paragraph describing the last of Min's personal examples:

> [Barry] attempted to explain his view toward the products of the future that was spoiling people not to do their necessary work. (*opening of essay*)

> One time in June that was the last day month for school. It was hot that the radio reported the outdoor temperature was 98°. The sun light liked hot arrows shot into people's skin. (*personal example*)

In the first excerpt, Min takes on the challenging task of summarizing in one sentence the central rhetorical act of the Barry passage. While substituting "allowing" for "spoiling" would create a collocation that worked grammatically, the substitution would not adequately convey Min's interpretation of Barry's viewpoint. The second excerpt shows difficulties with clause structure that occurred frequently in Min's university writing during his first two quarters: an incomplete understanding of the function of "that" to introduce complements and comparative structures. Min's phrasing in these excerpts and in other parts of his essay indicated to us a writer who lacked the language resources to express his ideas clearly in English. Comments that Min offers about his first-quarter university writing experience in an interview 4 years later support this evaluation:

> At first I think I have a lot to say but I cannot say it, you know, cannot express just the signal in—or whatever is in my brain is not just Chinese or English, it's just a mix. I want to express right but it just don't come out the way I expect it.

In addition to evidence of developing discourse level competence in writing, his essay, like Alex's, shows many of the problems common in the compositions of developing native English writers: a lack of elaboration in both the introduction and conclusion, supporting examples that are introduced by narrative rather than generalizations that would signal controlling ideas of paragraphs, a lack of transitions or subordination in some places to connect ideas within paragraphs and across examples, and inappropriate structuring of "old" and "new" information within sentences. There has been much discussion in ESL composition and contrastive rhetoric literature about the difficulty of judging whether rhetorical structures in nonnative English essays that differ from those essays written by experienced native English writers can clearly be attributed to transfer from native language or should be regarded as developmental difficulties. Mohan and Lo (1985) argued that analyses of classical and modern Chinese texts do not support claims of marked differences between Chinese and English written organizational patterns (e.g., Cai, 1999, cited in Connor, 1996; Kaplan, 1966; Matalene, 1985; Shen, 1989).

A growing body of research has contributed to identifying differences between Chinese and English rhetoric within specific genres; however, there is also agreement among researchers that identifying such contrastive features is very complex, especially with the increasing cross-cultural interaction among members of the same academic disciplines (Connor, 1996). Although a knowledge of the cultural orientations that may influence L2 writers is extremely valuable for mainstream and ESL classroom teachers working with these students, such information may be less useful for the placement of immigrant secondary students based on a single piece of writing. In other words, evaluators must be careful about designating ESL rhetorical features that may also characterize native English writing. As Benson et al. (1992) noted, "The issue of developmental learning is compounded by ESL students who have been educated in U.S. schools and sometimes have the combined difficulties of L2 and developmental students" (p. 70). Based on these considerations, it is primarily from evidence of linguistic difficulties in his essay, in addition to his length of residency and SAT verbal score, that we regard Min's placement into ESL composition, rather than into mainstream composition, as an appropriate one.

University Writing Development and Ongoing Assessment

In the first quarter of his freshman year, Min enrolled in the ESL composition section taught by Frodesen. This course was similar in some ways to the mainstream preparatory course in that students work on multiple drafts of essays based on readings, interact with peers in student response groups, and meet with the instructor in conferences. It also offered instruction in the kinds of grammatical and vocabulary problems that advanced learners of ESL experience in academic writing, including considerable editing practice in identifying and correcting errors in drafts, and provided specialized tutorial assistance. During the first weeks of the course, Min's high level of class participation was marked by thoughtful contributions to class discussion and enthusiasm about the writing process, but also showed significant problems in English pronunciation. At first, these pronunciation problems suggested a somewhat lower English proficiency level than Min actually had; as it turns out, he has a slight hearing disability, which apparently prevented him from distinguishing many sounds in his acquisition of spoken English. Min's hearing problem, along with the tendency for native speakers of Chinese to slight medial and final consonant sounds in English words, affected his interactions with other students.

During his first quarter of ESL, Min's most noticeable writing development between drafts and final papers submitted for his portfolio involved rhetorical features rather than language use. He engaged enthusiastically in conferences that concerned content and organization and produced final papers that were significant improvements over his first drafts. For example, in the second draft of his first paper, a literacy autobiography, he had extensively revised a description of how, as a young boy, he had been inspired to read a long classical Chinese novel after listening to a serialized radio story about one of the characters, named Monkey Su. But many of the structural errors persisted, with fragmented sentences such as "Monkey Su, a radio series story that I really enjoyed," and a high frequency of word-level errors as evidenced by the following description: " ... I was totally attractive by the action and character of Monkey Su. I paid special attention to the word that used to describe him."

Although Min completed faithfully all assignments that involved editing for grammatical and lexical errors, and he responded, with corrections, to the individualized feedback on errors in drafts, he seemed largely unconcerned and uninterested with the linguistic aspects of his writing other than vocabulary and idioms. He resisted repeated instructor recommendations to work with the class ESL tutor who had been assigned to the section from the campus tutorial center. The first time he was asked to meet with the tutor, during the beginning of the quarter, he responded that his roommate would "help" him instead. Told that having a roommate proofread and correct his errors was not an acceptable source of writing assistance because it would not help him identify and edit his own errors, Min refrained from getting corrections from his roommate but still would not work with a tutor.

By quarter's end, it seemed that Min was resistant to recognizing how significantly his grammatical problems distracted readers from his content. In retrospect, the resistance seems more a reflection of both Min's general confidence in himself as a good writer, stemming from his high school experience, and his lack of awareness of how his language inaccuracies affected reader comprehension. In subsequent interviews he described good writing in terms of knowing the subject and being able to take a stance about it. Although our research did not include formal investigation of Min's metacognitive model of writing, his descriptions, in interviews, of his concepts of good writing, combined with information he provided about teacher feedback on his writing in high school (primarily positive with little attention to language problems) helped us to understand better the nature of his writing development at the university and his general lack of attention to his language problems. In turning in his final in-class writing exam for the course, Min offhandedly told Frodesen that he did not have time to proofread it, even though she had previously emphasized in class how important it was for students to leave time for careful proofreading and correction of errors on the final to demonstrate their progress in language accuracy.

At the end of the quarter, Min turned in a portfolio of four essays (including drafts and final papers) and journal entries. Course grades (pass/no pass) and promotion to the next level are determined by portfolio assessment in which each student's portfolio is read by his or her instructor and several other ESL instructors. Although Min passed the course, he was not promoted to the mainstream composition course in the writing program because of the frequency and nature of language problems that persisted.

Disappointed but not discouraged by his failure to be promoted, Min turned his attention the next quarter to improving his linguistic competence in writing. He became a "convert" to working on his writing with tutors, a habit he retained through his senior year for every course that had a writing requirement. During this second quarter, in addition to repeating the ESL course with a different instructor, Min worked in one-on-one sessions with Frodesen twice a week to identify and edit grammatical and lexical problems in drafts and other writing assignments for his composition course. He worked with a tutor from the campus tutorial center on content development and organization 1 hour a week. On ESL program review of his portfolio and the progress he had made in developing editing strategies at the end of the quarter, he was promoted to the writing program.

Evidence for Min's successful transition to mainstream writing courses may be seen in the texts he produced, in comments from interviews with his composition instructor (the same one for both Writing 1 and Writing 2), and in his course grades: A- and A. Min's final exam for the first writing course demonstrates, along with his continued development of rhetorical skills, the development of syntactic complexity and a reduction in the frequency and types of errors, especially those in sentence structure. An excerpt from Min's Writing 1 final exam is given here:

> "The End of Play" is adapted from Marie Winn's book *Children without Childhood*. In this passage, she claims that "the old forms of play no longer seem to provide children with enough excitement and stimulation." She says that today's children have substituted television viewing and video games, and that they don't play doll, toy-soldier, jump-rope, and ball-bounce anymore.
>
> Base on my own experiences, and observations, however, I don't agree with her claims. Children are still childlike. I think today's children like doll play, toy-soldier play, and jump-rope play as well as television viewing and video games.

In reviewing Min's writing history at the university, we might ask on what basis we can claim that Min's placement in ESL was appropriate, and that his ESL course and tutorial work helped him make a successful transition to mainstream composition; that is, how do we know that his development of academic writing competence would not have been similar had he been placed into a mainstream course to begin with? Could we not also, from another perspective, view him as simply using an accommodationist coping strategy (Leki, 1995) in the face of those holding the gatekeeping power after he had been kept back in the ESL program? It is, of course, impossible to know what Min's writing would look like now had he not been placed into ESL, but we can hypothesize several things based on what we learned about his educational background and his beliefs about writing and about himself as a writer. Because he had been given little feedback on language problems in high school and because his concept of good writing at that time had little to do with linguistic accuracy, it is likely that Min would have paid even less attention to his grammatical problems other than asking a friend or roommate to "correct" his papers. Even an understanding mainstream composition instructor (which he did have) would have been, if not overwhelmed by the variety of errors, short of time and most likely the expertise to address them. In retrospect, it seems that one of the greatest benefits Min might have reaped from experience in ESL was his nonpromotion in that it motivated him to seek tutorial assistance, which he said he found extremely worthwhile throughout his college career. At the tutorial center, he worked consistently with one tutor, a graduate student, on papers for a number of courses with writing requirements. In addition, we can infer that Min regarded the assistance he got in ESL as valuable from the fact that he enrolled during his senior year for noncredit-bearing ESL tutorial courses to work on writing and oral skills in preparation for pharmacy graduate school interviews.

Implications for Placement, Ongoing Assessment, and Writing Instruction

After the initial placement of second language learners in either ESL or mainstream writing courses, the one-time assessment exam has served its purpose; however, the process of assessment and placement is ongoing. Based on our experiences, the recommendations that follow can be made.

Student Information. Using a questionnaire, at the beginning of each term, ESL and composition instructors gather information concerning students' linguistic and academic background, including ESL and writing courses completed. We suggest that instructors schedule conferences with students using the questionnaires as a springboard for discussion. In addition, an autobiography assignment focused on language and educational issues can provide insight into students' self-concepts as writers and their cognitive models of good writing.

Teacher In-Service Training. On campuses with ESL programs, articulation between ESL and mainstream composition in the form of coordinated meetings or workshops can help mainstream composition instructors understand the cultural, social, and educational influences that shape the writing of NNES. If opportunities exist for reading groups, as they do at our universities, composition teachers could read and discuss current research on these topics, such as McKay and Wong's (1996) case studies of junior high school Chinese students' writing development and Spack's (1997) cross-cultural, longitudinal study of a Japanese student acquiring academic literacy at a U.S. university. Workshops can also assist instructors in identifying some of the language problems, such as kinds of verb errors or clause structure errors that often distinguish developing bilingual writers from stabilized, functional bilingual writers and in providing classroom and conferencing strategies for helping both of these types of writer further develop academic language proficiency.

Continuity Between ESL and Writing Programs. On campuses where students enter mainstream composition courses from ESL programs, ESL and Writing Program instructors should meet to discuss student writing and placement decisions. Summary reports, and, if possible, portfolios, should accompany students when they make the transition from ESL to mainstream classes.

Course Design.   When possible, programs should design course sequences that allow for the continuity of instruction, assessment, and further placement. As North (1996) maintained, "we must make it possible for teachers to work with students often ... to gain a grounded sense of what happens with and to them as writers" (p. 156). In this way, functional bilingual writers have a better opportunity to learn and practice the kinds of strategies they need to develop further their academic language proficiency.

Support Services.   Recognizing the need for individualized instruction to help L2 learners develop their academic language proficiency, composition programs should establish and maintain appropriate tutorial support. If possible, students should meet with the same tutor throughout writing sequences. In addition, tutors and instructors should meet regularly to update the progress of students and make instructional recommendations.

The L2 writer profiles we have presented in our study underscore the complexity of acquiring academic written competence in a second language. They also demonstrate that, for composition instructors, some awareness of L2 writers' linguistic and educational backgrounds is important for placement decisions and critical for appropriate instruction. Although instructors cannot be expected to diagnose exactly where a student may be on the continuum representing incipient and functional bilingual stages of L2 development (in some cases, an accurate assessment seems possible only in retrospect when we can see that a student's level has remained stable), they can become more sensitive to the range of differences among bilingual writers through knowledge of their students' literacy experiences and through a better understanding of language features that reflect differing levels of L2 acquisition in academic contexts.

REFERENCES

Bartholomae, D., & Petrosky, A. (1990). *Ways of reading: An anthology for writers, 2nd ed.* Boston: Bedford, St. Martin's Press.

Benson, B., Deming, M., Denzer, D., & Valeri-Gold, M. (1992). A combined basic writing/English as a L2 class: Melting pot or mishmash? *Journal of Basic Writing, 11*(1), 58–74.

Braine, G. (1996). ESL students in first-year writing courses: ESL versus main-stream classes. *Journal of L2 Writing, 5*(2), 91–107.

Cai, G. (1999). Texts in contexts: Understanding Chinese students' English compositions. In C. R. Cooper & L. Odell (Eds.), *Evaluating writing* (2nd ed, pp. 279–297). Urbana, IL: National Council of Teachers of English.

Connor, U. (1996). *Contrastive rhetoric: Cross-cultural aspects of second-language writing.* New York: Cambridge University Press.

Frodesen, J. (1991). Aspects of coherence in a writing assessment context: Linguistic and rhetorical features of native and non-native English essays. *Dissertation Abstracts International, 52*(1), 150A.

Hamp-Lyons, L. (1991). The writer's knowledge and our knowledge of the writer. In L. Hamp-Lyons (Ed.), *Assessing second language writing in academic contexts* (pp. 57–68). Norwood, NJ: Ablex.

Hamp-Lyons, L. (1996). The challenges of second-language writing assessment. In E. White, W. Lutz, & S. Kamusikiri (Eds.), *Assessment of writing: Politics, policies, practices* (pp. 226–240). New York: The Modern Language Association of America.

Huot, B. (1996). Toward a new theory of writing assessment. *College Composition and Communication, 47,* 549–566.

Kaplan, R. B. (1966). Cultural thought patterns in intercultural education. *Language Learning, 16,* 1–20.

Leki, I. (1995). Coping strategies of ESL students in writing tasks across the curriculum. *TESOL Quarterly, 29,* 235–260.

Matalene, C. (1985). Contrastive rhetoric: An American writing teacher in China. *College English, 47,* 789–808.

McKay, S., & Wong, C. S. (1996). Multiple discourses, multiple identities: Investment and agency in second-language learning among Chinese adolescent immigrant students. *Harvard Educational Review, 66,* 577–608.

Mohan, B., & Lo, W. A. (1985). Academic writing and Chinese students: Transfer and developmental factors. *TESOL Quarterly, 19,* 515–534.

North, S. (1996). Upper-division assessment and the postsecondary development of writing abilities. In E. White, W. Lutz, & S. Kamusikiri (Eds.), *Assessment of writing: Politics, policies, practices* (pp. 148–157). New York: The Modern Language Association of America.

Shen, F. (1989). The classroom and the wider culture: Identity as a key to learning English composition. *College Composition and Communication, 40,* 459–466.

Spack, R. (1997). The acquisition of academic literacy in a L2: A longitudinal case study. *Written Communication, 14,* 3–62.

Valdés, G. (1992). Bilingual minorities and language issues in writing. *Written Communication, 9,* 85–136.

White, E. (1990). Language and reality in writing assessment. *College Composition and Communication, 41*, 187–200.

White, E., Lutz, W., & Kamusikiri, S. (Eds.). (1996). *Assessment of writing: Politics, policies, practices*. New York: Modern Language Association of America.

5 Language Identity and Language Ownership: Linguistic Conflicts of First-Year University Writing Students

Yuet-Sim D. Chiang
Mary Schmida
University of California at Berkeley

How can I give myself an American identity if I cannot even feel connected to the American language itself? By saying connected, I mean the feeling of owning the language and, therefore having full authority over it. It does not matter how frequently I use English, somehow I can never feel that I own it.

—Hai Nguyen

I am a native speaker of English because English is the language I know best.

—Peter Mack

I communicated with my sisters at home only through English in the midst of mom yelling, "Speak Korean! Are you Korean?"

—Jane Kim

Now, the only time I speak Vietnamese is to my parents. Unfortunately, I don't talk to them much, only when necessary; it's not very often that I speak their native tongue. I speak English fluently now and this is the reason why I don't talk to my parents very often.

—Christine Nguyen

Recently, a body of research has emerged that views language and literacy acquisition from a broad-based sociocultural perspective; a perspective that seeks to explain success or failure of learning from within a social and political context in which the language learning occurs (Lantolf, 1996; Peirce, 1995; Rampton, 1995; Siegal, 1996). It is within this theoretical framework that we align ourselves.

Our study is somewhat different than those conducted by researchers before us, however, in that this study deals *not* with immigrant populations learning the language of the dominant society, but with U.S. born children of immigrant parents who must define and negotiate the boundaries of language and identity.

Despite this new trend in considering the construction of identity in language and literacy acquisition, however, there is still a shortage of research-based studies that specifically examine the conflicting constructions of English literacy, language identity, and native language loss among speakers of non-English language background (NELB). The lack of study is not coincidental; rather, we argue that it is a culmination of several factors that include: (a) the traditional and unchallenged division of native and nonnative speakers, (b) an oversimplification of English learning at the college level into arbitrary categories such as (mainstream) English and English as a second language (ESL), and (c) a lack of theoretical discussion of the literacy practices of language users caught on the language borderlands of these three subcategories.

Although the linguistic gaps between first language (L1) learning and native language loss have been documented by linguists at a macro level, and acknowledged by leading Asian American writers (e. g., Fong-Torres, 1994; Tan, 1989) at a personal level, the social, cultural, and emotional tensions of the disharmony have yet to be framed carefully within the theoretical and pedagogical frameworks of applied linguistics studies.

THE STUDY

The Institution: College Writing Programs

This year-long study was conducted during the fall semester 1995 and the spring semester 1996 within the College Writing Programs (CWP) at the University of California (UC), Berkeley, where both researchers were instructors. The aim and scope of the CWP, as stated in the college writing handbook, is to help students ground their own literacy within the demands of the larger language community, while simultaneously helping them to develop fluency and control over their own language skills. In both the reading and writing activities, students' language experiences are an integral part of the classroom discourse. This six unit, one-semester course, College Writing 1A, fulfills the Subject A requirement as well as English 1A. Students who pass this course with a C or better may enroll directly in an English 1B course.

All freshmen entering the UC, Berkeley must fulfill an English proficiency requirement which is called the Subject A requirement. Students can meet the Subject A requirement before coming to Berkeley by passing the university's writing proficiency Subject A essay exam, which involves reading a short selection and writing an essay within 3 hours. Students who receive a combined score of 6 or below (out of a possible 12 points) must take College Writing 1A.

The Participants

In the state of California, the Asian population of NELBs is predicted to increase from 5.2 million in 1976 to 8.3 million in 2000, a jump of 36% (Oxford-Carpenter, Pol, Lopez, Stupp, Gendell, & Peng, 1984). Within the CWP, where this study was conceived and conducted, Asian American students make up approximately 56% of the student population (Simons, Perrow, Stritikus, Schmida, & Ponte, 1997). Because of these figures, this study was limited to Asian American students.

Although statistically it appears that the Asian population has maintained its home language (50% of the Asian American students in our study reported that they speak their ethnic language at home, vs. only 15% of the Chicano students), these categories do not tell the true story. It was through student interviews that the reality of language loss and the tension between linguistic identity and language ability emerged.

Research Questions

This study focused on the following questions:

1. How are the boundaries among English literacy, language identity, cultural identity, and native (heritage) language loss manifested, defined, and maintained?
2. What are the social, cultural, and emotional consequences/implications of the phenomena of language use and language identity for this particular linguistic group?
3. How do NELB students negotiate between the borders of English language use and L1 (e.g., Chinese) identity?
4. What is the impact of the disharmony among language use, language identity, and language ownership on their development as English language users?

Stages of Study

This study was conducted in two main stages. Stage 1 consisted of pretesting the survey questions that came out of an analysis of students' literacy experiences from Chiang's class. This student information was gathered over a period of two academic years (1995 and 1996) by compiling students' "Literacy Life History" essays, writing in which students examine their own literacy journeys. *Literacy journey* in this context refers to the students' relationships with literacy and language, both written and spoken. Twenty-five questions were posed to the students as writing prompts in this assignment, and included both open-ended questions (Writing is:____; English is:____;) as well as more directed questions (When were you first aware of using language? Who were the people involved? What is good writing?). The survey questions were later refined and then administered to the larger group of 471 students enrolled in any of the 14 sections of College Writing 1A.

The answers given by the students in the large survey were examined and from those, 20 randomly selected students who reported that they were Asian American were chosen to participate in individual open-ended interviews with the researchers. These taped interviews lasted anywhere from 1 to 2½ hours.

DATA ANALYSIS

Data analyzed consisted of responses from surveys from this section (termed *general response 1*), students' written responses in the survey, detailed transcriptions from the 20 interviews, and students' writing portfolios.

Method of Analysis

The constant comparative method outlined in Bogdan and Biklen (1982) was used in the analysis of the collected data. The constant comparative method allowed for the delimiting of the ongoing hypotheses in which tentative theories were generated and which, in turn, were either rejected or supported by the collected data, for example, surveys versus literacy biographies versus personal essays versus interviews.

Data collected from the program-wide written survey were coded quantitatively when appropriate; the open-ended survey and interview questions were coded according to themes that emerged from the students' responses. Themes included such categories as: emotional attachment to English, dominance of English in society, notions of what it means to be a nonnative or a native speaker of a language, code-switching, English as a tool, bilingualism, definitions of self, and cultural and linguistic bonds to a language.

Of the students surveyed, 60% of the Asian American students reported that they were nonnative English speakers (NNES), and 91% reported they were bilingual according to their responses on the survey. Interestingly, although 91% of the students designated themselves as bilingual, only 37% reported they spoke both their ethnic (heritage) language and English at home. And among the 40% of the Asian American students who labeled themselves as native speakers of English, only 28% of those same students reported learning English as a first language. What this points to is that 12% of the 40% students who labeled themselves as native speakers of English actually began speaking English as a *second* language (L2), not as a first language. Perhaps these students label themselves as native English speakers because they think that their primary language—the language of school and economic success in the United States—is and has been English.

RESEARCH FINDINGS

"The act of learning language[,] is also learning the culture through language. The semantic system which he is constructing becomes the primary mode of transmission of the culture" (Halliday, 1975, p. 66).

The scope of this chapter does not allow us to address the multilayered issues of language, identity, and literacy that have emerged from the study. Instead, we devote our discussion to a dominant theme captured in the study; namely, the conflicts between linguistic identity and linguistic ability, and how these conflicts are manifested in students' self-definitions of the following categories: bilingual identity versus bilingual literacy, native versus non-native speaker, and cultural identity versus linguistic identity.

Bilingual Identity Versus Bilingual Literacy

By the students' own definition, a *bilingual individual* is one who *identifies* with a language other than English. In other words, their self-definition does not necessitate an ability to speak, read, and write in their heritage language, but rather a traditional cultural *affiliation* with the heritage language. Throughout the study, we note that the students' self-definition is not grounded in a clear or competent ability to speak the ethnic language; instead, it is informed by a sense of cultural identification as the following attests:

Wong: I find it hard to speak to my grandparents, because I don't speak it [Chinese] anymore, and so I can't communicate with them what I want to.

Researcher: Why is that important to you?

Wong: I just think it is. I guess the most important reason is I want to be able to talk with my grandparents... and I remember a time when it was really easy for me to talk to [my grandmother]. Now, if I try to say the words, I have a very strong English accent and it's kind of a shock that I didn't realize I was losing my Chinese so quickly, but I was. I want to get it back, trying to get at least the sound right.

In fact, in many instances, language for these students is being used as a synonym for culture. This double-edged consciousness—culture as language—operates at a very complex level, often forcing students to position themselves as in between worlds in spite of the publicly self-proclaimed bilingual identity. The following excerpts capture the dilemma many students feel in terms of language use and the positionality of their two worlds:

Excerpt 1:

Student: You either speak really good English or you're kind of in between.

Researcher: What do you mean by "you're kind of in between?"

Student: It's like me. I can't really speak really well in English. Like right, you know? But I can't do really good in Chinese either. So I'm kind of in between.

Excerpt 2:

Researcher: You wrote in the written response that you're "bilingual." What do you mean by this?

Wong: I don't know if I am really bilingual because I don't really bond with—I don't really connect with the English culture. American culture. I'm kind of in between, I guess. I don't really speak [Chinese] that well, therefore I'm non-native Chinese. But language and the culture are kind of connected, I think.

Researcher: Do you consider yourself bilingual?

Wong: To a point.

Researcher: To an extent?

Wong: Yeah. But I think more English 'cause I don't use Chinese on a regular basis. ... I don't feel emotionally attached to it, but sometimes I feel guilty when I don't ... But I feel I should be Chinese. I, like I said, when I, I think in English. It's so, it's easy. When I think in Chinese, I have to think for a while. It's hard ... I never really thought in Chinese for really anything ... I feel like a, like a, you know if I were to use a term, a bamboo. Like um, yellow on the outside and white on the inside.

It seems that for this group of linguistic minorities, the collapsing of language and culture into one category allows them to name their allegiance to their ethnic heritage without impeding their linguistic ability in English. However, this seemingly benign conceptualization is problematic for it raises crucial questions of the core and essence of being literate. What these students are experiencing seems to be serious disjunctures between the way they conceptualize their linguistic identities. That is, on the one hand, they are not fully comfortable with speaking, reading, or writing their heritage language, whereas on the other hand, they are not fully integrated into the culture of mainstream, academic English by the virtue of the label, linguistic minority. Although at ease with their ethnic culture, these students do not possess the full linguistic facility to participate fully as members of a cultural group, particularly so if we view language learning as a transmitter of culture. Their inability to have full participation at the cultural level is captured in the following excerpt:

Soo Kim:	The only time I can talk to my parents is when I speak Konglish or in broken English.
Researcher:	When you talk about family problems, is English used then? Or Korean? In conflicts, what language is used?
Soo Kim:	Um. I think English is used when dealing with family problems and with other people. But if I have a problem, I'll talk with them in both Korean and English. Because sometimes I feel like when I talk to them in Korean, I can really get their attention. You know, really grasp hold of them when I talk in Korean because it's their whole language. Maybe it'll penetrate their psyche or something, you know.
Researcher:	What happens when you try to do so but you do not have adequate vocabulary and terms and all that?
Soo Kim:	I have to speak English. I find myself doing that. I would just start talking in English.
Researcher:	So then you have a combination of both?
Soo Kim:	Yeah. But that doesn't happen too often. I can usually talk to my parents in basic Korean most of the time.
Researcher:	What do you mean by basic Korean?
Soo Kim:	Just non-complicated vocabulary. There's nothing complicated. Just regular phrases, conversational dialogue, that kind of thing. Nothing complicated.
Researcher:	So for complicated or complex concepts, you use English?
Soo Kim:	Yes. I use English, yeah. I just ask them how to say it in Korean.

If, as Halliday (1975, p. 66) posited, "the act of learning language [is] also learning the culture through language. The semantic system which [the student] is constructing becomes the primary mode of transmission of the culture," and if indeed the semantic system is the primary mode of transmission of the culture, it raises questions of whose culture, and whose semantic systems are being privileged in English learning.

Another dominant thread is that these students identify with their heritage language, even if they do not speak it (indeed, they *all* reported that they were bilingual). It is as if by claiming the language, they claim a linguistic identity that perhaps exists in their minds, but not in their tongues. Even as they assert that they are native speakers of English, they are also asserting that they are bilingual (even if their heritage language use is devoid of any language transactions involving complex negotiations). One student said, "I am a Chinese American. So, I guess I'm bilingual," as if one begets the other, or vice versa. Language exists in the mind; for these students, it remains there, and they identify with it by considering themselves "bilingual" even when their bilingualism is not supported by a clear literacy competence (indeed, most of the students reported that they cannot read or write in their heritage language).

What is most troubling is that although school literate in English, these very students are not able to fully "bond" with the language because of the ways in which they perceive speakers of English in relation to themselves (as "they," "them," and the "other.") And although they feel connected to their home culture, they are not able to connect with it linguistically, often needing to resort to "konglish," "vietnamish," "chinglish," "broken English" or "English substitutions." More often than not, their linguistic lack in the heritage language compelled them to simplify the naming of their complexed realities to simple or broken English. They are faced with the double whammy of having a cultural home language in which they have the culture but not the full linguistic ability, and with English (for many a home and school language) in which they have the linguistic ability (however varying it is) but not the culture that, according to the students, means mainstream culture.

NATIVE VERSUS THE NONNATIVE ENGLISH SPEAKER

The constant waverings in the bilingual identification also seem to complicate the way students define themselves in terms of the native speaker identification. Although a majority of the students interviewed were either born here or came to United States at a preschool age, and in spite of the clear documentation (indeed, UC Berkeley undergraduates are from the top 12% of California schools) that they could only read and write English, many of them did not claim the native-speaker identity. The following three excerpts are typical of the spectrum of student responses when asked to elaborate on their native or nonnative affiliation:

Excerpt 1:

Chan: A native speaker— to me, I think it's somebody who can speak English very well. I mean, it doesn't matter where you were born. A couple of my friends came here when they were small and they speak English perfectly. So shouldn't that be native? ... I don't really know how to define myself. Am I a native speaker of English, too?

Researcher: How would you define a nonnative speaker?

Chan: Nonnative speakers. Hmm. Are they supposed to be less of an English speaker? Do they speak not as well as the people that are born here? I think that language is basically your culture, by your family. So when you're not born here, I think you don't speak well, maybe. Maybe that's how they define it. Nonnative: You're not born here and you don't speak as well because you don't culturally, like, bond.

Excerpt 2:

Researcher: How do you define the "native" speaker?

Nguyen: It [English] is just the way they speak in America.

Researcher: And what about Vietnamese?

Nguyen: My native language.

Researcher: What does the term nonnative speaker mean to you?

Nguyen: A person that English wasn't their first language.

Researcher: And how about when you hear the word "native English speaker?"

Nguyen: Like, they constantly use English, and I think, like, their first language.

Researcher: Are you a native or a nonnative speaker of Vietnamese?

Nguyen: I'm not sure. I don't know. [pause] I think I'm a nonnative 'cause my Vietnamese isn't that great.

Researcher: And what about English?

Nguyen: I think I'm native.

For many of these students, despite their sometimes contradictory ambivalence in the native and nonnative categories, we discovered that when questioned about their "thinking" language, English predominates:

Shun: I think the native speaker is probably either English was your first language or English is a language you're fluent at. But native sounds like to me, it's your first language. But that's complicated because I actually learned Korean first.... Then I took on English and then my fluency in English took off, whereas with Korean, it just gradually ... I don't know. It's complicated.

Researcher: So you consider yourself a nonnative speaker of English?

Shun: I don't think so. Probably because I'm so fluent at it. So if I said I was a nonnative speaker, it would sound funny because I would say, "Wait. But I speak it fluently." So I can't be. It just contradicts itself.

With other students, the ambivalence is less defined even as they "other" the native-speaker:

Researcher: So what is a native speaker?

Cheng: I ... I'm not sure. It's like other people in class, when they have to speak English, they have to think first right? So, their original language is like their natural instinct; that's how it is for me. English is, it's natural. I think in English.

These identification labels that the students create illustrate their dissatisfaction with the inherent binary categories with respect to their bilingual identity, which force them to categorize their identity into an either–or sort of framework, when in fact they may not perceive it in such clear-cut distinctions. At the beginning of the interview, Cheng talks about her bond to the Chinese culture, and how she understands it better than she understands U.S. culture. Dominating her literacy narrative is the self-imposed nonnative speaker. However, when asked to define a native speaker, she answers, "I'm not sure." In fact, her linguistic identity dramatically turns around when she talks about the "natural instinct" and how to her, "English is natural." Cheng even goes further to say that she "thinks in English" even as she holds on to a nonnative identity. It is as if to say that she could not be a native speaker of English because of her more primal bond to Chinese. Many of the students said that they hear the heritage language spoken at home, between parents and grandparents, or a family gatherings, and that because of this they feel a connection to the language. It seems that regardless of their linguistic inability to fully communicate with the language, the students' emotional connection to the heritage language remains deep and complex.

Another point of interest is that with some students, the native speaker label comes not by conscious choice, but by default as the following responses attest:

Shennie: I describe myself as a native English-speaking student because I was born and educated under the U.S. system. The English I've learned in public schools was the same for both White and non-White students, regardless of the home language.

Lee: I think I'm a native speaker of English because I'm proficient in it even though I learned a language before hand [meaning Taiwanese] but there's a cultural language which is Chinese; it's like my language that I can always be at, I can always like, I can always revert back to, because it is, it is innate in me in some ways, you know.... But to me a native language is a language that you continually speak, that you write an essay on it. You know like I just wrote an essay for College Writ-

> ing and, and there's no way I could have put those
> ideas into Chinese. So, and that's why I like, just creat-
> ing ideas and creating new thoughts is like what I
> think is a native language just because that's how you
> advance.

So despite the fact that these students use English to create "ideas and new thoughts" and that English is primary in their lived realities, they still distance themselves from English, often times reducing it to "a tool." "English is a great tool, a tool you know, tool for me that I use as a language, and you know, to write my papers and stuff like that, useful things" (Wong, Interview 1). And that despite the fact they could not read, write, and can barely speak in their heritage language, these students still see it as their bond to their cultural roots: "Chinese to me is uh, in the essence, it is me."

Perhaps because of their difficulty in labeling their own linguistic abilities, many of these students refer to English-speaking people, and the English-speaking world, in terms of "other." Although most of the students were born in this country, and English is primary in their lived realities, they are unable to fully assert themselves as native speakers. In fact, to many of these students, native speakers are the Americans, the "they" and the "them." Although English-dominant, these students are not as ready to identify with the language, in terms of the native label, as they perhaps do with their heritage language, although many are not speakers of that language.

BLURRED BOUNDARIES: REVISIONING THESE STUDENTS

The varying contradictions in students' definitions of bilingual identity, bilingual literacy, and their ambivalence toward defining themselves as a native versus a nonnative speaker raise some important questions of the way literacy experiences of linguistic minorities are defined. Our students do not neatly fit into clean-cut categories such as mainstream English speaker, ESL speaker, or bilingual students. Neither does it seem that their literacy journeys are duly served by the arbitrary and ill-challenged categories of language minority students, ESL, and international students.

Category 1: Mainstream English Speakers

The students we interviewed shared many of the literacy needs and orientations of mainstream students—literacy as an act of making meaning, literacy as an act of self-definition, and literacy as a way to engage with the world even as they are tagged with the nonnative English-speaking label. That many resisted enrolling in a nonnative English-speaking section (an option available to ESL students), and that all our students interviewed were from the native English-speaking section further attest to their mainstream affiliation. For many of the students, the reality is that English is more than a functional tool, or an L2; in many aspects, it is their primary language.

Although the needs of these students cannot be adequately addressed under the mainstream English speakers category, ironically, they are as mainstream as can be. The students we have are considered the model students. They are enrolled in three or four other classes in addition to their college writing class, and are successful in meeting the academic demands of the university. These are the students who are seen as having made it; whose education is smooth sailing, whose relationship with the English language has gotten them all As.

Paradoxically, another indication of their primary affiliation to English (part of the mainstream linguistic identity) is in their struggle with their linguistic and cultural loyalties. Perhaps, had these students not had such a primary and emotional bond with English, they would not have been so split in their struggles with, contradictions, and uncertainties about their cultural and linguistic identities.

Category 2: Language Minorities

The label *language minority* is used to group and homogenize language learners of non-English language background. The underlying sociopolitical assumption is that these "linguistic minorities" do not speak English as a primary language. Instead, what is often assumed in this reductionist term is that English is an add-on, that is, students are assumed to have primary affiliation with their heritage language—be it Spanish, Vietnamese, Cantonese—and a lesser/secondary affiliation with English. The complex juxtaposition of home language and the primacy of English in their lived realities is eclipsed by the term *language minority*.

The student responses suggest that English and the students' heritage tongue are not viewed in competition with one another. Home language and school language (i.e., English) are felt to coexist comfortably at various levels; English is understood to work in parallel with their mother tongue.

Indeed, although many of our students may be termed as *language minorities*, their literacy journey indicates that English is really their primary language even when they seem to flip flop between the two languages. The primacy of English reverberates throughout their literacy narratives. Significant, too, is the use of English when students articulate their need to combine two languages to express their complex thoughts:

> For everyday, routine speech, I would think in Chinese when I want to speak Chinese, and in English when I want to think in English. For abstract thinking, I would think in English or most of the time, and in Chinese for concepts that are not readily expressed by English. Therefore, when I "flip-flop" between Chinese and English, I am relying on *both* at the same time in order to help express my ideas.

Yet, in as much as these students are aware of that need to combine the heritage and the learned/school language, their sense of their own language deficiency plagues their journey, as the following excerpts revealed:

Excerpt 1:

Therefore, I do not have a well-founded mastery of either language but a super-ficial knowledge of both languages, with each language being only capable in expressing my basic thoughts. (It is only when I combine the two language that I can express my complex thoughts.)

Excerpt 2:

Because I do not have a solid language foundation in one language, I will have trouble communicating my complex ideas with using one language. [i.e., Chi-nese and English].... As a result, my weak language foundation affects my learning and writing English or Chinese.

Category 3: ESL Speaker

The biggest assumption (and perhaps the most homogenized category) is that of ESL. The embedded hierarchy indicates the secondary importance of English in relation to the native tongue. In other words, because English is their second language, students are assumed to have difficulties with the language. As noted by Reyes, "in classrooms and schools, as in larger societal structures, educators and policymakers are conditioned to ignore differences and to treat them as de-ficiencies" (Reyes, 1992, p. 437). The educational society expects them to make ESL mistakes; they are expected to stumble over the English language for it is not their native tongue. Students in our study often internalize this ill-defined assumption even when their affiliation to English is primary rather secondary. And this internalization often leads them to see themselves as incapable of owning the language as captured in the following:

I am unsure about writing. I am confused. I am frustrated. I think I will never become a good writer because I am Asian. It is excusable for me not to be good at writing. I am not supposed to be good anyway. People expect me to be geared to-ward science and math. This expectation gives me an excuse to avoid writing. "People don't expect me to do well anyway," or "Why bother? I will never learn how to speak and write like natives," I always say to myself.

It is further assumed that they have their first or native tongue to fall back to. Whereas they are not expected to have English mastery because it is their second tongue, they are presumed to have mastery in their native tongue. In many instances, this may be the case, but this is not true for all our students. Almost without exception, each expressed great difficulties in using their na-tive or mother tongue:

Because I learned both languages at a relatively early age, I spoke both English and Cantonese without any accent. However, my Cantonese vocabulary was limited to that of a five-year-old.

To compensate for their linguistic limitations in the heritage language, many students either resorted to keeping their thoughts simple so they have enough words to express them, or to the use of broken English to keep up communication when speaking to family members, or to combining English with the heritage language such as in "konglish," "Vietnamish," or "Chinglish." As Jane Kim describes in one of her portfolio pieces:

> I communicated with my sisters at home only through English in the midst of my mom yelling "Speak Korean! Aren't you Korean?" Then I would start to break out in "Konglish" whenever my mom was nearby. I felt my English had to compensate for what I lacked in my knowledge of Korean. Although I don't speak Korean with a heavy accent, it's still difficult to communicate in the language. My vocabulary is very limited and my reading and writing power is very weak.

> Many people are surprised that I can speak as well as I can for someone who has practically lived in America all her life. I'm still saddened at the fact that I can't communicate to my parents the same way my sisters are able. If I talk to my mom, it's usually just simple questions I need to ask her; otherwise I'd ask my sisters to ask for me.

Characterizing Jane Kim's English as her second language does not capture the full complexity of her linguistic experience. Kim's experiences with language and literacy, particularly in the home context, seem to depict someone who turns to English for stability and a sense of self.

Therefore, a further limitation in the ESL characterization is that English is really the primary medium students use to articulate their complex realities. They depend on it to help them weave in and out of their everyday communication interactions. Their race and/or ethnicity does not preclude them from relying on English to express their multifaceted realities and to make the necessary transitions between home and school.

CONCLUSIONS

What we strive to do in this chapter is to highlight the cultural and linguistic web of home language and English for students from NELB. Essentially, we hope that the insights of their multifaceted experiences provoke language educators to question and think beyond the narrow confines of a monolithic English ideology, and reorientate themselves to the sociocultural politics of English literacy in a multicultural and multilingual world.

In addition, we wish to suggest the following educational implications:

- The need for language teachers to be adequately trained and professionally prepared to recognize and attend to the increasingly blurred cultural and linguistic boundaries of linguistically diverse students. Whereas categories like ESL, bilingual, and linguistic minority do indeed serve to delineate some students, these categories are inadequate when it comes to capturing the literacy journey of students whose lived realities often waver between cultural and linguistic borderlands.

- The urgency to reexamine the categorization of native versus nonnative students and reconceptualize the labels. As our study has indicated, the nonnative labels are neither adequate in capturing the complexities of their literacy experiences, nor resonant in representing their paralleling cultural and linguistic ties to English and their heritage language. Perhaps the overarching question should be less whether these linguistically diverse students are native or nonnative, but rather how primary English fits their literacy and linguistic identity. The reorientation will not only serve in recentering the primacy of English literacy as an act of constructing one's social, cultural, and political place in the world, but it will also heighten the role of English as a world language.

- The need for greater interaction and exchanges among leaders of National Council of Teachers of English, Teachers of English to Speakers of Other Languages, National Association of Bilingual Education, and World Englishes and their obligation to provide more informed and cross disciplinary insights into the multiplicity of English learning in a pluralistic world. With the increasing dominance of English across the world, it is no longer sufficient to work within the narrow paradigms and specificities contained within each linguistic field. Instead, researchers need to view commonalties and contradictions and come up with new insights and models formed from multiple perspectives. This kind of interdisciplinary model will add to a fuller understanding of the literacy journey of a diverse student population.

- The need to not only acknowledge but accommodate the intersections of race, culture, and ethnicity in the sociopolitical constructions of English literacy. As pointed out by Peirce (1995), which our study supports, "the individual language learner is not ahistorical and unidimensional but has a complex and sometimes social identity, changing across time and space" (pp. 25–26).

ACKNOWLEDGMENTS

Preparation of this chapter was supported in part by a major grant from National Council Teachers of English "Grant-in-Aid" and by College Writing Programs, UC–Berkeley.

REFERENCES

Bogdan, R., & Biklen, S. (1982). *Qualitative research for education: An introduction to theory and methods.* Boston: Allyn and Bacon, Inc.

Fong-Torres, B. (1994). *The rice room: Growing up Asian American. From number two son to rock 'n roll.* New York: Hyperion.

Halliday, M. A. K. (1975). *Learning how to mean: Explorations in the development of language*. London: Edward Arnold.

Lantolf, J. (1996). SLA theory building: Letting all the flowers bloom! *Language Learning, 46*, 713–749.

Oxford-Carpenter, R., Pol, L., Lopez, D., Stupp, P., Gendell, M., & Peng, S. (1984). *Demographic projections of non-English language background and limited English proficient persons in the United States to the year 2000 by state, age, and language group*. Rosslyn, VA: National Clearing House for Bilingual Education.

Peirce, B. N. (1995). Social identity, investment, and language learning. *TESOL Quarterly 29*(1), 9–31.

Rampton, B. (1995). *Crossing: Language and ethnicity among adolescents*. New York: Longman.

Reyes, M. (1992). Challenging venerable assumptions: Literacy instruction for linguisticallly different students. *Harvard Educational Review, 62*(4), 427–446.

Siegal, M. (1996). The role of learner subjectivity in second language sociolinguistic competency: Western women learning Japanese. *Applied Linguistics, 17*(3), 356–382.

Simons, H., Perrow, M., Stritikus, T., Schmida, M., & Ponte, E. (1997). *Participating in academic conversation: An evaluation of college writing*. Unpublished report, University of California at Berkeley.

Tan, A. (1989). *The joy luck club*. New York: Putnam.

II

The Classrooms

6 Preparation for College Writing: Teachers Talk About Writing Instruction for Southeast Asian American Students in Secondary School

Beth Hartman
Elaine Tarone
University of Minnesota

Increasing numbers of limited English proficient (LEP) students whose native language is not English are moving through U.S. public schools and entering institutions of higher education. In Minnesota, for example, a recent front-page newspaper story read: "the number of students [in the state] who speak little or no English has more than tripled in the past 10 years to about 27,000—roughly the size of one of the state's largest school districts" (Smith, Minneapolis *Star Tribune*, May 24, 1997, p. 1). Of course, many of these students intend to enter colleges and universities, and will need to have good writing skills to earn postsecondary degrees. But what are the English language writing skills of these students? What sort of writing instruction do they need or receive, particularly at the secondary level? Few studies have examined the nature of LEP student writing instruction in high schools, or looked at literacy instruction across classroom contexts. Although there is an increasing amount of research on emergent literacy in bilingual children (e.g., Edelsky, 1982; Hudelson, 1984; Urzua, 1987), research on writing instruction for older students (middle school and high school) who are learning to write for academic purposes is much harder to find (but see Adamson, 1993; Harklau, 1994).

What is the nature of English as a Second Language (ESL) and mainstream academic writing instruction in the secondary schools? Does it prepare LEP secondary students to succeed in meeting writing requirements in higher education? Adamson (1993) points out that writing appears be among the most important language skills for academic achievement among second language (L2) learners. This is particularly true at the postsecondary level. Instructors at many U.S. colleges and universities have noted that the writing skills of LEP students who are graduates of U.S. high schools often significantly hinder their ability to compete with native-speaking peers in higher education.

Secondary school teachers may have a good deal to tell about the writing background of immigrant high school graduates who are now entering colleges and universities. This chapter focuses on the reported writing instructional practices of teachers of Southeast Asian American LEP students at a high school in the upper midwest. It is hoped that this discussion of high school teachers' teaching practices and beliefs about the teaching of writing to LEP learners will help college-level writing instructors better understand the writing backgrounds of LEP students who have been educated in U.S. public schools, the particular strengths and weaknesses they bring with them as academic writers in higher education, and the reasons why so many of them find it difficult to handle the writing demands at higher level institutions.

It is important to understand that immigrant LEP students' goals and needs for learning to write may be very different from those of international students studying in U.S. schools. International students will probably only write in English as part of their educational requirement and even then probably only in a specific academic field, whereas immigrant students need to be able to write in English for a wide range of purposes for the rest of their working and earning lives (Raimes, 1991). In addition to writing for academia, these students need to be able to write for a variety of social contexts, including the workplace, the business world, and the community in addition to academia. Secondary school teachers may need to prepare their students to write in their L2 for this wide range of contexts, and not just for academic purposes. But certainly, if LEP students are to succeed in higher education, they must be provided in the secondary schools with the fundamental writing skills they will need in college classes. What is the nature of academic writing, as opposed to other sorts of writing the LEP student is learning to produce? Indeed, what is the nature of academic language?

L2 researchers have looked at what it takes for an ESL learner to become proficient in the type of language used in school, as compared with the type of language used in everyday communication. Cummins (1983) draws a distinction between the proficiency required to use language for interpersonal communication and the proficiency required to use language for academic purposes. He points out that in interpersonal communication, language is context-embedded, with extralinguistic cues such as facial expressions to aid in communication. Academic language is typically context-reduced language, as in academic written texts and essays, where there are few extralinguistic cues to meaning and interpretation, and communication may depend solely on the ability to interpret and encode complex linguistic structures. Academic writing, then, involves more complex linguistic structures than other types of writing, a different set of rhetorical skills, and far less situational support for the L2 learner (cf. Swales, 1990).

Clearly, it takes longer to achieve mastery in the academic register of an L2 than in the interpersonal register of that language. Collier (1989) examines the length of time it takes to become academically proficient in an L2. In her survey of research literature, she finds that oral interpersonal language is often mastered in as little as 2 years, whereas proficiency in academic and literate language use takes much longer, about 5 to 10 years depending on the educational background and the instructional program of the student. The students who take the longest are those who arrive at a young age (i.e., before age 7 or 8) with little or no academic preparation in the first language and who receive no bilingual instruction. These students require from 5 to 10 years to achieve native speaker norms for academic language proficiency, if indeed they ever do.

Unfortunately, public school administrative guidelines often suggest that L2 learners should stay in ESL classrooms no longer than 2 years. This is long enough to gain proficiency in oral skills, but not long enough to become proficient in English literacy skills—literacy skills that involve not only the ability to handle complex decontextualized language but also the ability to participate in the culture of mainstream classrooms. When ESL students are moved to mainstream classes before developing the language, background knowledge, and cultural schemata these classes assume, they miss a great deal of information and are often inhibited from participating in a class where they must compete with those who are much more proficient than themselves (Miramontes, 1993). This is yet another interruption in the education of these students, many of whom have already had their education interrupted several times. Moreover, when students are moved from ESL to mainstream classes, mainstream teachers can have the impression that these students' language and academic preparation problems are solved, and believe that these students should be ready to perform on the same level as native-speaking students (Miramontes, 1993).

In her study on children writing in an L2, Urzua (1987) states that schools are economically hard-pressed to provide in service training for mainstream teachers and programs for LEP learners that might make the acquisition of literacy more effective. She calls on those in the field of ESL to:

> help all educators realize the time that learners will require to become competing members in their classrooms. In addition, it is necessary for us to know much more about the acquisition of literacy. Being more knowledgeable about this process will help educators make informed decisions about intervention strategies which will facilitate that acquisition. (p. 281)

In responding to Urzua's call for more research on the acquisition of literacy skills by LEP students, Downing and Tarone (1990) and Tarone et al. (1993) studied the writing skills of the largest group of immigrants in secondary schools in the Twin Cities (Southeast Asian American students). The writers studied included Southeast Asian American students at a St. Paul secondary school (including students with Vietnamese, Cambodian, Laotian and Hmong backgrounds) in the following groupings: (a) students placed in the two highest level ESL high school classes (Levels 3 and 4), and (b) students placed in 8th-, 10th-, and 12th- grade mainstream classes. In addition, the study included a group of Southeast Asian American university students in a special ESL writing course, and a group of international university students from a range of countries enrolled in an advanced level ESL composition course. Finally, there was a control group of native English-speaking university students enrolled in a university freshman composition course.

Writing samples obtained from all these groups of student writers were scored using a specific analytic rating scale focusing on the traits of grammatical accuracy, fluency, organization, and coherence. The results showed little difference among the scores of immigrant writers across the grade levels examined, from eighth grade through the college level. The writing scores of the college-level immigrant students were significantly below those scores obtained from the native-speaking college freshmen students. Tarone et al. pointed out that the lack of difference in writing scores from one grade level to the next among the immigrant samples might indicate that individual students were not improving in their writing skills as they moved from one grade level to the next. Whatever the reason, they noted that the writing skills of the university-level immigrant students were more limited than those of their native- speaking peers and concluded "certainly there seems to be a need for more focus upon writing skills in general if these learners are to be adequately prepared for the modern working world and for college-level work in particular" (Tarone et al., 1993, p. 24).

THE NEED FOR THE TEACHERS' PERSPECTIVE

Tarone et al. (1993) focused on the students' writing scores on the writing test that they administered. However, in order to understand why these students performed the way they did on that measure, more information is necessary. In particular, we need to know what attempts were made to teach writing to these students in their various classes in the secondary school: in their ESL classes, in their mainstream English classes, and in their mainstream content classes (e.g., science, math, social studies, etc.) What was the nature of their writing instruction? Many of the students in this earlier study and LEP students like them are now in our colleges and universities, and college writing instructors will benefit from understanding the writing preparation of such students. This chapter describes that preparation from the point of view of some fairly typical secondary school teachers who taught writing skills to LEP students prior to their entry into college or university.

THE STUDY

Downing and Tarone (1990) conducted interviews with these Southeast Asian American students' ESL and mainstream teachers in the secondary school complex studied. Due to constraints of time and space, an analysis of those responses did not appear in Tarone et al. (1993). By reviewing the interview questions and the responses of both ESL and mainstream teachers with regard to the way writing was taught to immigrant and native-born LEP students in different types of classes in this particular secondary school, we may gain a better understanding of why the students performed the way they did. In particular, we may obtain a snapshot of the teaching practices that existed in the school at the time of the study, and use this information to help inform college and university teachers attempting to help LEP students coming from similar public school experiences to become more academically proficient in the area of writing.

Research Questions

The research questions we address, then, are the following:

1. How do ESL teachers describe the way they teach writing to particular nonnative groups at the secondary level?
2. How do mainstream English teachers describe the way they teach writing to particular nonnative groups at the secondary level?
3. How do mainstream content teachers describe the way they teach writing to particular nonnative groups at the secondary level?

Data Collection

Written transcripts of oral interviews conducted for the Downing and Tarone (1990) study were examined for this chapter. The teachers interviewed were those in the school who responded to our request to interview them in fall 1989 and cannot be taken as representative of the school faculty as a whole. Thirteen teachers were interviewed: 3 ESL teachers and 10 mainstream teachers. Of the three ESL teachers, one taught ESL Level 1, another ESL Levels 1 and 4, and another taught Levels 2, 3, and 4. Of the 10 mainstream teachers, 5 were English teachers: an 8th-, 10th-, 11th-, 12th-grade teacher, and a 12th-grade Assurance of Mastery English teacher (for those who had not passed the English-language competency test required for graduation). The 5 other mainstream teachers were 8th-grade teachers of geography and history, home economics, and history; a 9th-through-12th grade home economics teacher; and a 12th-grade social studies teacher.

Interviews typically took about 30 minutes. The teachers of these classes were asked in taperecorded interviews to respond to the following set of questions. The interviewer covered all the questions in every interview, although not necessarily in the following order, and allowed the teachers to expand on issues which they felt to be related or important. The topics covered were:

What methods do you use to teach writing?
How often are writing assignments given?
What types of writing assignments do you give?
What do you look for in the writing of your students?
How do you evaluate your students' writing?
Can you make any generalizations about problems that the Southeast Asian students in particular have in their writing?

The interview questions and the teacher responses were transcribed[1] by the interviewer. We subjected the transcripts to a largely interactionist[2] analysis.

Results: Teacher Statements on the Teaching of Writing

In response to the question of how often writing assignments were given, teachers apparently took "writing" to mean any writing, from simply providing one-word answers to questions, to longer compositions. In the discussion that follows, then, *writing* refers to the expression of ideas in writing, an expression ranging in length from one word to sentences to longer compositions.

The following section describes the teaching of writing, thus defined, in ESL, mainstream English, and content area classes in the secondary school complex studied.

Teaching Writing in ESL Classes

Methods of ESL Writing Instruction.   Three ESL instructors were interviewed; one taught ESL Level 1, another ESL Levels 1 and 4, and another taught Levels 2, 3, and 4. These ESL teachers were asked about the kind of writing students did in their classes. The lower level ESL teachers responded that writing instruction in their classes consisted of written substitution drills and patterned practice exercises at the sentence level. One ESL Level 1 instructor reported that he had his students read first and then write what they read: "They are able to write the same words, they are able to write the same structures, they understand those structures. And then they substitute sometimes nouns, pronouns, adjectives." He then stressed the importance of getting the students to understand what they wrote by "drilling, doing it over and over again until I am sure myself that they are getting the structure. Now they can use it on their own. Fill in the blanks, fill in the gaps, substitution and drills, those are the main activities that I like to concentrate (on)".

Another Level 1 teacher responded to the same question by saying, "The lower the level class, the more we directly model what's done. So with lower level kids it becomes virtually a written version of an oral substitution drill, or

---

[1]Again, we thank Kimberly Taylor Townsend for her work transcribing the interview data. We were not able to ask the teachers or the interviewer for clarification or elaboration but drew our generalizations solely from the written transcripts of the oral interviews. It was unclear in the interviews just how much time was spent on the development of writing skills in the ESL and mainstream classrooms in comparison to the development of other skills.

[2]Interactionist approaches to interview analysis are described in Silverman (1993, 90–114). In this approach, "interviewees are viewed as experiencing subjects who actively construct their social worlds; the primary issue is to generate data which give an authentic insight into people's experiences" (p. 91). Thus, we are interested in the teachers' presentation of their own experiences in teaching writing, bearing in mind that those constructions may or may not accurately reflect reality. However, the interpretation of the interview data is also positivist in the sense of Brown and Sime's view that "an account is neither naive nor an apology for behavior, but must be taken as an informed statement by the person whose experiences are under investigation" (Brown & Sime, 1981, p. 160).

I provide a particular grammatical sentence structure that I am asking them to manipulate."

In ESL Levels 2 and 3, students reportedly moved from sentence writing based on a model to paragraph writing, also based on a model. Level 2 drills might include dictation, changing sentences from one type to another, copying a question and then writing the answer. The ESL Level 2 teacher noted that sometimes students at this level like to write longer amounts but she discouraged it until they could become more organized. She noted, "They can just get so disorganized in their writing it's not of any value." In ESL Level 3, students moved from paragraphs to longer essays (a maximum of two or three paragraphs), still following a model or format provided by the teacher. By ESL Level 4, writing was still very controlled: Students were constructing sentences using particular vocabulary words or taking a group of words and making a story or paragraph writing based on a model.

The ESL teachers were asked whether they did any "process kind of writing," or whether they required multiple drafts in their writing assignments. The ESL teachers did not mention any use of prewriting activities (such as concept mapping, brainstorming, or freewriting) in their writing assignments. Their responses suggested that "process writing" in ESL classes meant writing an initial draft and revising it once. ESL teachers reported that they rarely asked for more than two drafts of any given assignment. One teacher responded, "With the higher (level ESL classes) especially I do the rough draft, because they can change, they can make it better …. I usually don't go for the third of fourth draft. Life's too short, they can write about something else."

Another ESL teacher responded, "Yeah, they will correct things, but I can't tell you that I do that every time because you can get the sensation that you beat something half to death." He explained that it was usually the upper levels of ESL that worked on multiple drafts: "In the lower levels when I am dealing with writing, it's not with compositions and narratives as such, we're dealing with sentences and answering questions."

Kinds of ESL Writing Assignments. In discussing what kinds of paragraphs the students in ESL Levels 2 and 3 wrote, one teacher responded, "Probably I'll use a model, or use a model out of the book because the book is pretty good at that. And also I use, we make up paragraphs together as a class on the board, whatever the subject is going to be."

The Level 4 ESL teacher we interviewed taught a reading class and a writing class. In the Level 4 reading class, the teacher described writing as based on the readings they had done: "They have to construct sentences using particular vocabulary words, or they have to take a group of words and make a story and the more words they can get in the story, the more points they get." These students also did question-answer type exercises as well as longer essays. With the essays, this teacher mentioned that she tried to have them write about something in a content area, noting that this is where her students had the most trouble. In the ESL Level 4 composition class, the teacher explained that most often his students' compositions were descriptive, usually based on a model with which he was working where he might manipulate verb tenses. He added that they also wrote about personal experiences. When asked if his classes worked with other rhetorical modes, he replied that they did some comparison/contrast and wrote some business letters of request, but did very little argumentative writing.

Evaluation of ESL Writing.   When asked what they looked for in the writing of their students, ESL teachers responded that their primary concern was with grammar usage and structure. In the lower levels of ESL, where writing consisted of grammar exercises, it was evident that these ESL teachers might focus primarily on comprehension and correct grammar usage in student writing. But even in the upper levels of ESL, when the students were apparently writing longer amounts, the teachers seemed more concerned with form than with other factors of writing such as organization and content. When asked what the focus was in commenting on students' first drafts, one ESL teacher replied: "Grammatical mistakes, particularly things that deal with logical word order and proper verb tense." When asked if the key to getting LEP students to write well was to work on grammar a lot, he replied, "Structure is everything. The only way to teach it is by example." He then went on to say that many LEP students had learned that they didn't have to be totally grammatically correct when they spoke, and that this carried over into their writing. For this reason, he felt that modeling correct usage was important for writing at all levels of ESL.

ESL Teachers' Generalizations About the Writing of Southeast Asian American Learners.   When asked to make generalizations about the problems that Southeast Asian American students had in writing, the ESL teachers usually responded with comments on the difficulties these students had with grammar, listing problems with verb tense, article usage, and the use of idioms as examples. They made little reference to other writing problems such as vocabulary, content and organization.

The Teaching of Writing by Mainstream Teachers

The mainstream content teachers' comments revealed a great deal of frustration in dealing with LEP students that were placed in their classes without adequate academic language buildup. They knew these students needed more help and some felt guilty that they did not have enough time to provide that help. One content teacher was asked if she gave LEP students extra help, or if she thought that was the ESL teacher's job. Her response was, "It's whoever's job who has the time" A U.S. history teacher, asked the same question, said "sometimes I feel a bit guilty that I'm not working in that area, but I really feel I could spend too much time diverting from American History if I did that." The teacher of 12th-grade college prep English protested the fact that LEP students were mainstreamed into his class when many were not literate enough to answer essay questions on tests. He said:

This is a big problem because I am not in a position to take these kids aside and tutor them to get them caught up. So we're running into that enormous barrier of social promotion. They're sending kids into the senior year and out on the streets who are basically functionally illiterate ... I'm not concerned about the kids who are more or less home-grown products here but have S.E. Asian ancestry; they'll become Americanized if they haven't already. But the kids right off the boat can't be mainstreamed as quickly. This is a travesty. For crying out loud, spend some time tutoring them before you throw them to the wolves, as it were. I can't slow up!

Teaching Writing in Mainstream English Classes

The five mainstream English teachers who were interviewed taught 8th-, 10th-, 11th- and 12th-grade English, and 12th-grade Assurance of Mastery English.

Methods of Writing Instruction in Mainstream English.   The English teachers reported that the mainstream English classes had about one writing assignment a week. At all levels, process writing was the method of instruction. The comments of the mainstream English teachers showed a much broader view of this approach than the ESL teachers', including a lot of talk about prewriting activities such as brainstorming, jotting down thoughts, and so on., and the importance of revision in the students' writing. The 11th-grade English teacher commented,

> In general, we're trying to get the students to see that writing is never a totally finished process ... I try to get students to see that they need to do some kind of prewriting or freewriting activity using lists, brainstorming or clustering. I encourage kids to have other people read their work and tell them that they need to communicate to those other people ... And try to get them to see that revision is not just recopying.

Another teacher discussed the use of journals in her 10th-grade English class. She described it as an informal writing situation where she gave students a topic on the board to get them going on writing in journals. This journaling was used as a kind of prewriting exercise "to get ideas and to simply put down what's in their mind on paper. And out of those journal entries sometimes we'll take one and develop it into a more formal assignment."

Kinds of Writing Assignments in Mainstream English.   In mainstream English classes, descriptive writing was taught in the lower levels, and argumentation, literary criticism, and research paper writing were taught in the upper levels for college-bound students. The 10th-grade English teacher said, "Essays could be in conjunction with a piece of literature; they might have to write a character sketch, they might have to write a book report." She stressed that the book reports in her class were not just summaries, but literary

critiques. In 11th-grade English, a teacher said "I try to always present them with essay questions that are always open-ended, that there is not a right answer, but rather they stake out a position and show how they can defend that position, communicate the position." He also talked about having his students study literary criticism by "presenting that criticism to them and ... pulling some stories and talking about them in light of those criticisms. And so the two major papers are broken into two sections, one they have to explain the criticism in their own words and then apply it to a piece of literature."

A 12th-grade English teacher classified the kinds of writing assignments he gave as "expository, argumentation, persuasion; I cover the whole gamut of writing ... compare/contrast I do use a lot." He said his writing assignments were usually connected with the literature they were studying. For example, he asked students to deal with the notion of honor and how the concept of honor changed from the 15th century to the 20th century. He also described having his senior students learn how to write a term paper, taking them through every phase of the process: "how to research, how to develop the topic outline, how to limit your topic."

Evaluation of Writing in Mainstream English. In their evaluation of students' writing, the mainstream English teachers reported that they looked more for organization, clarity of thought, and critical thinking skills than grammar. The teachers were asked what their focus was when correcting the final drafts of their students' writing. The 8th-grade English teacher responded, "I guess my focus would be more on the organization. The grammar will come; there is a unit we will do. If I see a lot of problems we will talk about it, but I don't go that specific[ally] into grammar or mechanics of writing." She added that she thought asking students to be accountable for every part of writing would be too difficult for them because they would not be able to think about everything at once. Another English teacher said he pointed out grammatical and mechanical errors, but added, "My basic comments ... tend to be on organization and clarity of thought." Another said, "Yeah, I look at sentence structure, but then overall in the paragraphs, I want some analysis. I'm looking for signs that they know something about critical thinking." On the value of teaching grammar to Southeast Asian American students, one mainstream English teacher noted:

> My experience has been that you can take a Southeast Asian student and give them a grammar worksheet and they will do very well; they'll realize the pattern, but with a composition type of exercise they will often make those same type of mistakes because they are dealing more in the creative use of the language rather than that structure.

Another English teacher remarked, "They (Southeast Asian American students) usually get high scores on their grammar quizzes ... one part of speech at a time. Now, when they're all together it's more confusing for them."

***Generalizations of Mainstream English Teachers About Writing
Problems of Southeast Asian American Students.***   When mainstream English teachers were asked to make generalizations about the writing problems of the Southeast Asian American students in the study, there
was some reference to grammar and spelling difficulties, but their main concern was that these students could not seem to get their ideas across in their
writing. One teacher did attribute this to their "unique syntax" that she
found confusing. Another talked about a lack of logical process in their writing and pointed out that although logic was also a problem in the writing of
many students, it was particularly difficult for Southeast Asian Americans.
He believed they had trouble thinking in a logical mode:

> It's just a different way of thinking, I think what they are pulling is something
> from their own experience, but it doesn't necessarily fit with what they are try-
> ing to say. But a lot of what I think is cultural because they're in American cul-
> ture and I'm thinking as an American and to me it's very clear (but to them, it's
> not) ... To set up a paragraph with the main idea is very difficult for them.

Another mainstream English teacher felt that these LEP students lacked
the vocabulary to express their ideas, let alone the expression of critical thinking skills required in his classroom. Thus, both these teachers seemed to be referring to a lack of critical thinking skills apparent in LEP student writing; one
of them seemed to assert that the problem with these skills might be cultural.

Finally, the 10th-grade English teacher revealed how ESL students with
these poor writing skills were able to pass a mainstream English class: "If the
class has a limited number of writing assignments, then the students can pass
on the easy stuff: objective tests, promptness in handing in assignments, attendance and class participation."

The Teaching of Writing by Content Area Teachers

The five content area teachers who were interviewed taught 8th-grade geography and history, 8th-grade history, 8th-grade home economics,
9th-through-12th-grade home economics, and 12th-grade social studies.

Methods of Writing Instruction in Mainstream Content Classes.
In these content area classes, teachers reported that writing activities were
taking notes, writing answers to short essay questions, and writing compositions. There was very little writing instruction apart from occasionally pointing out grammar and spelling errors.

Kinds of Writing Assignments in Mainstream Content Classes.
In these classes, teachers stated that writing styles were not taught, but students needed to be able write short essay answers to test questions and display higher order thinking skills in their writing using comparison/contrast,

critical analysis, and argumentation. They might also have had to research and produce a short term paper.

Evaluation of Writing in Mainstream Content Classes.

These content area teachers had a slightly different focus in evaluating the writing of their students. They looked for knowledge of content material in grading: "Does the student understand the subject material he or she is writing about?" They corrected only the glaring grammatical errors and generally did not consider grammar in grading.

Generalizations of Mainstream Content Teachers About the Writing of Southeast Asian American Students.

In their generalizations about the problems with Southeast Asian American student writing, the content area teachers noted that these students often lacked the vocabulary to comprehend subject matter and to express what they did know in an organized manner.

When asked if the Southeast Asian American students in the study spoke up in class, several mainstream teachers responded that these students were very hesitant to do so but an ESL teacher noted that in her class they participated quite actively. One mainstream teacher commented that she saw very little verbal interaction in a large group but when she divided them into smaller groups, particularly in their own languages, they communicated beautifully.

In these interviews, mainstream teachers were asked if they could make any recommendations for helping the LEP students write better. The most common suggestion was one-on-one tutoring. These teachers listed several possible sources for this type of tutoring including volunteers from a local college and the community. One teacher expressed hesitancy in using peer tutors for assistance in ESL writing saying that many native-speaking students are themselves not very good writers, but mentioned possibly using "top-notch seniors."

A few teachers noted that the students seemed to learn language and concepts better when they could communicate in their native language. One teacher noticed that when she divided her students into small groups where they could speak their own language they communicated very well and handed in better assignments. Another teacher talked about his success when he was able to explain a particular grammar point in Thai, which some students understood and were able to explain to the others in Hmong.

Discussion of Teacher Responses to the Questionnaire

There seem to be consistent patterns observable in the teachers' responses that we can analyze in terms of several themes. These themes are: the role of explicit grammar instruction in the teaching of writing, the importance of teaching the writing process, the role of academic content in writing assignments, the amount of variety in the types of writing assignments given, the role of one-on-one peer tutoring in writing instruction, and the use of the native language in the teaching of writing.

The Role of Grammar in Teaching Writing to Southeast Asian Students.

It was apparent from the teachers' responses that ESL teachers saw themselves primarily as grammar teachers and that their focus in the teaching of writing was on grammar and structure; in contrast, the mainstream teachers in the survey were more concerned with the LEP students' ability to communicate, to show critical thinking skills and to display content knowledge in their writing. The ESL teachers' focus on form was evident in the degree of control they maintained in the writing activities of their students and in the attention they gave to errors in grammar compared to other problems in writing. There is certainly a difference in disciplinary emphasis here; it is more typical for secondary level ESL teachers to have training in grammatical analysis than for secondary level English teachers to have that training. Frodeson (1991) points out that ESL writing teachers know from experience that certain grammar problems cannot be ignored. Grammar mistakes often lead to error in communication and can affect the reader's overall perception of the quality of the ESL writer's composition.

This orientation of the ESL teachers to grammatical accuracy in writing was consistent with that in published ESL textbook materials. Hudelson (1984) criticizes ESL reading and writing texts (for children) that claim that "ESL reading and writing should be strictly controlled so that errors do not occur ... that writing, especially at the initial stages, should consist of copying, filling in blanks, and taking dictation rather than creating one's own messages" (p. 222). Kroll (1991) and Paulston and Bruder (1976), before her supports an ESL writing curriculum that follows a continuum from controlled to guided to free writing. And indeed, this seems to be the process the ESL teachers said they would prefer.

However, it would appear that in this secondary school ESL program students did not progress far along the controlled to freewriting continuum. The mainstream English teachers observed that although the LEP students often performed well on grammar worksheets, there was no indication that these students actually transferred that usage to their writing. Was this because they had not had enough time doing freewriting in their ESL classes? Or was it because of problems inherent in the controlled to freewriting approach itself? These questions are also raised by Leki (1992), who points out that although many LEP students are able to do grammar-based guided compositions, they still produce "peculiar non-English sounding texts" when asked to write creatively. This ESL program relied on a controlled to freewriting approach. Within that framework, it would appear that more time needed to be spent in these ESL classes with students doing more freewriting. The ESL teachers felt their students were not in ESL classes long enough for them to progress to the point where they could function at the "free end of the continuum" and gain the experience they needed to be successful in mainstream classes.

Importance of Teaching the Writing Process.   The ESL teachers described very little process writing in the ESL classes, even at the upper levels, and even then this was usually just one draft that was corrected and revised. This lack of quantity of process writing contrasted sharply with the situation in the mainstream English classes, where teachers reported using the process approach, including prewriting exercises and multiple revisions, routinely at all grade levels.

A particularly important step in the writing process is prewriting. Zamel (1982) reviewed case studies of successful college-level ESL writers and noticed that all of those students talked about the value of classroom discussion of a particular composition topic before they were asked to write about it. She stresses that this is a crucial aspect of teaching composition, and notes that methods based on the traditional read–analyze–write model ignore this step. However, although mainstream English classes did stress prewriting activities, these did not appear to be of primary importance in either the ESL classes or in mainstream content classes. Mainstream content teachers indicated in their comments that they did not have the time to give these students the attention they needed in prewriting, and we have already noted that the concentration of ESL writing instruction on the controlled end of the continuum seemed to preclude much process writing, including prewriting activity.

The ESL classroom would be a particularly good place for the use of prewriting activities, because in these activities the students can get the help they need in clarifying their ideas, learning culturally appropriate ways of expressing them, and developing suitable vocabulary—in other words, in prewriting discussions, students have the opportunity to learn the values and assumptions of the culture of the mainstream classroom, and strategies for communicating successfully in writing in that culture, and ESL teachers are particularly good resources for that learning.

The revision aspect of process writing was also quite different in the ESL classes and the mainstream English classes. The ESL teachers appeared to be focused on grammatical and structural errors in asking students to revise their writing, rather than on teaching writing revision as a process of discovering meaning or learning to couch their message in more culturally appropriate forms. From the comments made by the ESL teachers in the interviews, revision was apparently viewed more as a correction process than a learning one, a process focused primarily upon identification of error. Taylor (1981) says:

> A major result of a writing program which focuses primarily on form is an insufficient emphasis on content which would create the opportunity for students to experience the process of discovering meaning and then of struggling to give it form through revision. (p. 9)

Kroll (1991) points out that editing or correcting grammar errors on the first draft can be a counterproductive activity, possibly exacerbating whatever insecurities students might have about their writing and drawing their attention away from other kinds of revision work such as communication of ideas and organization. She recommends correcting grammar errors on the final draft after the content has been corrected. When teachers view revision as primarily a process of error correction, the students may develop the idea that revision is a punishment for failure to do it right the first time rather than learn that revision is a valuable process in learning to write.

Writing as a way of discovering meaning and revision as a method of learning to express it more clearly is especially valuable to LEP students. Feedback during the revision process can provide L2 learners with valuable input as they plan and organize their writing at the conceptual level, learning new cultural models for expressing their thoughts. Indeed, Leki (1992) suggests that LEP writers need more work with writing (i.e., idea expression) than they do with accuracy of language forms. She stated that native-speaker students need a concept- and strategy-focused stage in the revision process to help them become socialized to the majority culture's norms and values for academic mainstream classes.

> the self-reflection taught in process approach classes functions in part to socialize young native students into their own society, to help them situate themselves in current social and political debates, and thereby to prepare them to take up various roles in this society.(p. 7)

We suggest that immigrant students could also benefit from such self-reflection.

The Role of Academic Content in Writing Assignments.   Although it is important that immigrant students learn the writing process, it is also important that they be exposed to authentic writing tasks from the content areas so they become aware of the schemata, purposes, and rhetorical conventions these classes assume (Reid, 1992). In this survey, the teachers in the mainstream content classes indicated that there was a variety of writing styles LEP students needed to be able to use in their classes. These included short-answer questions for tests, comparison and contrast, critiques, and term papers. Mainstream content teachers also indicated that they did not teach these writing styles.

Current ESL pedagogy stresses the importance of using content material in the ESL classroom. However, only one ESL teacher in our interviews indicated that she used content material in the teaching of writing in her ESL class, and she noted that this is where these students seemed to have the most difficulty.

More efforts to teach writing in ESL classes by using content material from mainstream classes would probably help to shift the focus on form to more concern with the communication of ideas and the knowledge of subject matter that these students need to be able to demonstrate in their mainstream classes. LEP students may have problems writing for these classes because of poor language skills or lack of knowledge about content material. However, even if students have strong language skills and content knowledge, they may still have a "limited or skewed perception" of what is expected of their writing in mainstream classes. The problem of communicating successfully may be due to their lack of familiarity with the culturally accepted forms or modes of academic prose (Reid, 1992). In this survey, one of the mainstream English teachers notes the difficulty Southeast Asian American students have with writing in a "logical mode," and feels this may be due to cultural differences (cf. Atkinson, 1997, for a discussion of the nature of "critical thinking skills" and the pitfalls involved in trying to teach them).

Mainstream teachers commented that LEP students were hesitant to speak up in class. However, an ESL teacher stated that her students always spoke up in class quite readily. Possibly small homogeneous groups gave these students more confidence to speak up in ESL class. Possibly the ESL class allowed them to develop their English proficiency in a less competitive setting. Such an opportunity to express themselves on academic subjects would be an important factor in the development of writing skills (Miramontes, 1993) Adamson (1993) urges ESL teachers to teach language through content while these students are still in ESL so they may gain the confidence they need to become more active participants in mainstream classrooms.

An effective way to teach language through content might be by providing adjunct courses for upper level LEP students (Murie, 1998). In an adjunct course, LEP students are concurrently enrolled in ESL and content courses. The ESL and content teachers work together to coordinate a program based on the language requirements of the LEP students in content courses. The activities of the language classes are then determined by the requirements of the content courses. Such courses would provide ESL teachers with a more accurate notion of what students are struggling with in mainstream classes, and provide the opportunity for a wider range of contextualized writing assignments.

Variety of Types of Writing.   The ESL teachers stated that in ESL classes students were exposed primarily to descriptive or narrative writing, and little if any argumentative or analytical writing. According to mainstream teachers, in mainstream English classes and mainstream content classes, students are required to do comparison–contrast, analytical, definitional, cause–effect, and even some research project type writing.

At the university level, a focus on critical writing and thinking skills appears to be a top priority in the language curriculum according to a survey by Snow (1988). ESL teachers in secondary schools such as the one studied here should provide learners with more exposure to a wider range of types of writing. Here again, it is possible that students would need to spend more time in ESL classes and adjunct ESL/content classes in order to be exposed to this wider range of writing instruction.

Role of One-on-One Tutoring in Writing.   When mainstream teachers were asked to make recommendations for improving the writing skills of the Southeast Asian American students, the most common recommendation of these mainstream teachers was one-on-one tutoring for the students, possibly with some of the better senior class students. It is interesting that none of the ESL teachers made this recommendation.

To our knowledge, there is very little research on the use of native-speaking peers in assisting LEP students in learning written language skills. Adamson (1993), in his review of the successful academic strategies of LEP learners, found that learners benefited greatly from peer interaction. With one student, it was the most important factor in his learning. In a study of peer interaction and the oral language proficiency of Spanish-speaking elementary children, Johnson (1983) found that interethnolinguistic peer tutoring increased students' verbal interaction in English and resulted in increased vocabulary comprehension—but this was oral, not written, second language development. However, if one area where these LEP writers need help is with vocabulary and concepts (in addition to grammar and mechanics), then one-on-one peer interaction might help with this area during the process of writing, particularly in the prewriting phase. Such interaction might be of less help with the final draft, where issues of grammatical accuracy would come to the forefront, and where ESL teacher input might be necessary.

Use of the Native Language in Teaching Writing.   Some teachers mentioned situations where use of the native language was an especially effective learning strategy for the Southeast Asian American students. The use of the native language as a helpful tool in learning a second language is well supported by other studies. Auerbach (1993), in a survey of ESL literacy studies, looks at the positive results achieved when use of the native language is allowed in the ESL classroom, and calls on the field to give up the idea that instruction must be entirely in English. Perhaps we should look at the advantages of native speaking instructors or tutors and a more bilingual approach to literacy at the secondary level. Being able to discuss vocabulary and concepts in the native language is a strategy that Adamson (1993) found to be very successful in one of his case studies and is also noted by Saville-Troike (1984) as a tactic used by those students who performed best in content areas.

IMPLICATIONS FOR TEACHING

Based on the patterns in the teacher responses that we have outlined we believe there are clear implications for the teaching of writing to nonnative speakers of English (particularly Southeast Asian Americans) at the secondary and at the college or university level.

1. Allow and encourage LEP students to spend more time in ESL classes to develop their literacy skills to higher levels before being mainstreamed. A consistent theme for all the ESL teachers was that they did not have enough time to teach students to write well. This would have gone far in enriching the academic proficiency of the Southeast Asian American students in the study and

helped them perform better and become more active participants in their mainstream classes. At the advanced level, as LEP students are ready to move to mainstream classes, provide a bridge for the transition by offering very advanced adjunct ESL courses designed in cooperation with content area teachers.

2. Spend more time on the problems these students have with organization and content in their writing. These are the areas with which mainstream teachers are most concerned. If possible, the teaching of grammar should be integrated into all areas of the students' learning.

3. Include more process writing in the ESL writing instruction. This method of teaching writing can be valuable as a way of learning language and discovering meaning. Students need to be encouraged to see it in that light rather than solely as a correction process. Rather than teaching writing skills prescriptively by presenting models first, allow the students to build from their own ideas and show them the models and language forms to use as they are writing to help them express their ideas.

4. In ESL classes, if a controlled to freewriting model continues to be used, move more quickly from the controlled end of the teaching continuum to the freewriting end, giving the students more opportunities to learn organizational and thinking skills by drawing from their own ideas in writing.

5. In teaching writing in ESL, use content material that the LEP students are likely to encounter in mainstream classes. Teaching writing through content with the use of simplified texts on high-interest topics will likely result in more attention paid to content and organization and on grammar in context than on grammar and structure out of context. An adjunct course provides an excellent setting for teaching writing through content.

6. LEP students need to be able to present their ideas in a logical manner not just in descriptive writing, but in a wider variety of complex rhetorical modes such as comparison–contrast, cause–effect, and argumentation in order to be ready for their mainstream writing assignments.

7. Consider using peer tutors in roles that make sense. Many of the mainstream teachers in this survey seemed to think one-on-one tutoring would be very helpful. With some organization and selection, it might be good to use native-speaker students within the school to help nonnatives, especially with the prewriting phase of a process writing assignment; such native tutors might prove an economical resource and possibly a rewarding experience for the students.

8. Allow and encourage wherever possible the use of the native language. A specific example is the use of writing techniques like "reformulation."[3] Reformulation gives the learner a more active role in comparing his or her own writing with that of specific target equivalents while permitting the use of the native language. In general, the strategic use of the native language appears to be beneficial in helping ESL students understand language and concepts and this is essential for the development of academic competence.

ACKNOWLEDGMENTS

We are grateful to Kimberly Taylor Townsend, the graduate research assistant who conducted interviews, gathered and transcribed the data that we analyzed in the chapter. We would like to thank Andrew Cohen, Bill Johnston, and the editors of this volume for their constructive comments and suggestions. Any problems, inconsistencies, or clarity issues that remain are our responsibility.

REFERENCES

Adamson, H. D. (1993). *Academic competence. Theory and classroom practice: Preparing ESL Students for content courses.* New York: Longman.

Atkinson, D. (1997). A critical approach to critical thinking in TESOL. *TESOL Quarterly, 31(1),* 71–94.

Auerbach, E. (1993). Reexamining English only in the ESL classroom. *TESOL Quarterly, 27(1),* 9–13.

Brown, J., & Sime, J. (1981). A methodology for accounts. In M. Brenner (Ed.), *Social method and social life* (pp. 159–188). London: Academic Press.

Collier, V. (1989). How long? A synthesis of research on academic achievement in a second language. *TESOL Quarterly, 23,* 509–531.

Cummins, J. (1984). *Bilingualism and special education.* San Diego: College Hill.

Downing, B., & Tarone, E. (1990). *The writing of S.E. Asian-American students in secondary schools* (final report). Minneapolis: University of Minnesota Composition Research Center.

Edelsky, C. (1982). Writing in a bilingual program: The relation of L1 and L2 texts. *TESOL Quarterly, 16,* 211–228.

Frodeson, J. (1991). Grammar in writing. In M. Celce-Murcia (Ed.), *Teaching English as a second or foreign language* (pp. 264–276). Boston: Heinle and Heinle.

---

[3]Gilbert (1996) provided a description of the use of the technique of reformulation in learning low intermediate writing skills in a second language. In this technique, there is a principled role for the use of the native language in combination with specific target language models.

Gilbert, S. (1996). *Reformulation of written German from the learner's perspective. CARLA Working Paper #3*. Minneapolis: Center for Advanced Research on Language Acquisition, University of Minnesota.

Harklau, L. (1994). ESL versus mainstream classes: Contrasting L2 learning environments. *TESOL Quarterly, 28*, 241–272.

Hudelson, S. (1984). Kan yu ret and rayt en Ingles: Children become literate in English as a Second Language. *TESOL Quarterly, 18*, 221–238.

Johnson, D. M. (1983). Natural language learning by design: A classroom experiment in social interaction and second language acquisition. *TESOL Quarterly, 17*, 55–68.

Kroll, B. (1991). Teaching writing in the ESL context. In M. Celce-Murcia (Ed.), *Teaching English as a second or foreign language* (pp. 245–263). Boston: Heinle and Heinle.

Leki, I. (1992). *Understanding ESL writers*. Portsmouth, NH: Boynton/Cook.

Miramontes, O. (1993). ESL policies and school restructuring: Risks and opportunities for language minority students. *The Journal of Educational Issues of Language Minority Students, 12*, 77–96.

Murie, R. (1998). Strengthening the bridge: A high school–university partnership. *MinneTESOL/WiTESL Journal, 15*, 1–11.

Paulston, C. B., & Bruder, M. (1976). *Teaching English as a second language: Techniques and procedures*. Cambridge, MA: Winthrop.

Raimes, A. (1991). Out of the woods: Emerging traditions in the teaching of writing. *TESOL Quarterly 25*, 407–430.

Reid, J. (1992). Helping students write for an academic audience. In P. Richard-Amato & M. Snow (Eds.), *The multicultural classroom* (pp. 210–221). Reading, MA: Addison-Wesley.

Saville-Troike, M. (1984). What really matters in second language learning for academic achievement. *TESOL Quarterly, 18*, 199–219.

Silverman, D. (1993). *Interpreting qualitative data: Methods for analysing talk, text and interaction*. London: Sage Publications.

Smith, L. M. (1997, May 24). The language challenge. *Minneapolis Star Tribune*, p. 1.

Snow, M. (1988). Content-based language instruction: Investigating the effectiveness of the adjunct model. *TESOL Quarterly, 22*, 553–574.

Swales, J. (1990). *Genre analysis: English in academic and research settings*. Cambridge, England: Cambridge University Press.

Tarone, E., Downing, B., Cohen, A. D., Gillette, S., Murie, R., & Dailey, B. (1993). The writing of Southeast Asian-American students in secondary school and university. *Journal of Second Language Writing, 2*, 149–172.

Taylor, B. (1981). Content and written form: A two-way street. *TESOL Quarterly, 15*, 5–13.

Urzua, C. (1987). "You stopped too soon." Second language children composing and revising. *TESOL Quarterly, 21*, 279–297.

Zamel, V. (1982). Writing: The process of discovering meaning. *TESOL Quarterly, 16*, 195–209.

Zamel, V. (1987). Recent research on writing pedagogy. *TESOL Quarterly, 21*, 697–715.

7 Classroom Instruction and Language Minority Students: On Teaching to "Smarter" Readers and Writers

Linda Lonon Blanton
University of New Orleans

Concerned about the current state of college preparatory writing instruction, especially for language minority students, this chapter maps out some of the problems and some solutions. To begin with, I take an unsympathetic look at academic writing and claim that much of it is not a good target toward which to aim writing instruction for *any* students.

Next I define what I mean by *language minority* students, characterize their academic backgrounds, and explain instructional problems they frequently have with existing institutional practices. These include problems with our placement of them, curricular designs of writing courses, and pedagogical practices that fail to help them become stronger readers and writers, practices I characterize as *flawed*. Then I focus on critical literacy, not writing skills, as the desired goal of college preparatory writing instruction for all learners, including language minority students.

Finally, moving inside the classroom, I offer a view of how academic writing instruction can be better accomplished through different handling of our evaluation of student writing, better understanding of authority and power as major issues for second-language (L2) writers, and greater efforts to engage students in the practices of intertextuality, as what academic writers do with texts. I end with a hypothetical conversation among four women, all concerned with writing and its power in and over our lives.

AN UNSYMPATHETIC LOOK AT ACADEMIC WRITING

In ordinary life, when a listener cannot understand what someone has said, this is the usual exchange:

Listener: "I cannot understand what you are saying."

119

Speaker: "Let me try to say it more clearly."

But in scholarly writing in the late 20th century, other rules apply. This is the implicit exchange:

Reader: "I cannot understand what you are saying."

Academic Writer: "Too bad. The problem is that you are an unsophisticated and untrained reader. If you were smarter, you would understand me."

The exchange remains implicit, because no one wants to say, "This doesn't make any sense," for fear that the response, "It would, if you were smarter," might actually be true (Limerick, 1993, p. 3).

A colleague of mine, a literature scholar, took such offense at Limerick's (1993) view of academic writing that she wrote the author, defending *our* honor. To my colleague, I wondered aloud what academic journals, and, even more so, what academic textbooks *she* had read over the years. To me, Limerick's sentiments triggered a replay of my own undergraduate days, slogging through textbook after textbook, bleary-eyed, and desperate to come away from assigned readings with a modicum of understanding. Like Limerick's reader, I thought if only I were smarter I would understand.

Since then, experience, confidence, and cynicism have taught me to recognize dull, unnecessarily difficult prose when I see it. And when a text is necessarily difficult—when, for instance, I don't have the background knowledge to understand it with a realistic amount of effort—I know what the problem is. It may well be my lack of knowledge, but it's not *me*.

But what about language minority students in prefreshmen (English as a Second Language, and/or basic) writing programs in our institutions of higher education? Surely many of them must think it *is* them. Why else, after receiving diplomas from U.S. high schools, would they be directed to take college preparatory writing courses, while their supposed peers move steadily toward baccalaureate degrees? Why else would they be excluded from the mainstream curriculum? If only they knew more words. If only they knew more grammar. If only they were smarter.

Why *is* so much academic writing so awful? Well, Limerick (1993) claimed that when academics write for each other, they write inaccessibly to create a kind of camouflage. (Nobody can claim you are wrong or even raise questions, if they cannot even *tell* what you have said.) Timid and fearful people, the ones nobody wanted to dance with in high school, academics pad themselves with protective gear and convince themselves defensively that the unintelligibility of their prose insulates them from bland ordinariness, says Limerick. Anticipating counterclaims to being the most popular dancer at the prom, I'd say that academics write the way they do because that is what everyone thinks is expected, and that is what gets published. After all, *they*—those who publish in prestigious venues, the ones who speak with such assurance—must know, and who are *we* (especially we in the academically marginalized and gendered fields of composition and ESL) to say otherwise.

Like our students, we have not wanted to say, "This doesn't make any sense," for fear we might be told it would if we were smarter. Worse yet, we may fear discovering *they* as a creation of our own collective intellectual insecurities.[1]

So, like the emperor's courtiers, we perpetuate the fraud. Intimidated by writing *we* don't understand, we say nothing for fear that we're the only ones who can't see the royal robes. Even if undaunted, we rationalize that others will judge our students' writing by what we assume to be *their* standards. So we teach writing in ways we think is in students' best interest, maintaining tight control over their forms of expression, and thereby continuing the charade.

Why don't language minority students—at least the ones that have moved beyond preparatory programs and count themselves as "English readers"—see their problem in managing volumes of assigned reading as what it often is, that is, trying to make sense of incoherent writing? In part because preparatory teachers keep the secret well. In ESL or basic (remedial) reading courses, students are often shielded from awful writing, exposed only to "model" readings in the form of engaging short stories or evocative essays. Understandably, teachers may do this to generate interest and stimulate discussion, but also to expose students to writing of the sort they want them to emulate.

Even when teachers could find more broadly authentic academic pieces (e.g., academic reports, journal articles, textbook chapters) that *are* decently written—and some of them are—they exclude them as too difficult, or as part of someone else's discipline, leaving students to wrestle later with texts of this sort, on their own. No wonder students are overwhelmed when they finally do face academic reading and writing demands across the disciplines. Failing, often enough, to prepare students for even the decent stuff, teachers surely don't prepare them for the awful stuff. I too have not wanted to say, "Look, I know this writing is horrible, but this is what you're up against, so let me help you figure out ways to deal with it." Let's call it what it is, and go on from there. Difficult though the work of reading these texts might be, students will be enormously relieved to know it's a problem with the texts and not with them.

In practice, then, we don't usually tell it like it is. Thinking that students' future writing teachers will expect detached, obscure prose, as will their professors in other disciplines, we writing teachers continue the cycle, with everyone thinking "the other guy is the one who demands that kind of awful writing" (Limerick, p. 23). Helplessly, we abandon language minority students (and other students) to their fate. As Hairston (1986) explained, "Intimidated by writing they can't understand, particularly if it appears in a textbook or under the name of some famous person, [students] assume that obscure and wordy writing must be good academic style" (p. 12).

What we should do, to expose the fraud, is become impatient enough to say, "What does this mean? I don't understand." We can't push the responsi-

---

[1] I am grateful to Linda Harklau for this insight.

bility onto students. Even if students see it as it is, rarely do they feel empowered to ask what *it* means—or to assert that they will write otherwise—for
fear that their grades will suffer, or others will think them stupid or unprepared.

If, in actuality, students leaving preparatory (ESL and basic/remedial)
writing programs do find teachers across the disciplines who expect that kind
of writing, do I advocate sacrificing students' academic success—that is, decent grades—to advance a campaign for good writing? Of course not. But
helping students trust their own voices and gain experience in formulating
their ideas clearly as they connect to the ideas of others is to help students
build strength as readers and writers, help them build a base for dealing with
the awful stuff when it comes along.

Just as importantly, helping students write well and recognize and enjoy
good writing is a way to help them avoid becoming silenced by awful writing,
by a "style with its flaws concealed behind a smoke screen of sophistication"
(Limerick, 1993, p. 24). Preparatory writing teachers can help students experiment in accommodating different audiences, writing for a variety of purposes, and adjusting to public discourse without losing their own unique
voices and identities. Help them find a meaningful and acceptable role for
personal experience in academic communication, and teach them to account
for others' ideas without effacing their own.

Writing teachers can help student writers by liberating them of the burden
of thinking they have to write the awful stuff because that's what we've led
them to believe good academic writing is. We can also relieve them of the notion that there exists a template for academic writing, a template that, unfortunately in some writing classes, configures itself as *the* expository essay, or,
worse, the five-paragraph theme. I remember some recent ESL writing students of mine, who, on reading a classmate's essay on parental discipline—an
essay I said I liked very much—were dumbfounded that the essay began with
a lengthy illustration. But how could that be *good*, they wanted to know.
Look, the writer didn't state her thesis up-front. She didn't even begin with
generalizations. She didn't announce the topic to her readers. She didn't use
deductive logic to make her point. She didn't write a summary conclusion.
And, most damning of all, she consistently used "I."

I responded by pointing out alternatives, as we went through other classmates' essays, often very different but still successful, I thought. Some students in the class, chafing under the yoke of conformity to anonymity, were
enormously relieved to hear they had choices—and could have a voice. Others, secure in the certainty of a formula for school writing, were aggrieved to
consider up to then unknown complexities and choices.

Am I being fair about the sorry state of much academic writing and its cor-
rosive influence on writers, writing, and learning? I think so. There simply *is*
a lot of poor prose out there, and we *are* mistaken if we validate it by emulat-
ing it, by holding it up as a standard. But don't get me wrong: writing that requires work, even struggle—difficult writing, and critical writing *is* difficult—is not the same thing as awful writing (although *any* text can be writ-

ten badly). And we would mislead students and ourselves by trying to save everyone the struggle.

For students' own success in college, we must help them develop as critical writers, but in the complex institutional world of higher education, we must also help them survive by developing enough rhetorical flexibility to accommodate expectations (some of which seem more legitimate than others) that differ across disciplines, as well as among individual teachers. Will preparatory students have to read awful academic writing? Probably. Poorly written textbooks and turgid discipline-specific texts are not simply going to disappear. So let's help students develop reading and writing strategies to survive. Above all, let's make sure they don't misread their difficulties as assurance of their own inadequacies.

LANGUAGE MINORITY STUDENTS: WHO ARE THEY?

Armed with diplomas from U.S. urban high schools, thousands of students whose home language is not English enroll in urban colleges across the country every year. Many of these students immigrated to the United States with their families some years back, when they were in the elementary grades. Others arrived more recently but in enough time to receive most, if not all, of their secondary schooling here. Some, of course, may have been born here.

Many young immigrants or children of immigrants acculturate and assimilate well. And by the time *they* leave high school, their language and literacy capabilities and their academic records place them in a strong position for the most competitive of U.S. colleges. Students like these went to my daughter's high school—immigrants from India, Argentina, Korea, Vietnam, China, and other places—and they had their pick of postsecondary schools. As noted in her school's roster of graduating seniors, these particular classmates of hers chose Georgia Tech, Carnegie Mellon, Vanderbilt, Emory, LSU, Dartmouth, NYU, UT/Austin, UCLA, Rice, Wake Forest, Tulane, and Texas A&M. And given their accomplishments in high school, they are almost certain to be stars in college. These are the success stories, however, and are definitely *not* the students in need of remediation or any other preparatory services as they enter college.

For reasons not always clear to us, other students, whose home language is also not English, tell different stories. They too graduate from U.S. high schools, but then find their educational possibilities limited by their high school experience and records, by their failure to perform well on entry exams or placement tests, or by all of these. Students fitting this latter profile crowd into urban community colleges and city/state universities and are shunted into preparatory programs. These students are ones I have worked with for several decades and have written about (Blanton, 1992a, 1992b, 1993, 1994), ones I refer to here as *language minority* students.

When these students reach college, they may feel strongly that they shouldn't be placed differently from other U.S. high school graduates, and are offended when labeled *ESL*. They are, after all, not *foreign*. In most cases, they either hold green cards and are official residents, or they are U.S. citizens. They and their families are also likely to be taxpayers in the locale where they attend college. They probably dress and look like other American students.

Many language minority students speak English with fluency, whether or not it is accented with the imprint of their home language. Some may even sound native-like. Others, for reasons not always in accord with the number of years in the country or length of schooling, may have gotten stuck in a sort of interlanguage. These latter students have difficulty being understood, their pronunciation is "flawed," and their grammar is nonstandard. They may have received the same amount of schooling as the former students, but, for reasons perhaps more related to personal identity or to learning style, it has had little effect on their speech (Ioup, 1996).

Regardless of the state of their spoken English, language minority students, as defined in this discussion, write below par and are designated ESL or basic/developmental/remedial in their college placement. Yet these students are often more literate and schooled in English than in their home language, leading to their unfortunate characterization by some teachers as remedial in two languages.

PROBLEMS WITH PLACEMENT

If administrative procedures, placement exams, and particularities of their writing preclude language minority students from being mainstreamed,[2] where do we place them? It is not always a solution for them to be placed with basic/remedial writers whose home language *is* English, in part because teachers of these classes often throw up their hands, claiming they are not trained or equipped to work with ESL problems. And, in fact, the writing of language minority students often does show evidence that English is not their mother tongue. A reasonable programmatic response is to train basic writing teachers to integrate language minority students into their classes, but reason does not always prevail.

To complicate matters further, it is also problematic for language minority students to be placed in ESL programs, in part because they take it as an act of discrimination. Why *should* they be separated from other U.S. high school graduates and not allowed to take regular courses, they reason. They assume that writing courses enrolled in by students whose home language is English are more legitimate and will move them toward their major courses more quickly. This, in fact, may be so, because the writing of students in ESL programs is often held to a standard of grammatical perfection not applied to the writing of non-ESL-enrolled students.

---

[2]Although I use *mainstream* to refer to the curriculum that language minority students are not permitted to enter on arriving at college, I see the metaphor as problematic. It sets these students apart, as if their writing and reading needs represent *differences of kind*. Rather, I assume along with Farr and Daniels (1986) that the teaching of writing/reading to students of all linguistic backgrounds must be guided by the same general principles.

Language minority students are also uncomfortable, they say, when placed in ESL classes with "foreigners," that is, international students with F-1 visas who arrive in the United States to complete their higher education and then return home. Not surprisingly, language minority students have little in common with international students, either in terms of future plans, prior school experience, or degree of familiarity with the surrounding community. To add insult to injury, they may be given textbooks that require them, for example, to compare aspects of life in "their" countries to those in the United States. And they may suffer the indignities of being introduced to instructional details, such as which side of their notebook paper to write on, or to cultural aspects of U.S. life, such as, say, the frequent use of first names among casual acquaintances, as if they were newcomers to the country. (See Harklau, in press, for a detailed discussion of the cultural orientation, commonplace in ESL instruction, that is inappropriate for language minority students.)

When placed in preparatory classes with "internationals," language minority students naturally assume that they are mistaken for foreign. Their membership in the community is challenged. Their status as residents or citizens is ignored. And their right not to be treated differently from other U.S. high school graduates is denied. With such resentment—submerged as it may be—draining away their energies, no wonder some language minority students have difficulty concentrating on learning. They are insulted. They have lost face.

ILL-SUITED INSTRUCTIONAL DESIGNS

Whether language minority students are placed in ESL programs with internationals or in basic/remedial writing classes with (other) Americans, classroom instruction is often ill-suited to their literacy needs. Let's take ESL instruction first. Traditional pedagogy in ESL classes assumes a focus on linguistic structures, understood as part of the language acquisition process. As such, classwork targets language forms, such as modals and verb tenses, if sentence-oriented. If discourse-oriented, instruction targets more global elements such as, say, connectors as part of paragraph cohesion or introduction-body-conclusion essay development. Either way, grammatical, syntactic, and rhetorical elements—that is, language structures—form the pedagogical focus.

More advanced instruction, in traditional ESL pedagogy, translates into students' presumed need to acquire *more* English, which may indeed be the case for international students with prior limited exposure to the language. Even with the pedagogical focus shifted away from speaking English to reading and writing it, ESL teachers, relying "almost exclusively on linguistics for their conception of literacy" (Rodby, 1992, p. 2), teach reading and writing as language structure/form. When not concentrated on comprehension exercises and vocabulary work, reading activities may focus on unraveling syntax that readers might stumble over, or on analyzing an essay writer's use of discourse elements to achieve a particular rhetorical effect. In writing class—and reading and writing continue to be handled separately—students write on assigned topics in order to practice using language correctly. Because, in a traditional paradigm, writing improvement is assumed to result from correction, student writing is turned in to the teacher, who corrects it and hands it back, thereby providing necessary feedback for better writing on the next assignment.

Conflating literacy acquisition with language acquisition, ESL instruction marches ahead, teaching "more" English to students, some of whom have spent much of their schooling, if not most of their lives, in the United States. Evaluated in their ESL classes according to the norms of a discourse community that marginalizes them, even threatens to exclude them (Harklau, in press), language minority students' frustrations mount.

The problems then are these. To begin with, the administrative practice of placing internationals and language minority students in the same classes, without regard to individual circumstance or instructional need, ignores the assault of that practice on the identity and pride of language minority students. Worse, program decisions in those joint classes usually privilege the internationals: teaching goals, textbook choices, and instructional talk are all founded on everyone's "newness" to things "American" and to everyone's need for greater English-language fluency.

Next, let's discuss basic/remedial writing instruction, which is often on an institutionally parallel track with ESL writing instruction. When placed in basic/remedial writing courses with non-ESL students, language minority students don't always fare much better than in ESL courses with internationals. Traditionally, basic/remedial courses are designed for native English speakers, primarily nonmainstream dialect speakers who have experienced little success with school writing. The institutional crux of the matter is that while traditional writing pedagogy presumes that basic/remedial students have little need for language development—and, if they did, teachers of basic writing generally have little linguistic training—basic writing programs, traditionally taught, demonstrate little understanding of literacy either.

Shaughnessey's (1977) and Rose's (1989) insights to the contrary, eradicating the nonstandardness of students' written English remains the paramount goal of most basic/remedial programs today. Get their writing cleaned up and get them through the proficiency test that stands between them and further college study: that's the pressure placed on basic writing teachers by administrators, who don't want noncredit-bearing programs siphoning off scarce resources, and state legislators, who oppose appropriating funds for remedial education.

Akin to the recent congressional debate on welfare, the debate on remedial education is a blame game. If secondary schools were doing their jobs, if parents were taking proper responsibility for their children's learning, if students were more serious about school, then we wouldn't have students, particularly immigrant students, entering college in need of remedial English (and math). So we must take a stand against all that permissiveness and personal irresponsibility—*us* paying for *them*—and either cut off funds for remedial programs altogether, or give students a small window of opportunity—one to two semesters, at most—to get up to speed. Move them on or move them out.

No wonder that teachers, like drill sergeants, march students through training in standardizing the forms they use in writing. But even before heightened anti-immigrant sentiments and new funding pressures, basic writing textbooks were written according to a traditional pedagogy that made them little more than grammar exercise books. The focus was almost exclusively on the most frequent and "egregious" errors basic writers make in using English-language forms: lack of subject–verb agreement, sentence fragments, run-on sentences, spelling and punctuation mistakes, and nonstandard verb tenses.

Even when traditional basic/remedial writing instruction takes a more rhetorical slant, it, like traditional ESL writing instruction, sticks to a form-centered pedagogy (Blanton, 1995), simply shifting the focus to overall paragraph or essay structure. Writing practice then centers on matters such as, say, thesis statements, topic sentences, or supporting examples. Infused with an antiquated perception of English discourse as "fitting" rhetorical modes (Bain, 1866), like muffins in a tin, remedial writing lessons model, say, expository essay structure or cause–effect arrangement. With little concern for reading, except for analyzing texts as models of rhetorical modes, traditional pedagogy gets students operating in conceptual frames that, true, can manifest themselves in English discourse (whether academic or not), but—herein lies the fundamental instructional problem—with form externally imposed on writerly efforts, effectively stifling a writer's possibility to generate thoughtful prose.

Before discussing further the literacy needs of language minority students—and, I would add, the needs of all students preparing for college writing—I want to briefly outline some of the unsuccessful instructional practices that are commonplace in ESL and basic/remedial writing programs today. For ease of expression, I often use the term *preparatory* to refer to both ESL and basic/remedial programs, because language minority students may be institutionally tracked along either route.

FAILED INSTRUCTIONAL PRACTICES

Instead of grappling with the inescapable complexity of critical literacy, preparatory writing programs often opt for simplified solutions (Salvatori, 1996). These so-called solutions are, in effect, flawed practices that hamper a program's effectiveness in helping students become stronger and "smarter" readers and writers. Some of the flawed instructional writing practices are these:

1. Modeling preparatory writing courses after single-genre-oriented freshman English writing courses, a practice that ignores students' need to gain varied literacy experiences that translate

across the disciplines. In my institution, the first semester of freshman English teaches *the* expository essay; the second, *the* argumentative essay. The failure in this programmatic arrangement is multilayered: if freshman English doesn't prepare students for writing across the curriculum, then the prefreshman program modeled after it—with its sole objective to place students in freshman English—obviously won't prepare students for college success either. Worse, if preparatory writing students spend their instructional time prepping for a single-genre writing course or for the test that gains them entry, then preparatory writing instruction easily slips into teaching a template for writing. Teaching in preparation for, say, expository essay writing easily becomes teaching the five-paragraph theme, a genre specific only to the writing classroom (Heath, 1987).

2. Positioning language as subject rather than as medium, creating a void for talking, reading, and writing. It works this way. Lessons *about* language—on, say, verb forms or paragraph structure—provide students with information that can possibly aid them in editing their writing (Krashen, 1985), but provide no power to generate exploratory, expansive, analytic, and communicative language. Language of this latter sort cannot be taught, although it can be learned, but learned only when writers are provided "opportunity for trials, and chances for having successful communication in writing" (cf. Freedman, 1985; cited in Heath, 1987, p. 91). It requires, at a minimum, intellectual engagement with complex ideas that captivate a writer enough so that she is willing to wrestle with them.

3. Ignoring students' lived experience, effectively cutting them off from their individual possibilities as readers and writers. And this is only half of a larger problem. Preparatory writing programs commonly push student writers to one extreme or another. Either they are given assignments limiting them to writing about themselves as topic, producing necessarily self-referential writing that precludes their engagement in the intertextual arena that characterizes academic writing. Or they are instructed not to involve themselves in their writing, not even to use "I." Either extreme hampers writing development. Self-referential writing is unsuccessful because it strikes academic readers as nonauthoritative, as "high schoolish" (Braun, 1996, p. 33). At the other extreme, writerless writing contributes to the awful stuff discussed earlier.

4. Treating reading as the retrieval of information, denying students the opportunity to construct meaning as real readers do. Look at ESL reading textbooks on the market today: most treat reading as information retrieval. Reading so construed becomes a reductive activity, because responding to others' right or wrong questions

requires decoding, not interpretation or analysis or any of the other turns of mind that comprise critical literacy.

5. Treating writing as a solitary act, denying students the chance to engage in the kinds of collaborative conversations that characterize thinking, reading, and writing in the academy. Intertextual writing of the sort that validly characterizes academic discourse emanates from lived intertextual experiences, from an active exchange of ideas. Without it, a writer's writing remains self-referential, limited to reporting about one's self.

6. Packaging writing as preconceptualized assignments, robbing students of individually arrived at purposes for writing and sheltering them from the tough and messy mental work of constructing, shaping, and connecting ideas. Let's say you were to assign me to "write about the person who has influenced you the most." This is not *my* mental construct, does not fit into a scheme of thinking that interests or includes me, and from it I can churn up no *felt sense* (Perl's term, 1994, p. 151) with which to go forward. Aside from the questionable value of your assignment in preparing me for college study, that it has been conceptualized by someone else leaves me with little mental room to maneuver: I fill in *who* and *how*. When, later in my college study, I am suddenly expected to develop my own "take" in a subject area, I am hard-pressed. After all, my instructional experience has been limited to writing from someone else's mental vantage point. Let's say that, in an introductory anthropology course, I am given this assignment, which is surely more representative of what is expected of me in college: "Read two articles from the reference list on language and culture. Then, after summarizing them, relate them to each other, and apply one aspect of your discussion to your own experience." I am flummoxed. What *am* I supposed to write about? I have no clue because reflection, synthesis, and application—turns of mind highly valued in critical writing (and needed for the anthropology assignment)—both fuel and are fueled by the activity of constructing one's own conceptualization, which I have no experience in doing.

7. Treating texts as models of styles or strategies, preventing inexperienced reader-writers from gaining the reflective and intertextual experience necessary to achieve critical literacy. Mimetic work produces, guess what, imitation, and not at all the "highly constructed" mental activity required for critical writing (Salvatori, 1996, p. 443).

Further discussion of the problems created by these practices and the instructional needs these practices leave unmet are interwoven throughout the remainder of the chapter.

CRITICAL LITERACY AND CLASSROOM INSTRUCTION

As discussed elsewhere (Blanton, 1994), my experience with language minority readers is of treating texts as "dead on the page." As readers, they are not aware of the possibility of interacting with texts, yet this is the very behavior that researchers put at the heart of formal learning and academic success (Bartholomae & Petrosky, 1986; Carson, 1993; Heath & Mangiola, 1991; Leki, 1993; Salvatori, 1996; Spack, 1993; Wall, 1986; Zamel, 1996). Being unaware of textual interaction does not make language minority students "illiterate." Not at all. But their literacy is functional, not critical.[3]

Functional and critical literacy are different behaviors. Briefly, functionally, but not academically, literate readers decode texts, but seem unaware they can and should (from the academy's perspective) bring their own perspectives to bear in creating a reading. When the last word on the last page is decoded, the reading is finished. To functionally literate readers, "poor" reading, then, is failing to remember the words of a text.

If remembering the words were possible, even a decoding relationship to texts would be difficult with poor writing of the sort discussed earlier, with texts written by and to no one in particular. When a reader's mind "hydroplanes" over the surface of a page because it doesn't connect with anything *on* the page (Hairston, 1986), then even functional reading becomes undoable.

So students' failure becomes multilayered. They can't remember the words of a text because no one can. Even if it were possible, they couldn't remember poorly written texts because their minds wouldn't connect with anything on the page. And, with better-written texts, where a connection—and an interaction—is theoretically possible, these readers have no experience connecting and interacting. Unlike Alice, they don't know there *is* a looking glass to step through, into a world of "talking reading and writing" (Heath & Branscombe, 1985, p. 15).

Students who have no experience talking reading and writing claim no individualized perspective on texts. They don't factor themselves into the picture. And they reduce textual and intellectual complexity to a reductive simplicity. If you ask them questions that can be answered from a reasonably accessible text, you'll get answers. If you ask questions that can't be answered from the text, you'll still get answers from the text, or you'll get silence. Awhile back, I realized that I, too, had once been that kind of reader, the result of years of schooling where all my answers to others' questions were either right or wrong. And I am aware that at times I still have to stop myself from

---

[3]Throughout, I discuss the absence of what I call critical literacy as an educational problem for language minority students; and, indeed, I believe it is, given academic expectations in postsecondary U.S. schools. I do not, however, see the absence of critical literacy as an intellectual failure on students' part. Critical literacy, despite its privileged status in U.S. academia, is a way of being/knowing in the world, and, like all ways, it is socially constructed and culturally derived. If we knew more about the social and linguistic backgrounds of language minority students, we might well discover that, like Heath's (1983) Roadville and Trackton children, these students' literate ways simply do not synchronize with school ways; and *that* is the point of failure.

attempting to commit to memory the words of a text, as if I can't trust myself to assign significance.

Whatever else teachers do with language minority students to prepare them for academic study, we must create opportunities for them to interact with texts: Create opportunities to know that a text can function as a fulcrum to bring reader and writer together; to know that the reader has the responsibility of giving voice to the writer's argument, in the writer's absence, and then engaging in conversation with that voice; to have the confidence to match voices with the text's author; and to recognize, as in poorly written academic texts, when an author has failed to make a conversation possible (Salvatori, 1996).

In reading–writing classrooms, creating opportunities to interact with texts means engaging in tasks that require talking and writing about them. In particular, classroom activities need to engage students in questioning texts, linking them to each other, connecting them to their readers' experience, using them to support or explain their readers' ideas, using texts to illuminate their readers' experience, and using their experience to illuminate texts (Heath & Mangiola, 1991). These are the practices that accomplish critical literacy.

According to Heath and Mangiola (1991), these practices can be independent of any particular academic discipline, but underlie success in all fields of study. This idea accords with Spack's contention (1988) that language minority students should not work with ESL or basic writing teachers in the various disciplines. Rather, they need from preparatory teachers the kind of instructional work that can transfer to all disciplines.

Critical literacy needs to be distinguished from literacy *skills*, which lie outside of texts as wholes. Literacy skills are "mechanistic abilities that focus on separating out and manipulating discrete elements of a text—such as spelling, vocabulary, grammar, topic sentences, and outlines" (Heath & Mangiola, 1991, p. 40). Literacy skills can be learned from lessons and workbook exercises on, say, commas and verb agreement, but they do not accomplish critical literacy.

Critical literacy is more than learning to read and write, and more than know-how in using language conventions. Readers and writers achieve it through textual interaction because that, in fact, is what *it* is: ways of interacting with texts. Although literacy skills undoubtedly transfer to students' future coursework—especially in enabling them to offer up acceptable-looking assignments—critical literacy practices, and not skills, make the crucial difference in academic success.

ACCOMPLISHING GOOD WRITING

Surely good *academic* writing is, at its core, *good* writing. School writing programs operate according to the tacit assumption that good writing can be defined and recognized. They have to. Otherwise, how could teachers work at helping students write better and then evaluate their writing?

Unfortunately, in writing courses—and especially in college preparatory writing programs—writing gets codified into absolutes that read as formulae (e.g., "The introduction ends in a thesis statement"). The desire for certainty is understandable, because writing—the doing, learning, and evaluating of it—*is* so very complex. Absolutes give comfort, especially to language minority students and others who have had little success with school writing. And they give something to teachers to "teach." But absolutes create a false picture of what writing is and how writers accomplish it. Writing by formulae results in, well, formulaic writing, writing as canned as music in elevators. Writing by the numbers, like painting by the numbers, does little to forward students' intellectual and expressive development. Worse, it makes it next to impossible for students to accomplish good writing.

What *is* good writing? A better question is *when* is writing good? And the answer has to be "I dunno, it depends." Not an altogether comforting answer, but true nevertheless. Good writing is context-bound. What is good writing for one purpose and one audience is not necessarily good writing for a different purpose or audience. Put us in the context, explain to us the writer's purpose, give us the writing to read, and we'll tell you if it's good or not: we'll know it when we see it (Leki, 1995).

So, to provide students with realistic direction, I tell them "it depends." As readers of their writing, their peers and I have to know *who* and *why*: who they are writing to and why that particular audience needs to know what they have to say. Only then can we review their writing with any intelligence and give feedback that might be useful. When I am wearing my evaluator's hat, I need the same information. Like beauty in the eye of the beholder, the quality of a piece of writing is determined by those who read it. In order to read smart, readers need a context for reading.

One of the trickiest aspects of learning writing in school is that the reader is not always the audience. If, for instance, a student is writing to parents, advocating a certain approach to disciplining young children, and the writing—because it happens to fulfill a school assignment—is going to be reviewed by the student's peers and later evaluated by a teacher, then the writer has to make explicit the purpose and audience in ways that would not be necessary if the writing was appearing in a newsletter published expressly for parents. If, on the other hand, a student-writer's classmates and teacher *are* the true audience, then the writer does not have to work at creating such a fiction.

Failing to account for a credible audience in generating and shaping writing, and having no real purpose, students write for no reason to no one. But without audience and purpose, a writer can construct no motivation (Rodby, chap. 3, this volume), can generate no *felt sense*, which is that physical force that directs and guides a writer as he or she presses along, bringing words together to move the thinking forward (Perl, 1994).

No wonder teachers get questions such as "How many words does it have to be?" and "What do you want me to say?" No wonder that teachers of writing, not understanding they often get what they ask for, resort to evaluative responses such as "unfocused," "unclear," and "your point?" If we assign preconceptualized topics, take away a credible audience, remove any real purpose for writing, our students-trying-to-be writers will move words around on the page to reach the requisite 300th word. And not a word more.

EVALUATING WRITING AS GOOD

To evaluate students' writing, I must have my own clear sense of what good writing is, and I have to let students in on it. From a reader's perspective, given a knowledge of the writer's audience and purpose, I ask myself these questions (revised from Hairston, 1986, pp. 11–20):

1. Is the writing significant? That is, does the writer make it worth the reading? (It might be worth my reading, for instance, if the writer's perspective is unusual, or the writer tells me something I didn't know or hadn't thought about quite in that way.)
2. Is the writing clear? In other words, given a reasonable amount of effort, can I, the reader, follow along?
3. Is the writing unified? Does it stick to a topic and develop the topic in some sort of way that makes sense to me, a reader of English?
4. Is it grammatically acceptable? Because this is school writing, does the writer use standard usage expected by any educated reader?
5. Is it economical? Can I breeze through fairly easily without having to wade through what Zinsser (1980) called "clutter" (cited in Hairston, p. 16)?
6. Is the writing vigorous? Can I feel some life, some energy, that helps to move the writing along?
7. Is there a voice? In other words, can I sense the communicating presence of a real human being, a mind at work?

Because these questions form my basis for evaluation, my students need to ask themselves the same questions in revising and editing their work. If they revise and edit their writing by the same criteria used to evaluate it, then—it stands to reason—they are working smarter. Yet how often in writing programs do students work in the dark, their writing judged by criteria known to the teacher but hidden from them? No wonder they ask, and ask again, "What do you want?"

In addition to knowing the evaluation criteria, students need to know that these criteria are socially constructed. All criteria are. There are no universal "truths" here. Evaluation criteria are constructed by the teacher from his or her professional and writerly experience, and reconstructed from the constructions of others with whom the teacher feels philosophically and pedagogically compatible. They are not written in stone. Nor are they handed down on clay tablets. The criteria that I use work for a reader of English, but only for some readers of English. They work for me now, but I have not always operated by the same criteria.

The chemistry professor across the campus from me may not want vigor and authentic voice in the laboratory reports he assigns. And students need to know that their professors in different disciplines—and even in the same discipline—may have different expectations and operate by different standards of evaluation.

The situation may be complex, but writers have no choice but to be sensitive to varying contexts. That assumption, after all, lies at the heart of viewing writing according to socially based criteria, because texts are, in fact, situated in the very interaction between writer and reader. (See Blanton, 1995, for discussion of a reader-based/social paradigm for writing instruction.) And readers' expectations are fluid, in that they are socially constructed, culturally derived, and altered by a writer's intentions, as well as by the reader's own.

Consequently, additional evaluative ground rules need to apply because it is writing for school purposes that students are doing. For one, the subject matter, audience, and purpose need to be considered appropriate for public discourse. (See Joos' 1961 discussion of registers.) This ground rule doesn't make me the language police. It simply recognizes that all language users socially contextualize language. School is not home. Classmates are not intimates. If, for instance, a student wrote an outpouring of her own intensely personal childhood tragedy as a victim of sexual abuse, and, for some reason, wanted me to read her writing, I would not refuse. Neither would I evaluate it. I would express my sorrow and concern. I would invite her to drop by my office and talk, if she wanted. I would advise her of available counseling services, if she were seeking help. But I would *not* evaluate her writing. How could I? If, on the other hand, a student were researching crimes against children, and she chose to use her own experience as a victim of sexual abuse to authenticate her claims, I think I could evaluate the effectiveness of her efforts.

As evaluators of writing, teachers do not always face decisions that involve such gut-wrenching matters. Rather than writing so intensely emotional that it requires us to set aside our evaluator's role, we may instead see writing that strikes us simply as sophomoric. What this may mean is that the writing topic is either so personalized (e.g., "Grandfather's influence on my life") as to preclude interaction by a public reader, or so episodic and closed ("a tragic accident"), as to exclude interaction altogether (Braun, 1996). Either way, public readers are left empty-handed, even miffed, because school writing is publicly situated, right? Yet this is not obvious to ESL/basic writers whose prior instruction considered no social basis for writing.

Guarding against assuming that *my* intentions when making assignments are necessarily a student's intentions when fulfilling them (Horvath, 1994)—and trying to rule out faultiness in the assignments I give—I respond to the issue of appropriateness in a way that, I hope, allows students to do two things: socially contextualize their language, and, when they fail, save face. Simply stated, my next evaluation question, added to the other seven, is this:

8. Is the writing socially appropriate, given a public audience?

To my growing list, I add two final criteria, which, like question 8, are especially shaped to help student writers meet the expectations of academic readers. These concern authority and intertextuality, and are discussed separately.

AUTHORITY AND POWER: READER-WRITERS SITUATING THEMSELVES IN THE ACADEMY

I have written elsewhere that academic writers are expected to write with something called "authority," the absence of which is powerlessness (Blanton, 1994). In part, powerlessness results from being cut off from one's self, from instruction where answers to others' questions are right or wrong (Bartholomae & Petrosky, 1986). Taking the broad view, powerlessness comes from being educated according to transmission pedagogies—where, in other words, instruction is designed to transmit knowledge to the unknowing (Cummins, 1989; Freire, 1983).

From the perspective of academic reading, what is perceived as powerlessness results from students never having opportunities to bring their own views and experience to bear on texts (Salvatori, 1986; Wall, 1986), or even knowing that such a transaction is possible. Viewed from a slightly different angle, such readers are powerless because they unwittingly concede their power to others—to teachers, to writers of printed texts, to other readers who they think are smarter. Readers perceived as powerless are those also perceived as functionally, but not critically, literate. These are, not coincidentally, the students in college preparatory writing programs today.

Within this construct, readers performing critically are, conversely, not powerless. *They* engage in reading and writing as transactional processes. Empowerment as a critical reader, then, comes about through the practice of interacting with texts, and through developing individualized responses to them (Bartholomae & Petrosky, 1986). Reader-writers who develop individualized responses to texts—who can "talk" to them and about them, who can agree or disagree with them, who can relate their own response to texts and write about them—are empowered to practice literacy as academics do (Heath & Mangiola, 1991). Reader-writers with individual responses to public issues speak with certainty about something they own.

Further, voices of certainty *assume* authority as their ideas and perspectives are shaped by an awareness of audience and balanced with that audience's expectations. Authority is, then, a stance that writers assume in regard to the matter of audience (Wall, 1986). Assuming a stance of authority does *not* mean giving up one's unique identity and assuming an institutional identity, an institutional voice, which is no identity, no voice, at all. (Institutional writing, like institutional food, is generic. It's that awful stuff. Academic writing doesn't need to be disembodied and voiceless, disowned by its author.)

In fact, when academic readers consider a piece of writing authoritative, what they are admiring is actually the writer's success in achieving a balance between the uniquely individual and the audience's expectations of a broader, public discussion (Wall, 1986). Given this point of view, mature academic writing is not even possible without the reader-writer's individual and personal involvement or, conversely, without the reader-writer's inclusion of the individual. So, to my list of criteria for evaluating student writing, I add another. Not only "Is there a voice?," but

9. Can I hear a voice of authority, a voice balancing the individual self and the larger situated context?

As language minority students wrestle with the authority demon, they are necessarily conflicted (Mortensen & Kirsch, 1993). Connecting to themselves, to written texts, to audience expectations, and to academic standards and demands, they engage in a struggle for no less than their own identities. (All writers do.) At best, they achieve an ever-changing, ever-delicate balance. Audiences change, from writing to writing. Texts change, from course to course and from discipline to discipline. Standards change from discipline to discipline, and maybe even from teacher to teacher. Expectations and standards change, as students advance in their studies. And all the while, individuals change, as they nurture and develop themselves, and make their way. If all goes well, the academy also changes, unless, as is often the case, representatives of the academy take for granted that life there is governed by a single set of norms—theirs—that everyone else must adopt (Pratt, 1991).

At worst, language minority students succeed academically but lose themselves, lose the struggle to hold on to *their* selves, and, like Rodriguez (1982), disconnect from the richness of their heritage, from their past. Like Chin's (1994) narrator, they may find the price for comfort is their mother tongue. Or they think the price too high, and they abandon the struggle altogether, leaving academia embittered and defeated. Some will think my characterization overly dramatic. I don't think so.

INTERTEXTUALITY: INTERWEAVING WRITING AND READING

Interweaving ideas, the writer's own with the ideas of others, is expected in writing for school purposes, and increasingly so as students advance in their studies. This interwovenness, or intertextuality, can be thought of in various ways. As a kind of accounting for ideas articulated by others and related to a writer's subject. As showing that one is well-enough-read in a subject area. As accomplishing writing in ever broadening contexts to learn and engage ideas outside one's own experience. As exercising one's ability to go beyond the receptive comprehension of texts in order to transform them for one's own writing purposes (Flower, 1990). As writers allowing their reading to influence their writing—in a "hybrid act of literacy" (Spivey, 1990, p. 259). As a means of engaging in self-reflection and self-awareness, which is the very essence of critical thought (Salvatori, 1996). Or as all of the just mentioned.

Intertextuality involves, then, certain kinds of literacy practices, a certain collegial comportment, rhetorical display, and intellectual work. It manifests itself in writing, but is predicated on a writer's engagement with other texts before and during the emergence of his or her own. The outgrowth is critical thinking, intellectual growth, and greater literacy. These are life-long endeavors, but they must be, can be, accomplished through textual interaction, even in the beginning stages. This means, in effect, that over time they accomplish themselves. Literacy accomplishes literacy (Rodby, 1992). Critical literacy accomplishes critical literacy.

Yet if critical minds engage in intertextual thinking, if students—advancing in their studies—engage in intertextual research, and if academic writers engage in intertextual writing, where do inexperienced reader-writers begin to work at it? Preparatory writing programs, and even freshman writing programs, seldom give students the opportunity to learn intertextuality. In freshman writing at my institution, students in the second semester are expected to write *a* research paper, a separate assignment from the rest of their writing, which, by definition, requires no research. In the ESL program where I teach, students do not write from sources, at least not for evaluation purposes, because "How could we know what is the writer's own?" Not privileging interconnection to others' ideas enough to evaluate it, we do not build intertextual thinking and writing into the curriculum. My students and I work at it anyway, but it is a tough go.

Guiding ESL/basic writers through the early experience of remembering others' work, referencing it, pulling it in at just the right place in one's own emerging text, transforming it to fit and smoothing it in, shaping it to serve one's own ends, and giving it space without privileging it over one's own words—all of this must be accomplished, as a series of approximations, like the driving that evolves in driver's education. Once behind the wheel, you get the hang of it in doing it, little by little, but there are white knuckle moments.

Some of the greatest complexities of intertextuality are not the linguistic and rhetorical ones, but the psychological ones. Reader-writers must muster the confidence to appropriate ideas and information from others' texts and adapt them to their own ends. They have to see themselves as joining the intellectual discussion (Greene, 1992). Not only are they joining it, they must take the lead and exercise authority over other texts: what to use, what not to use, how to mold it, how much credit to give it. These are heady matters.

Developing reader-writers have to also gain the confidence to foreground their own ideas, and use information from sources as background to explain and support those ideas. Using themselves as conduits for others' ideas, inexperienced reader-writers, those with little confidence, at first let others speak *for* them, assuming perhaps that others' words create a better text than one's own (Campbell, 1990). I have known how they feel, and the struggle to reframe someone else's ideas, in effect to appropriate them, takes a kind of assurance, a kind of public assertiveness, that many of us have to invent. That struggle, I sense, is evident in the writing of this language minority student:

Gandhi made a difference. He accomplished his goal to bring freedom to his people "without firing a shot." "He also showed that a highly spiritual concept—nonviolence—can be an intensely practical tool in the quest for peace, even in the twentieth-century world of realpolitik, power, and violence," remarked Barash. Rosa Parks is another example.

Most of every paragraph in this writer's text is a quotation, but it *is* a beginning. Texts written by second language writers and studied by Campbell (1990) also foregrounded others' words, rather than using them to explain or support the writers' own.

Even more invisible and complex is the intense and intellectually taxing textual interaction that precedes the emergence of a writer's text. In reading others' words, a reader must, as far as possible, make the text speak, absent its author. Then, with an awareness that develops only through reflexivity, the reader articulates a response to the author's argument and critiques the two (Salvatori, 1996). Only through responding to texts, and then through responding to one's responses, through selecting what one considers significant, and articulating why one assigned to that particular idea a certain significance, only through these and other practices can inexperienced reader-writers gain experience. Elsewhere I have written about Berthoff's (1981) double-entry notebooks and their use in helping students read critically (Blanton, 1995).

Pedagogically, intertextualizing presupposes using reading as a means of teaching writing. It is not possible when reading and writing are taught as separate classes, as is often the case in ESL programs. Neither is it possible when the writing curriculum does not include reading, does not provide texts for writers to engage, as may be the case in basic/remedial writing programs. It does not work even when reading and writing are combined, if reading gets privileged over writing, or if readings get atrophied to "models" of style or rhetorical strategy (Salvatori, 1996). If reading becomes a pretext for writing, or if reading gets reduced to a set of disparate vocabulary, grammar, and "comprehension" exercises, then little is gained in reading *or* writing (Zamel, 1992).

So, because college students are expected to perform intertextually, I add a final criterion to my list for evaluating school writing:

10. Is the writer working "across texts?" That is, is the work intertextual?

More is involved here, of course, than adding to a list, although that is important because it tells student writers what to expect. And even that will help them work smarter. But what is at issue here is the very foundation for academic literacy. Although the task of teaching critical reading and of teaching composition through reading—of teaching critical writing—is daunting, it must form the pedagogical and intellectual core of preparatory reading-writing programs.

CONCLUSION

I conclude with a hypothetical conversation among four people, who, I dare say, never spoke to each other before my efforts to orchestrate a meeting. I envision them, like the women around the *mah jong* table in Tan's novel (1989a), gathered to talk and enjoy each other's company. From the reflective heart of their experiences, they teach us about writing, learning, and teaching:

Shirley: See the crystal, look, there in the window. Notice the light. The essay, the luminous essay, is like that crystal. Its permanence in our memory cannot be fractured. A critical essay holds together because the essayist tells the reader the structure that is to come and builds a temporary frame for the content that passes through it. Like light through a crystal. Each is unique, with a vitality that defies formulae, defies conventional form (Heath, 1987).

Min-zhan: I wish I could speak about writing as beauty. As a crystal. For me, writing has meant struggle. In my life, school language was separated from home language. I had to work at keeping them separate. When my own thoughts, *my* questions, crept in, I became silent. Silent to protect myself. Otherwise I would be found out. My metaphor is writing as tool, as survival tool. I felt obligated to reproduce the stance of the discourse I read. I forced myself not to participate in reading and writing conversations, forced myself to be a bystander. When my voices tried to interrupt, I silenced them. They made me afraid. I see disturbing signs in my daughter's writing instruction, signs of the metaphor of writing as tool dominating the understanding of language. The voices of the world outside the classroom are made to seem irrelevant (Lu, 1987).

Mina: Some of those voices outside are of *my* students, Min-zhan. When they enter writing class, they know their outside voice—the voice that those inside have made irrelevant—will not do, but they have no other voice, no academic voice, to put in its place. For them, writing is fear. What they say is wrong, but they don't know what to say right. It is the "mystery" of error that intimidates them, has them in its power. Too often they are afforded the chance to prove, once again, they do not belong there, as they keep failing to do even simple things right, things that are simple only to those who already know them. And when they are offered "solutions," it is too often formulae for writing, not the possibilities of creating something uniquely theirs, like Shirley's crystal (Shaughnessy, 1977, 1994).

Mrs. Tan (insisting on *Mrs.* and the last word): Too much talk here. Only one thing important. Easy to read. Tell writer, give me easy to read. What that business, hard to read? Say, Mr.-So-Smart, listen here. Do again. Don't forget reader. He not remember reader—again? Then he Mr.-Not-So-Smart. Tell him that (Tan, 1989b).

ACKNOWLEDGMENTS

I am indebted to my colleague Elizabeth Penfield and to Linda Harklau, for critical readings of earlier drafts of this chapter.

REFERENCES

Bain, A. (1866). *English composition and rhetoric: A manual*. (American edition, revised.) New York: D. Appleton.

Bartholomae, D., & Petrosky, A. (1986). Facts, artifacts and counterfacts: A basic reading and writing course for the college curriculum. In D. Bartholomae & A. Petrosky (Eds.), *Facts, artifacts and counterfacts: Theory and method for a reading and writing course* (pp. 3–43). Upper Montclair, NJ: Boynton/Cook.

Berthoff, A. E. (1981). *The making of meaning: Metaphors, models, and maxims for writing teachers*. Montclair, NJ: Boynton/Cook.

Blanton, L. L. (1992a). A holistic approach to college ESL: Integrating language and content. *ELT Journal, 46*(3), 285–293.

Blanton, L. L. (1992b). Reading, writing, and authority: Issues in developmental ESL. *College ESL, 2*(1), 11–19.

Blanton, L .L. (1993). Reading as performance: Reframing the function of reading. In J.G. Carson & I. Leki (Eds.), *Reading in the composition classroom: Second language perspectives* (pp. 234–246). Boston: Heinle & Heinle.

Blanton, L. L. (1994). Discourse, artifacts, and the Ozarks: Understanding academic literacy. *Journal of Second Language Writing, 3*(1), 1–16.

Blanton, L. L. (1995). Elephants and paradigms: Conversations about teaching L2 writing. *College ESL, 5*(1), 1–21.

Braun, M. J. (1996). *Freshman composition: An investigation into university literacy*. Unpublished master's thesis, Department of English, University of New Orleans.

Campbell, C. (1990). Writing with others' words: Using background reading texts in academic compositions. In B. Kroll (Ed.), *Second language writing: Research insights for the classroom* (pp. 211–230). New York: Cambridge University Press.

Carson, J. G. (1993). Reading for writing: Cognitive perspectives. In J. G. Carson & I. Leki (Eds.), *Reading in the composition classroom: Second language perspectives* (pp. 85–104). Boston: Heinle & Heinle.

Chin, M. (1994). *The phoenix gone, the terrace empty*. Minneapolis: Milkweed.

Cummins, J. (1989). The sanitized curriculum: Educational disempowerment in a nation at risk. In D. M. Johnson & D. H. Roen (Eds.), *Richness in writing: Empowering ESL students* (pp. 19–38). New York: Longman.

Farr, M., & Daniels, H. (1986). *Language diversity and writing instruction*. New York: ERIC and Urbana, IL: National Council of Teachers of English.

Flower, L. (1990). Introduction: Studying cognition in context. In L. Flower, V. Stein, J. Ackerman, M. J. Kantz, R. McCormick, and W. Peck (Eds.), *Reading-to-write: Exploring a cognitive and social process* (pp. 3–32). Oxford, England: Oxford University Press.

Freedman, S. W. (Ed.), (1985). *The acquisition of written language: Response and revision*. Norwood, NJ: Ablex.

Freire, P. (1983). Banking education. In H. Giroux & D. Purpel (Eds.), *The hidden curriculum and moral education: Deception or discovery?* (pp. 283–291). Berkeley, CA: McCutcheon Publishing.

Greene, S. (1992). Mining texts in reading to write. *Journal of Advanced Composition, 12,* 151–170.

Hairston, M. (1986). *Successful writing* (2nd ed.), New York: W.W. Norton.

Harklau, L. (in press). Representing culture in the ESL writing classroom. In E. Hinkel (Ed.), *Culture in second language teaching and learning*. New York: Cambridge University Press.

Heath, S. B. (1983). *Ways with words: Language, life, and work in communities and classrooms*. Cambridge, England: Cambridge University Press.

Heath, S. B. (1987). The literate essay: Using ethnography to explode myths. In J. A. Langer (Ed.), *Language, literacy, and culture: Issues of society and schooling* (pp. 89–107). Norwood, NJ: Ablex.

Heath, S. B., & Branscombe, A. (1985). "Intelligent writing" in an audience community: Teacher, students, and researcher. In S. W. Freedman (Ed.), *The acquisition of written language: Response and revision* (pp. 3–32). Norwood, NJ: Ablex.

Heath, S. B., & Mangiola, L. (1991). *Children of promise: Literate activity in linguistically and culturally diverse classrooms*. Washington, DC: National Education Association.

Horvath, B. K. (1994). The components of written response: A practical synthesis of current views. In G. Tate, E. P. J. Corbett, & N. Myers (Eds.), *The writing teacher's sourcebook* (3rd ed., pp. 207–223). New York: Oxford University Press.

Ioup, G. (1996). *Can form-focused instruction have an effect on fossilized grammatical rules?* Unpublished manuscript.

Joos, M. (1961). *Five clocks*. New York: Harcourt Brace.

Krashen, S. D. (1985). *The input hypothesis: Issues and implications*. London: Longman.

Leki, I. (1993). Reciprocal themes in ESL reading and writing. In J. G. Carson & I. Leki (Eds.), *Reading in the composition classroom: Second language perspectives* (pp. 9–32). Boston: Heinle & Heinle.

Leki, I. (1995). Good writing: I know it when I see it. In D. Belcher & G. Braine (Ed.), *Academic writing in a second language* (pp. 23–46). Norwood, NJ: Ablex.

Limerick, P. N. (1993). Dancing with professors: The trouble with academic prose. *The New York Times Book Review,* 3, 23–24.

Lu, M. (1987). From silence to words: Writing as struggle. *College English, 49*(4), 437–448.

Mortensen, P., & Kirsch, G. E. (1993). On authority in the study of writing. *College Composition and Communication, 44*(4), 556–572.

Perl, S. (1994). Understanding composing. In G. Tate, E. P. J. Corbett, & N. Myers (Eds.), *The writing teacher's sourcebook* (3rd ed., pp. 149–154). New York: Oxford University Press.

Pratt, M. L. (1991). Arts of the contact zones. *Profession 91,* 33–40.

Rodby, J. (1992). *Appropriating literacy: Writing and reading English as a second language*. Portsmouth, NH: Boynton/Cook Heinemann.

Rodriguez, R. (1982). *The hunger of memory*. Boston: Godine.

Rose, M. (1989). *Lives on the boundary*. New York: Penguin.

Salvatori, M. (1986). The dialogical nature of basic reading and writing. In D. Bartholomae & A. Petrosky (Eds.), *Facts, artifacts and counterfacts: Theory and method for a reading and writing course* (pp. 137–166). Upper Montclair, NJ: Boynton/Cook.

Salvatori, M. (1996). Conversations with texts: Reading in the teaching of composition. *College English, 58*(4), 440–454.

Shaughnessy, M. (1977). *Errors and expectations*. New York: Oxford University Press.

Shaughnessy, M. (1994). Diving in: An introduction to basic writing. In G. Tate, E. P. J. Corbett, & N. Myers (Eds.), *The writing teacher's sourcebook* (3rd ed., pp. 321–326). New York: Oxford University Press.

Spack, R. (1993). Student meets text, text meets student: Finding a way into academic discourse. In J. G. Carson & I. Leki (Eds.), *Reading in the composition classroom: Second language perspectives* (pp. 183–196). Boston: Heinle & Heinle.

Spack, R. (1988). Initiating ESL students into the academic discourse community: How far should we go? *TESOL Quarterly, 22*, 29–51.

Spivey, N. N. (1990). Transforming texts: Constructive processes in reading and writing. *Written Communication, 7*, 256–287.

Tan, A. (1989a). *Joy luck club*. New York: Ivy Books.

Tan, A. (1989b). Mother tongue. *Threepenny Review*.

Wall, S. V. (1986). Writing, reading and authority: A case study. In D. Bartholomae & A. Petrosky (Eds.), *Facts, artifacts and counterfacts: Theory and method for a reading and writing course* (pp. 105–136). Upper Montclair, NJ: Boynton/Cook.

Zamel, V. (1992). Writing one's way into reading. *TESOL Quarterly, 26*(3), 463–485.

Zamel, V. (1996). Transcending boundaries: Complicating the scene of teaching language. *College ESL, 6*(2), 1–11.

Zinsser, W. K. (1980). *On writing well* (2nd ed.). New York: Harper & Row.

8 One Size Does Not Fit All: Response and Revision Issues for Immigrant Student Writers

Dana R. Ferris
California State University, Sacramento

As process-oriented composition teaching approaches, with their empha-
ses on multiple drafts, feedback, and revision, have permeated U.S. college
classes, teacher commentary has become a much more vital and significant
aspect of writing instruction. Early first-language (L1) and second-language
(L2) process advocates (e.g., Hillocks, 1986; Krashen, 1984; Zamel, 1982,
1985) argued that teacher feedback is much more effective at intermediate
steps of the writing process than at the end of it (Leki, 1990). Although the
process approach has also led to an increased focus on other forms of response, such as teacher–student conferences (Carnicelli, 1980) and peer feedback (Ferris & Hedgcock, 1998; Mittan, 1989), neither type of feedback is
identical to written teacher commentary and neither, for a variety of reasons,
can or should replace it. Thus, because written teacher commentary is likely
to continue as a crucial part of composition instruction, it is important that
we carefully examine the nature and effectiveness of such responses.

Unfortunately, research on teacher response to L2 writing (whether written or oral) has been scarce and, for a number of reasons, inadequate. Such research as there is has been limited by the absence of systematic data collection
and/or analysis procedures, of longitudinal research designs, and of adequate
consideration of the larger pedagogical context (Ferris, Pezone, Tade, & Tinti,
1997; Leki, 1990; Mathison-Fife & O'Neill, 1997; Reid, 1994). Because of this
insufficient database, much of the advice given to ESL writing teachers about
response to L2 student writing tends to follow directly from that given to
teachers of native English-speaking (NES) writers, a trend that has been increasingly questioned and challenged by L2 writing researchers and theorists
(Ferris et al., 1997; Leki, 1990; Silva, 1988, 1993; Zhang, 1995). Furthermore,
examinations of teacher response and student revision in L2 contexts have
been almost exclusively concerned with either foreign language (FL) students
(specifically NES college students studying French, Spanish, or German in the
United States) or with international students pursuing their education in

United States academic settings. There is little published research available on teacher feedback to immigrant student writers and none at all (as of this writing) that attempts any direct comparisons between this group of students and international or FL novice writers.

This chapter begins by highlighting several key differences between international and immigrant English as a Second Language (ESL) students with respect to issues of teacher response. It then describes several recently completed studies on the immigrant student population, which were intended to address some of the gaps in the previous literature. Based on this discussion, key issues and strategies for future research on this important but relatively neglected aspect of ESL composition instruction are highlighted. The chapter concludes with implications for responding to L2 writers, focusing particularly on strategies for student writers who are long-term United States residents.

BACKGROUND: DIFFERENCES ACROSS
L2 STUDENT POPULATIONS

In large part because there has been so little research of any kind about teacher feedback and its effects on L2 student writers, previous reviews of research considered all studies of L2 writers together, regardless of differences across contexts and student populations (cf. Leki, 1990; Silva, 1993; Truscott, 1996). For instance, Cardelle and Corno (1981) warned teachers against giving students too much praise in their commentary, arguing that it may cause students to become complacent or may actually discourage them from revising ("My teacher liked this part of my paper, so I shouldn't change it."). But their subjects were NES students studying Spanish at the college level; it could certainly be argued that U.S. undergraduate students and ESL writers have different affective responses to positive feedback from their teachers. It has also been argued that FL students and instructors have different attitudes toward composition in the FL class than do ESL instructors and students, with the former group seeing writing primarily as language practice and the latter seeing it as a necessary survival skill for L2 academic settings (e.g., Cohen & Cavalcanti, 1990; Hedgcock & Lefkowitz, 1994, 1996). This difference in perceptions and goals influences teachers' response strategies and students' willingness and ability to consider their teachers' feedback carefully and to revise. It is not appropriate, therefore, to lump all L2 writing research together as if the studies and findings were comparable simply because subjects were writing in a second language.

In addition to considering differences between ESL and FL contexts, it is crucially important in analyzing and considering response to draw distinctions between international ESL students and immigrant students or other long-term United States residents. These distinctions have been examined in some detail in this volume and elsewhere (e.g., Ferris & Hedgcock, 1998; Leki, 1992; Reid, 1997; Spack, 1994); this discussion focuses on the implications of these differences for teacher response. Although some generalizations about these two groups of college students are made in this discussion, it must always be remembered that international and immigrant students are two internally diverse and heterogeneous groups of writers.

International Students

Depending on their specific linguistic, cultural, and educational backgrounds as well as their prior experience with U.S. higher education, international students may resist the notion of multiple drafting and revision and may not, at least initially, see the purpose of teacher commentary on preliminary essay drafts. Like U.S. FL students, writers whose primary English education has occurred in their home countries may not value either composing as a means to discover ideas or writing as a means to accomplish instrumental academic or professional goals, having experienced L2 writing mostly as a way to practice new vocabulary or grammar constructions (Reid, 1997). International students may also lack the pragmatic and cultural awareness that teacher feedback is meant to be taken seriously and considered carefully, regardless of whether it is in statement or question form, or whether hedges (such as "maybe") are used. Indirectness on the part of the teacher may be perceived as a lack of confidence or competence and cause the student to lose respect for the instructor (Leki, 1992; Levine, 1983, cited in Scarcella, 1990, p. 94).

Immigrant Students

Students who have been partially, primarily, or wholly educated in the United States will likely be more familiar and comfortable with teacher–student communication patterns, feedback, and the notion of revising after receiving feedback (Ferris & Hedgcock, 1998; Reid, 1997). They may also be more aware of U.S. pragmatic phenomena and thus able to correctly interpret a comment like "Could you maybe give an example here?" as "I would like you to provide an example at this point."[1] However, they may struggle with two important issues in relation to teacher feedback. First, even immigrant students who have resided in the United States for a number of years may still be acquiring academic literacy skills, although they may be highly fluent in everyday English. Like many of their NES counterparts, they may have failed to acquire the critical thinking skills prized by university instructors and assumed by teachers' higher order questions on their papers that challenge their logic (Atkinson & Ramanathan, 1995; Collier, 1989; Ferris & Hedgcock, 1998; Leki, 1992; Reid, 1997). Second, because they learned English in U.S. communication-oriented immersion–submersion settings, such students often lack the knowledge of metalanguage used by teachers to make comments about rhetorical aspects of student writing ("thesis," "topic sen-

---

[1]In an earlier study (Ferris, 1997), I found that the presence or absence of hedges in teacher commentary had no noticeable effects on the number and quality of revisions made by the student writers.

tence," etc.)—terms used in academic ESL textbooks that international students may have encountered in their home countries or in intensive English programs in the United States—and especially about grammatical and mechanical problems (Ferris & Hedgcock, 1998; Reid, 1997).

Examples of the possible gaps in immigrant students' formal grammatical knowledge were observed in a recent study by Ferris, Harvey, and Nuttall (1998) on the effects of a grammar training program on immigrant student writers' linguistic knowledge and accuracy. The researchers found that the subjects—junior-level university students taking an advanced "Writing for Proficiency" course—were able at the beginning of the program to label only 8% to 12% of common errors (noun plural/possessive, verb tense/form, run-ons, etc.) in a student essay excerpt. Unfortunately, most discussions of teacher feedback strategies and accompanying teaching materials overlook immigrant ESL students' lack of knowledge of formal grammar terminology. For instance, in preparing materials for the same grammar training project on the topic of subject–verb agreement for advanced university ESL students who were long-term United States residents, I consulted six grammar/editing books. All six assumed students' prior knowledge of the terms *subject*, *verb*, and *agreement*, and assumed that the students simply needed to know rules for avoiding errors in agreement. But when asked what they knew about subject–verb agreement, students in the program responded, "If the noun has an 's,' then the verb must also have an 's,' so they agree."

The foregoing discussion of immigrant students and teacher feedback leads to several questions that lend themselves to empirical investigation:

1. How do immigrant ESL writers react to teacher feedback?
2. What kinds of revisions do immigrant students make after receiving teacher feedback?
3. What kind of grammar feedback is most helpful for immigrant student writers?

The following sections discuss recently completed research that addresses these questions. In some cases, comparisons between research that has focused on international students and other studies that have focused on immigrant students are discussed. In other instances, no such comparisons are possible because relevant research does not exist. This discussion is followed by a summary of findings and of ways in which future researchers should consider investigating questions that remain.

RESEARCH ON FEEDBACK TO IMMIGRANT STUDENT WRITERS

How Do Immigrant Student Writers React to Teacher Feedback?

Early studies of ESL students' reactions to or preferences regarding teacher response typically reported that student writers disregarded teacher feedback and/or had limited strategies for utilizing it in subsequent writing tasks. It was also found that L2 student writers had strong preferences for grammar-focused feedback over responses to the content and organization of their essays (Cohen, 1987; Cohen & Cavalcanti, 1990; Leki, 1990, 1991; Radecki & Swales, 1988). However, these studies were conducted in single-draft settings in which students were not expected to revise their work after receiving feedback or in English as a Foreign Language (EFL) contexts or with international students in the United States.

Recently, several researchers examined student reactions to teacher feedback in settings where some or most of the student subjects were long-term U.S. residents (Ferris, 1995b; Hedgcock & Lefkowitz, 1994; McCurdy, 1992). In these studies, students reported that they consider teacher feedback very seriously and find it extremely helpful in revising their work and in later writing projects. In a previous study (Ferris, 1995b), for example, 155 university ESL students at high intermediate to advanced levels of English proficiency, nearly all of whom were long-term U.S. residents, were surveyed about their attitudes toward written teacher commentary on intermediate and final drafts of their essays. The students claimed to attend to teacher commentary on both preliminary and final drafts of their essays and to value feedback on both content and grammar issues. More than 96% of the respondents felt that their teachers' feedback helped their writing to improve. At the same time, the students reported experiencing at least occasional confusion over their teachers' questions in margins or endnotes and over grammatical symbols, corrections, and terminology. These results therefore support the previous generalizations that immigrant students are comfortable with feedback-and-revision cycles, that they perceive the value of improving their writing and of teacher feedback in achieving that goal, and that they may experience some confusion with regard to specific teacher response strategies.[2]

With regard to student reactions to teacher feedback, a helpful comparison may be made between Cohen (1987) and my earlier study (1995b), because my study was a third-generation replication of the former. Cohen reported that his student subjects had a "limited repertoire of strategies for processing teacher feedback" and that teacher feedback "may have a more limited impact on the learners than the teachers would desire" (pp. 65–66). In contrast, my subjects reported utilizing "a variety of resources to deal with teacher commentary" (p. 44). I attributed the differences to the process-oriented, collaborative nature of the writing classes being studied. However, the contrast may also be explained by the fact that the subjects in the my study had more extensive experience in U.S. academic settings and that they felt more highly motivated to revise and improve their work because they saw development of their writing skills as important to their future academic and career pursuits.

---

[2]It may also be the case that international student writers are equally confused by teacher questions and by various types of grammar feedback; however, there is no research on this point which directly compares the two general populations.

What Kinds of Revisions Do Immigrant Students
Make After Receiving Teacher Feedback?

There have been few studies of ESL students' revision patterns and even fewer that have specifically linked teacher feedback to student revision (see Ferris, 1997, for a review). L1 researchers have reported that inexperienced student writers are primarily focused on microlevel changes in their writing, seeing "revision" as mechanical correction and cleanup (Beason, 1993; Faigley & Witte, 1981). Similarly, research on L2 writers' revisions has generally found that student writers make primarily surface-level changes and relatively few macrolevel, content-focused revisions. However, most of those studies have focused on international students or EFL writers, who may have limited experience with or training in strategies for substantive revision and/or insufficient motivation for making major changes in their papers.

In contrast, in a longitudinal discourse-analytic study, I (Ferris, 1997) examined the effects of teacher feedback on a sample of 220 student papers (first draft/revision pairs), nearly all of which were written by immigrant ESL students, and more than 1,500 teacher comments provided on students' preliminary essay drafts. The results indicated that students utilized a great majority of the teacher's comments to make substantive and effective revisions. However, it was also found that some types of feedback were more likely than others to lead to effective student revisions.

A similar study (Patthey-Chavez & Ferris, 1997) utilized a case study approach to examine the effects of teacher–student writing conferences on the subsequent writing of several highly competent university international students. Data examined included students' first drafts, audiotapes and transcripts of teacher–student conferences, student revisions of the same paper, and first drafts of papers from the next essay assignment. Quantitative and qualitative differences were found between the conferences of the stronger and weaker writers, and the stronger writers produced more extensive and effective revisions. It was possible to trace effects of the conference discussions not only in the revisions of the paper that had been discussed, but also in the first drafts of the next assignments. Like the immigrant students whom I studied (Ferris, 1995b, 1997), the international students in this context also appeared highly motivated to improve their writing, as all of them had to pass an in-class essay examination at the end of their respective writing courses. In addition, the ESL and composition programs in which they were enrolled placed great value on multiple drafting and teacher feedback (cf. Atkinson & Ramanathan, 1995). Finally, it was apparent from the conference transcripts and from the revisions that there was mutual respect between teachers and students and that the students valued teacher feedback and appreciated the time their teachers took to meet with them.

In summary, these studies suggest that teacher feedback (whether oral or written) can have significant, positive effects on student revision when the feedback is thoughtful and focuses primarily on student ideas, when students are motivated to revise, and when they respect their teachers' efforts on their behalf. However, as I noted previously (Ferris, 1997), the findings "suggest two conflicting but coexisting truths: that students pay a great deal of attention to teacher feedback, which helps them to make substantial, effective revisions, and that students sometimes ignore or avoid the suggestions given in teacher commentary" (p. 330).

In an attempt to examine the characteristics of teacher commentary that lead to more or less effective student revisions, I (Ferris, forthcoming) examined 24 pairs of student first drafts and revisions completed by eight ESL student writers (seven immigrant students and one international student). It was found that the subjects were able to effectively address questions that asked for specific information from their own experience or from assigned course readings, feedback that suggested microlevel (word or sentence) revisions as opposed to global changes, and verbal summary feedback about specific patterns of grammatical error, combined with underlined in-text examples of these patterns. They were less able to cope with higher order questions or statements (Carlsen, 1991; Dillon, 1982; Kusnick, 1996) that challenged their logic or argumentation, and tended to either ignore or avoid such advice or to make ineffective revisions which failed to improve or even weakened their original texts.

Because there have been no direct comparisons to date between immigrant and international ESL students as to their ability to utilize teacher commentary in revision, it would be inappropriate to suggest that either group is more or less capable of or willing to incorporate teacher feedback in their revisions. What can be said, based on the fairly substantial sets of survey and discourse-analytic data collected from immigrant students in my earlier studies (Ferris (1995b; 1997), is that teacher feedback can have a very significant influence on students' revisions and that this feedback may at least occasionally be problematic for students. If nothing else, this conclusion suggests that teachers need to construct their feedback to immigrant student writers very carefully, knowing that their students will likely do their utmost to respond to teacher input in their revised texts.

What Kind of Grammar Feedback Is Most Helpful for Immigrant Student Writers?

A recent review essay by Truscott (1996), arguing that ESL writing teachers should dispense with all error correction, has caused researchers and teachers to focus on the issue of whether teachers should give grammar feedback to their students at all, and if so, what form(s) it should take. As with most other ESL writing research, the studies cited by Truscott to support his thesis focus almost exclusively on FL students or international students. As of this writing, no study has examined differences between international and immigrant students in their ability to process and benefit from error feedback and grammatical explanations. However, in her discussion of the differences between "eye" learners (international students) and "ear" learners (immigrant students), Reid (1997) pointed out that, although immigrant students have learned English "principally through oral trial and error" (p. 4), international students "know, understand, and can explain English grammar" (p. 6). These generalizations would imply that immigrant students may need different types of grammatical explanation and error feedback than do international students.

One weakness of Truscott's argument against error feedback in L2 writing classes is his lack of definition of the term *error correction*. One need only to survey different editing textbooks and error correction studies to conclude that the term *error correction* does not mean the same thing to all teachers and researchers. International students, for instance, may benefit from a very precise system of error correction that identifies and labels various error types so that they can access their previously learned knowledge of grammatical rules in editing their writing (see Lane & Lange, 1993, for an example of such a system). On the other hand, immigrant students may cope better with indirect feedback (Ferris, 1995c; Ferris & Hedgcock, 1998; Hendrickson, 1980) that simply locates errors for them without offering labels or corrections. This system allows them to use their acquired oral competence in the L2 to self-correct errors (Brown, 1994) in much the same way as NES self-edit, without reference to a system of grammatical terms and rules to which they may never have been formally exposed.

Although there is little hard evidence as to what types of error feedback work best for immigrant students, several recent studies report results that at least suggest support for indirect error correction methods. In an earlier study (Ferris, 1995a), 30 immigrant ESL students were systematically taught to self-edit their work over the course of a 15-week semester (using a pedagogical approach outlined in Ferris, 1995c). Error feedback consisted of verbal commentary (in an endnote) about one to three major patterns of error observed in a given paper, paired with underlined examples of each error type in the students' texts. At the end of the semester, examination of two in-class essays and three revised out-of-class essays showed that 28 of the 30 subjects showed at least some reduction in error frequencies of targeted patterns of error. Furthermore, as already noted, the discourse-analytic data reported in my earlier work (Ferris 1997) showed that the teachers' verbal end comments on students' errors (again paired with underlined textual examples) were highly effective in helping students to produce improved revisions.[3]

In Ferris et al. (1998), we addressed immigrant students' lack of prior grammatical training by assessing the effects of a 10-week grammar/editing tutorial program. This program consisted of minilessons (including definitions of key terms, examples, discovery and error correction exercises, and editing strategies) on writing problems common to the immigrant student population in that context (a large suburban 4-year public university in Northern

---

[3]In both studies, students had also received input from their teachers about grammatical rules and editing strategies in the form of in-class minilessons and/or out-of-class individualized assignments in an editing handbook. In other words, indirect teacher feedback about errors was not the only form of grammar/editing information given to students.

California).[4] Pretest data confirmed that the 40 students who began the program had very limited ability to identify the types of errors addressed in the tutorials, either in isolated sentences or in connected discourse. However, they showed dramatic improvement on these tasks on posttests. This study provides at least limited confirmation both that college-level immigrants lack specific types of formal grammatical knowledge and that they can benefit from focused instruction on grammar terms and rules and editing strategy training that addresses the gaps in their knowledge while building on their acquired competence in the L2.

To summarize, previous studies of immigrant student writers on issues related to teacher feedback and student revision have suggested the following conclusions:

- Immigrant student writers take teacher feedback very seriously and value it highly (Ferris, 1995b);
- Immigrant student writers are capable of utilizing teacher feedback to improve their papers during revision (Ferris, 1997; see Patthey-Chavez & Ferris, 1997, for similar findings with international students);
- Immigrant student writers utilize specific types of teacher feedback in revision more successfully than other types (Ferris, forthcoming);
- Immigrant student writers can utilize indirect error feedback from their teachers to produce more accurate texts (Ferris, 1995a, 1997);
- Immigrant student writers have limited formal knowledge of formal grammar terms and rules, but can benefit from instruction and practice which takes advantage of their acquired L2 competence (Ferris et al., 1998).

However, there still remain a number of unanswered (and largely unexplored) questions with regard to teacher feedback to immigrant student writers. First, it is important to consider feedback and revision by a wide spectrum of teachers and students. Given the discussion in this chapter, it is especially important to study and describe different populations of immigrant student writers, both to contrast them with international students and to identify various factors in immigrant students' backgrounds (linguistic and cultural differences, educational experience, etc.) that may affect not only the response and revision dynamic but the students' development as writers in general. Second, in designing research on teacher feedback, it is crucial that we provide precise descriptions of what teachers do as they comment and how students process those comments, and that we consider more carefully

---

[4]Topics covered were subject–verb agreement, nouns (types, plurals, possessives, articles/determiners), verbs (present vs. past tense, past vs. present perfect, modal auxiliaries), and sentence structure (types of clauses, punctuation of clauses, avoiding run-ons and fragments).

the students, settings, and tasks being studied. Previous response-and-revision research has been justly criticized for not adequately considering contextual variables. Studies of teacher response need to take a variety of factors into account, including, but not limited to, the following classroom variables: the type of assignment/genre of writing being completed, the point of the term at which the feedback is given, the number of drafts/papers being written and the relative weight given to each in the final evaluation, other types of response (e.g., peer, tutor, self-evaluation) received by students, turnaround time between submission of drafts and teacher feedback, the availability of in-class explanation of teacher response strategies and in-class opportunities for students to process and ask questions about teacher feedback, in-class instruction that could affect the form and content of the teachers' comments and the nature of the overall relationship between the teacher and his or her class. In addition to discourse-analytic, survey, and experimental techniques that have already been used, ethnographic interviews and teacher and student think-aloud data may be helpful at getting at these issues in greater depth.

IMPLICATIONS FOR COMPOSITION INSTRUCTION

Though the review of the literature presented in this chapter points out a number of limitations and gaps in the previous research, it also yields some preliminary insights and generalizations potentially useful for L2 writing pedagogy as it relates to response and revision for ESL writers, particularly those who are long-term United States residents. These suggestions fall into two general categories: implications for teachers as they construct responses to their students' papers, and implications for helping students to process teacher feedback and to utilize it effectively in constructing subsequent texts.

Considering Students' Competence

In writing comments to students, teachers need to consider carefully the knowledge and abilities of their students. For instance, as previously discussed, immigrant students may have little formal knowledge of grammatical terminology; marginal or terminal comments or error-labeling corrections may therefore have limited effects on their ability to produce more accurate papers. On the other hand, such students, particularly those at advanced levels of proficiency, may have a great deal of acquired competence in English and may be able to self-correct errors if they are pointed out (Brown, 1994). Similarly, teachers should not assume that their students are familiar with composition jargon such as "thesis statement," "topic sentence," or "transition." Before providing any feedback about content, organization, or grammar/mechanics, teachers should consider administering some form of survey or test to find out what their students already know (or do not know) of this metalanguage (cf. Ferris et al., 1998).

Considering Students' Preferences

In addition to considering students' knowledge, instructors should also explore students' expectations regarding feedback: Do they prefer oral or written? Would they like comments in the margins, at the end, on a separate sheet, or some combination of these? Do they expect comments of praise or constructive criticism? Would they rather have content and form issues addressed together or on separate drafts? Do they want all errors corrected or pointed out, or only a select few? With such information, teachers can either provide students with the types of feedback they prefer or explain to students their rationale for *not* doing what the students want. In either case, the students will likely feel more empowered and listened to than if the teacher merely imposed his or her own feedback style on them.

Assessing the Effectiveness of Commentary

Teachers should assess the effectiveness of their own responses by getting feedback from students as to what they appreciated or were confused by in the teacher's comments and by examining subsequent student papers to see whether or not the teacher response was helpful to students as they revised. Some practical steps toward such self-assessment could include providing in-class time for students to ask questions about and write brief summaries of the teacher comments after returning marked drafts (Ferris, 1995b), and requiring students to turn in all previous drafts with their revisions, perhaps with a cover letter explaining how they addressed the teacher's feedback on the prior draft or why they chose not to (Ferris, 1997).

In examining student revisions to assess the effects of commentary, teachers should pay particular attention to the effects of their own questions, especially higher order questions designed to challenge students' logic or stimulate critical thinking (Carlsen, 1991; Dillon, 1982; Ferris, 1997; Kusnick, 1996). Carlsen's (1991) review of educational studies of classroom questioning found little evidence of a relationship between higher order questions and student achievement. In a recent article on teacher questions, Kusnick (1996) noted that "despite our widespread cultural belief that questioning is an essential part of teaching, educational research has never demonstrated that asking students questions enhances learning" (p. 2). In my own recent research (Ferris, 1995b, 1997, in press), it was found that ESL students expressed confusion about the intent of teacher questions and that both L1 and L2 students were less likely to make effective revisions in response to higher order questions than to other types of comments (e.g., statements, imperatives, or lower order questions asking students to provide specific information). Although I am not advocating that teachers abandon such questions altogether, it is important to assess whether students are understanding and utilizing this type of feedback, and, if not, to help them to do so during the revision process.

Assisting Students With Revision

An important but overlooked step in the process of teacher response and student revision is actively helping students to utilize feedback, whether from teacher or peers, in shaping their revisions. Teachers all too often simply assume that students will understand the feedback itself and how to incorporate suggested changes skillfully in their revisions. However, recent research findings suggest that immigrant student writers may ignore or avoid comments when they do not feel competent to make the changes necessitated by those comments, even deleting material rather than attempting to improve it (Ferris, 1997, forthcoming), or making the change without the corresponding rhetorical or syntactic adjustments needed to make the revision flow smoothly. Teachers can provide practical help in the following ways:

1. Pairing their higher order questions or statements with concrete suggestions that could help students know how to address those comments.
2. Discussing revision strategies with the whole class, including showing a marked student essay and talking about what types of changes the teacher comments suggest and how those suggestions could be implemented in this paper.
3. Providing individualized assistance to students, via teacher–student conferences, to help them process the feedback and revise successfully.

CONCLUSION

Several major points have been advanced in this chapter:

1. Teacher response is an important part of the writing class and therefore needs careful examination by researchers.
2. Differences exist between immigrant student writers and other groups of L2 student writers that have implications for teacher response strategies.
3. Research findings suggest that both teachers and students need to consider response and revision much more carefully and systematically and in much more depth.

In closing, it is important to echo the warnings of L2 researchers and theorists that we not apply uncritically the findings and prescriptions of L1 composition research to the endeavor of responding to L2 student writing (Ferris et al., 1997; Leki, 1990; Silva, 1988, 1993, 1997). Not only do L2 writers need "more of everything" (Raimes, 1985, p. 250) in terms of linguistic and rhetorical information, but they are widely diverse in their cultural expectations of and educational experiences with teacher-student relationships, feedback, composing, and revision. Because of this diversity, it is important not only that we recognize differences between L1 and L2 writers but that we examine and carefully consider contrasts across L2 student populations—especially between immigrant and international students—in designing research and instruction and in constructing responses to student writing.

REFERENCES

Atkinson, D., & Ramanathan, V. (1995). Cultures of writing: An ethnographic comparison of L1 and L2 university writing/language programs. *TESOL Quarterly, 3,* 539–566.

Beason, L. (1993). Feedback and revision in writing across the curriculum classes. *Research in the Teaching of English, 27,* 395–421.

Brown, H. D. (1994). *Principles of language learning and teaching* (3rd ed.). Englewood Cliffs, NJ: Prentice-Hall.

Cardelle, M., & Corno, L. (1981). Effects on second language learning of variations in written feedback on homework assignments. *TESOL Quarterly, 15,* 251–261.

Carlsen, W. (1991). Questioning in classrooms: A socio-linguistic perspective. *Journal of Educational Research, 61,* 157–178.

Carnicelli, T. A. (1980). The writing conference: A one-to-one conversation. In T. Donovan & B. McClelland (Eds.), *Eight approaches to teaching writing* (pp. 101–31). Urbana, IL: National Council of Teachers of English.

Cohen, A. (1987). Student processing of feedback on their compositions. In A.L. Wenden & J. Rubin (Eds.), *Learner strategies in language learning* (pp. 57–69). Englewood Cliffs, NJ: Prentice-Hall.

Cohen, A. D., & Cavalcanti, M. C. (1990). Feedback on compositions: Teacher and student verbal reports. In. B. Kroll (Ed.), *Second language writing: Research insights for the classroom* (pp. 155–177). New York: Cambridge University Press.

Collier, V. P. (1989). How long? A synthesis of research on academic achievement in a second language. *TESOL Quarterly, 23,* 509–531.

Dillon, J. T. (1982). The effects of questions in education and other enterprises. *Journal of Curriculum Studies, 14,* 127–152.

Faigley, L., & Witte, S. P. (1981). Analyzing revision. *College Composition and Communication, 32,* 400–414.

Ferris, D. R. (1995a). Can advanced ESL students be taught to correct their most serious and frequent errors? *CATESOL Journal, 8*(1), 41–62.

Ferris, D. R. (1995b). Student reactions to teacher response in multiple-draft composition classrooms. *TESOL Quarterly, 29,* 33–53.

Ferris, D. R. (1995c). Teaching ESL composition students to become independent self-editors. *TESOL Journal, 4*(4), 18–22.

Ferris, D. R. (1997). The influence of teacher commentary on student revision. *TESOL Quarterly, 31,* 315–339.

Ferris, D. R. (forthcoming). Teaching Writing for Academic Purposes. To appear in J. Flowerdew & M. Peacock (Eds.), *The EAP Curriculum.*

Ferris, D., & Hedgcock, J. (1998). *Teaching ESL composition: Purpose, process, and practice*. Mahwah, NJ: Lawrence Erlbaum Associates.

Ferris, D., Harvey, H., & Nuttall, G. (1998, March). *Assessing a joint training project: Editing strategies for ESL teachers and students*. Paper presented at the annual meeting of the American Association for Applied Linguistics, Seattle, WA.

Ferris, D., Pezone, S., Tade, C., & Tinti, S. (1997). Teacher commentary on student writing: Descriptions and implications. *Journal of Second Language Writing, 6*, 155–182.

Hedgcock, J., & Lefkowitz, N. (1994). Feedback on feedback: Assessing learner receptivity to teacher response in L2 composing. *Journal of Second Language Writing, 3*, 141–163.

Hedgcock, J., & Lefkowitz, N. (1996). Some input on input: Two analyses of student response to expert feedback in L2 writing. *Modern Language Journal, 80*, 287–308.

Hendrickson, J. (1980). Error correction in foreign language teaching: Recent theory, research, and practice. In K. Croft (Ed.), *Readings on English as a second language* (pp. 153–173). Boston: Little, Brown, and Co.

Hillocks, G., Jr. (1986). *Research on written composition: New directions for teaching*. Urbana, IL: ERIC Clearinghouse on Reading and Communication Skills and the National Conference on Research in English.

Krashen, S. (1984). *Writing: Research, theory, and application*. Oxford: Pergamon Press.

Kusnick, J. (1996). Classroom questions. *Teaching Newsletter, 8*(2), 1–4.

Lane, J., & Lange, E. (1993). *Writing clearly: An editing guide*. Boston: Heinle & Heinle.

Leki, I. (1990). Coaching from the margins: Issues in written response. In B. Kroll (Ed.), *Second language writing: Research insights for the classroom* (pp. 57–68). New York: Cambridge University Press.

Leki, I. (1991). The preferences of ESL students for error correction in college-level writing classes. *Foreign Language Annals, 24*, 203–218.

Leki, I. (1992). *Understanding ESL writers*. Portsmouth, NH: Heinemann.

Mathison-Fife, J., & O'Neill, P. (1997). Re-seeing research on response. *College Composition and Communication, 48*, 274–277.

McCurdy, P. (1992, March). *What students do with composition feedback*. Paper presented at the 27th annual Teaching of English to Speakers of Other Languages Convention, Vancouver, B.C.

Mittan, R. (1989). The peer review process: Harnessing students' communicative power. In D. M. Johnson & D. H. Roen (Eds.), *Richness in writing: Empowering ESL students* (pp. 207–219). New York: Longman.

Patthey-Chavez, G. G., & Ferris, D. R. (1997). Writing conferences and the weaving of multi-voiced texts in college composition. *Research in the Teaching of English, 31*, 51–90.

Radecki, P., & Swales, J. (1988). ESL student reaction to written comments on their written work. *System, 16*, 355–365.

Raimes, A. (1985). What unskilled ESL students do as they write: A classroom study of composing. *TESOL Quarterly, 19*, 229–258.

Reid, J. (1994). Responding to ESL students' texts: The myths of appropriation. *TESOL Quarterly, 28*, 273–292.

Reid, J. (1997). "Eye" learners and "ear" learners: Identifying the language needs of international student and U.S. resident writers. In J. M. Reid & P. Byrd, (Eds), *Grammar in the composition classroom: Essays on teaching ESL for college-bound students* (pp. 3–17). Boston: Heinle & Heinle.

Scarcella, R. (1990). *Teaching language minority children in the multicultural classroom.* Englewood Cliffs, NJ: Prentice-Hall.

Silva, T. (1988). Comments on Vivian Zamel's "recent research on writing pedagogy": A reader reacts …. *TESOL Quarterly, 22,* 517–520.

Silva, T. (1993). Toward an understanding of the distinct nature of L2 writing: The ESL research and its implications. *TESOL Quarterly, 28,* 657–677.

Silva, T. (1997). On the ethical treatment of ESL writers. *TESOL Quarterly, 31,* 359–363.

Spack, R. (1994). *Blair resources for teaching writing: English as a second language.* Englewood Cliffs, NJ: Prentice-Hall.

Truscott, J. (1996). The case against grammar correction in L2 writing classes. *Language Learning, 46,* 327–369.

Zamel, V. (1982). Writing: The process of discovering meaning. *TESOL Quarterly, 16,* 195–209.

Zamel, V. (1985). Responding to student writing. *TESOL Quarterly, 19,* 79–102.

Zhang, S. (1995). Reexamining the affective advantage of peer feedback in the ESL writing class. *Journal of Second Language Writing, 4,* 209–222.

9 Opening Our Doors: Applying Socioliterate Approaches (SA) to Language Minority Classrooms

Ann M. Johns
San Diego State University

Throughout this volume, contributors have spoken of the special character-istics and needs of language minority students in English-medium colleges and universities. Caught among different worlds, these students require pedagogies that will assist them in sorting out their languages and cultures and in approaching new, and often foreign, literacy demands with strategies for success. In my view, it is the responsibility of composition instructors to help these students acquire a literacy strategy repertoire and develop the con-fidence that enables them to approach and negotiate a variety of literacy tasks in many environments. However, it appears that many composition in-structors do not view these goals as their responsibility. Instead, they turn their classes inward, toward the students themselves and away from the lit-eracy lives that have constructed, or will construct, them.

Expressivist and personal identity approaches to teaching, perhaps the most inward-looking, still predominate in many classrooms.[1] In these ap-proaches, the focus is almost exclusively on developing individual voice and identity, personal interests, and personal meaning making, generally through a limited number of pedagogical and literacy genres, such as the personal es-say or works of literature. The expressivist experience is undoubtedly a plea-sure for some students[2] because much of what they write is considered suc-

---

[1]Although expressivism was most popular in the 1960s, it appears to be making a comeback in various forms in composition classrooms. At a recent College Composition and Communication Conference, the number of papers devoted to writer identity, expressivism, and composition as therapy far outnumbered papers in which an epistemic voice was discussed (MacDonald, 1998).

[2]Although it may be very difficult for others. In a useful article on personal voice, Ramanathan and Kaplan (1996) argued that "voice ... [is] largely a culturally constrained notion, relatively in-accessible to students who are not full participants in the culture within which they are asked to write" (p. 22).

cessful and interesting by their composition teachers. However, their very success and pleasure can present problems later, as Leki (1995) pointed out:

> if writing successes come too easily, they may be insufficiently challenging to serve the purpose of giving students writing experiences they can later refer back to in attempting to address tasks across the curriculum. Although the [composition] class should no doubt be a psychologically nurturing place, surely being a safe refuge is not enough. (p. 256)

In other parts of the world, such as among Australian genre theorists and literacy teachers, expressivist and personal identity approaches are viewed as damaging to the language minority student. Martin (1985), one of the major Australian theorists, contended that many types of identity-based, student-centered classrooms do not assist the culturally and linguistically diverse students to understand literacy practices in the world around them. Thus, these classrooms "[promote] a situation in which only the brightest, middle-class monolingual students will benefit" (Martin, 1985, p. 61). Christie (1993) spoke of these approaches as "cruelly unfair" to language minority students (p. 100) because they are not encouraged to examine the unfamiliar social and rhetorical contexts in which they will be attempting to succeed while working within their second or third languages and cultures.

What I advocate is something quite different from personal identity and expressivist approaches, resembling, but not duplicating Australian curricula. I call it a socioliterate approach (SA).[3] SA is based on the contention that texts are social; important written and spoken discourses are situated within specific contexts and produced and read by individuals whose values reflect those of the communities to which they belong. The principal focus in an SA is not on the individual and his or her identity or meaning making as separate from culture, language, and context, but on understanding how all of us are shaped by the social nature of language and texts. Certainly students understand, at some level, texts' social nature, and the purposes of SA classes are to bring this understanding to the forefront and to encourage student flexibility and creativity in negotiating and processing texts in new social settings.

How might an SA classroom be organized? First of all, the teacher provides leadership, because the teacher has both expertise and years to his or her advantage. The teacher sets goals for students, makes a variety of assignments that encourage an understanding of the social construction of texts, and promotes text analysis and peer review in light of the social forces that surround the particular discourses at issue. Students read and write texts in more than one genre,[4] preferably a variety of texts from genres that are familiar and unfamiliar. Throughout the class, students are encouraged to

---

[3]See Johns (1997) for a much more complete discussion.

[4]*Genre* is defined in a number of ways. Here is my definition: "complex, evolving mental abstractions held by individuals within communities or larger cultures who share social and textual experiences" (Johns, 1997, p. 22).

bring texts from their first languages and cultures and to discuss the nature and purposes of these texts in light of the social environments in which they have been produced.

What kinds of texts do language minority students bring to class? Some bring flyers in English and their home languages that they find at the grocery store, the laundromat, or in their siblings' schools. These flyers are then analyzed for their purposes (e.g., to inform, invite, make a claim, promote a candidate), for their uses of language, for their layout, and for how the visual presentation is organized to meet the writer's purposes. Using flyers, students can discuss reader and writer's roles and values, context, and the effect that particular texts from the genre have on them and their families within their own communities. Other students bring their favorite magazines, such as *Low Rider*, which include a number of accessible texts for analysis: letters to the editor, editorials, feature articles, and advice columns. These common magazine genres are then compared with comparable texts in magazines directed to other populations. In some classes, students draw from their previous literacy experiences by bringing texts that have influenced their literacy lives.[5] They bring papers they have written for classes in high school, or books they read as children. All of these texts are viewed as social, influencing the students' literacy theories and approaches to reading and writing.

Instructors can also bring examples of their own writing to demonstrate the importance of social factors in the construction of texts. Huckin (1997), for example, used a letter he wrote to a state legislator, and this elected official's standard and inappropriate response, as texts for analysis of roles, language and the uses of power, and purposes and contexts for writing. Throughout his classroom analysis, Huckin spoke of the ways in which style, format, and text organization are employed by both reader and writer in attempting to achieve their ends.

After students have examined familiar or teacher texts, they can work on a variety of reading and writing tasks to expand their genre repertoires. If the class consists of undergraduates who will be processing pedagogical genres, students can study and write various types of summaries and abstracts.[6] They can also write short timed essays to very specific prompts, much like those required in discipline-specific classes[7] (Horowitz, 1986). Students can bring readings or papers from other classes to compare them for a number of features. In addition to using the standard pedagogical genres, instructors can ask students to write a memo to a faculty member discussing why they want to drop a class or were late turning in an assignment. Students can write letters to the editor of the college newspaper and be awarded a high grade if their letters are published. It is important to note that in a socioliterate class, students often analyze a number of texts from the target genre before beginning their writing pro-

---

[5]See chap. 8 of Johns (1997).

[6]Ratteray (1985) contended that there are at least six different types of academic summaries that vary in terms of organization and content.

[7]I use the term *discipline specific* rather than content based for nonliteracy classes. Literacy classes should be, by their very nature, cross-disciplinary.

cesses. This analysis, of both text-external and text-internal features, assists students in understanding that no text is autonomous and that the various textual elements are influenced by social and personal factors.

Throughout the class, students are asked to draft and redraft their papers, peer reviewing each other's work in light of social and linguistic factors. Students also pay close attention to their strategies for literacy practices: for deconstructing prompts, for approaching timed and process writing of various types, for understanding roles and purposes as readers and writers, and other factors.

Reflection is essential to student internalization of the social and personal factors influencing text processing for a particular genre. In my classes, for example, students have to take timed tests as the final examination. Before the final, they are administered practice exams that somewhat approximate the real test. Because timed tests are central to their academic progress, I encourage students to reflect critically on their strategies for writing under pressure and other factors influencing their success. Here, for example, is a comment by a Chinese American student about her reaction to and planning for the prompt on a timed practice examination:

> The practice exam has a good topic. However it seems that people need to take some time to really understand what the question is. I took about ten minutes to understand the question and spent another ten minutes to think my essay contents. Even though the topic was great, I misunderstood the question. I wrote another thing which seems not the main point of the question.

A Vietnamese American student compared the two of the practice examinations that she was administered, discussing how the topic of an examination prompt influences her writing success:

> I have took two practice exams, and both of them left me two different impressions. First at the early exam, the question came out with a description and explain a favorite person. I was totally not interested because I did not have any favorite friend. Conversely, the second one was more interesting which was mentioned about living in several places. It was related closely to a real life so it made me more easier to write and demonstrate my writing skill.

Another student, from the large, local Chaldean community, was annoyed by what he saw as the superficial nature of the topic in the practice examination, and his written response was unsuccessful because of this annoyance:

> I was surprised by the question. I thought that they would bring something more sophisticated and more complex. The subject was too wide and big to write about in the first place. [Because of this] I got confused about how much should I write about, and what exactly to focus on.

In addition to examining their strategies for approaching particular genres and comparing topics for assigned writings, students are asked to reflect on organization, language, values, and other social features of the texts they read and write. Students are also asked to compare texts within a genre for a number of features, so that they could understand that texts within a genre can—and often do—vary considerably depending on a number of factors such as context, content, and reader and writer roles (see, e.g., Johns, 1997, pp. 20–37).

The purposes of an SA are for students to free themselves of their sometimes limited theories of pedagogical and other genres, to analyze and value the genres from their first cultures, to approach all texts as socially constructed, and to reflect on their experiences with text processing.

SOME GOALS FOR A SOCIOLITERATE CLASSROOM

What are the specific goals of a socioliterate classroom, and how can they be realized? Below, I outline and discuss these goals in some detail.[8]

Goal 1: Draw From Student Knowledge of Genres and Apply That Knowledge to Analysis and Critique of Known and New Texts.

Our language minority students already know a great deal about socially constructed discourses, and, as the contributors to Murray's volume entitled *Diversity as Resource: Redefining Cultural Literacy* (1992) pointed out, the students themselves are valuable resources in teaching and learning. A central element of socioliterate classrooms is student discussion of familiar texts from their languages and cultures. Through this discussion, students recognize the conflicts and convergences among some first culture texts—and with those in the majority academic culture. What they know about the social construction of texts can, and should, provide topics for discussion and student research.

Goal 2: Perpetually Revise Theories of Genre.

One possible liability of an SA is that students will (again) attempt to discover a simple text template for certain common genres. This is a major problem for more traditionally taught students who may believe that every paper should look like a five-paragraph essay.[9] In our classes, we need to expose students to more than one text from a genre, therefore demonstrating that texts with the same name, and thus within the same genre category (e.g., "essay," "research paper," "lab report") tend to differ in various ways—because the situations in which the texts are produced are considerably different.[10] In a useful discus-

---

[8]See Johns (1997) for a more thorough discussion of these goals and suggestions for pedagogical approaches to realize them.

[9]Some of my students from high school and community college classes have been told just how many sentences should be in the introduction, what the topic sentences in each of the internal paragraphs should look like, how a conclusion should be formed, and so forth. They have rigidly followed an essay template over and over in their composition classes, and they find it very difficult to break from it to produce papers in other genres.

[10]In an interview with a finance instructor, my colleagues and I discovered that he referred to analyses of law cases as "essays." In my view, this is not helpful to students; however, naming of every pedagogical paper "an essay" is very common in discipline-specific classrooms.

sion of this important feature, Berkenkotter and Huckin (1995) spoke of "centripetal forces" that contribute to text conventions within a genre that are carried across situations—and "the centrifugal forces" that force changes in content, reader and writer roles, use of language, or other features. One example of these influences can be found in a pedagogical genre called *the summary*. Although we know that a summary is shorter version of the original, and that in many cases, the summarizer is encouraged to combine sentences and ideas in the final product, the other conventions of summarizing depend on the particular rhetorical situation in which the literacy event is taking place. When interviewing a faculty member from philosophy, for example, I discovered that there are specific ways to summarize texts from his disciplinary canon. Because of this, he devotes considerable time in his first-year classes to modeling the construction of summaries and he requires summarizing on every examination. His summaries are considerably different from those assigned by a history professor with whom I work. She is most interested in a single sentence summary of the argument, followed by analysis or critique.

Goal 3: Assess, Expand On, and Revise Strategies for Approaching Literacy Tasks.

No doubt many composition instructors devote considerable time to discussion of varying strategies for reading and writing. It is important to ask questions in which students distinguish among strategies, such as "What strategies did you use to approach this assignment? How were these strategies different from—or the same as—strategies that you attempted for our previous assignment?" In this way, students begin to understand what the research on good writing tells us: Individual processing of texts is complex and strategies may differ considerably from task to task. From this discussion of strategies, teachers can point out that there is no one "writing process"; instead, there are a myriad of processes depending on the importance of the text to the writer, his or her purposes and roles, the audience, the task, the topic and the context (see, e.g., Prior, 1995). If we provide our students with assignments that vary in terms of task complexity and constraints, context, roles, purposes, genre and other features, they will have an opportunity to reflect on the differences in their strategies—and on what does and does not work when approaching different types of literacy tasks.

Goal 4: Develop Abilities to Research Texts, Tasks, Roles, and Contexts.

If language minority students are to be successful in the many, unpredictable and foreign environments in which they will be attempting to read and write texts, they must become researchers, constantly asking good questions of texts, tasks, and of themselves. The last question most discipline-specific faculty want to hear from a student about an assignment is "What do you want?" However, there are many other ways to approach what faculty have assigned that are productive for students. Students can ask to look at a paper written by a successful student in the past; they can bring their drafts of a paper to the professor in order to elicit his or her comments; they can ask how the professor might approach the assignment. And they can also negotiate assignments to fit their needs and interests (see, e.g., Leki, 1995). A number of writing problems faced by language minority students are related to independent reading of assigned texts,[11] as some of the contributors to the Carson and Leki (1993) volume entitled *Reading in the Composition Classroom* pointed out. There are a number of identified reading strategies, of course, outlined in texts for teachers (see, e.g., Davies, 1995; Feathers, 1993; Grellet, 1981). These can and should be discussed and practiced in our classrooms. And, as researchers of disciplinary practices, our students can pose questions to the faculty member who made a reading assignment: "How would you read this assignment?" "What kinds of notes do you take when you read?" or "What will we be asked to do with this reading?"

Goal 5: Cultivate a Metalanguage About Texts and Textual Experiences.
One of the most challenging aspects of teaching language minority students is that although they may be completely bilingual and biliterate, they may not have the metalanguage necessary to discuss texts. Unless we share a language about their texts and can discuss the grammar and lexicon in some way, we operate at a distinct disadvantage. Thus, a class goal should be to encourage student development of a metalanguage in which they can discuss the language of their texts, by using handbooks or by developing, within the class, their own terms to discuss the language, structure, and social purposes of texts.

USING SOCIOLITERATE PRACTICES IN THE CLASSROOM

What happens when we attempt to use an SA? In this section I discuss a few assignments from a class in which I attempted to follow the goals just listed.

The class was a remedial or developmental course for students who had not passed the lower division writing competency examination at the university. The 25 students, all language minority, had been educated in U.S. high schools and, in most cases, community colleges. They had been in the United States for a minimum of 4 years although most had been in the country much longer. About 15 spoke Vietnamese, but others spoke Spanish, Arabic, or Southeast Asian. The students had a variety of majors, with a preponderance in technology and business. Marketing, engineering, computer science, and nursing were the most popular. Not surprisingly, none had chosen a major in the social sciences or humanities. Thus, the content of many of the typical English as a second language (ESL) or composition texts was unfamiliar—and sometimes not very interesting—to them.

---

[11]Many first- and second-year students at colleges and universities have had few chances to do independent reading, especially of expository prose. In California and a number of other states, most of the high school reading is of literature and it is completed within the students' classes.

Administratively, these remedial classes are organized in the following manner: The instructor is free to use any textbook or approach available until the last 2 weeks of class, at which time, the students purchase a required pamphlet of readings on a single topic, such as overpopulation. The information from that pamphlet provides the basis for the timed essay examination administered during the final examination week. Students pass the class if they complete the classwork and pass the holistically scored final examination with a composite of eight or more (two scorers, each using a 1 to 6 rubric much like those employed by the Educational Testing Service). If the students' instructors believe that a student has not been appropriately graded by the finals scorers, they may appeal the final examination score using texts written during the semester.

In a class such as this, which seems to be typical of many remedial classes throughout the country, the instructor and the students are in a bind: The students are anxious to pass the final examination so that they can proceed with their academic work[12], yet the teacher knows that the composition class may provide one of the students' few formal experiences with writing instruction. How can we assist these language minority students to acquire some of the tools that they need to approach any writing task, yet provide sufficient practice in the timed composition class essay to insure that students pass the final examination?

After I discussed my research on problems students from science and technology disciplines face when confronting final examinations developed by English teachers (Johns, 1991), the class and I decided to treat their entire experience as a laboratory for the study of the social construction of texts and the ways in which individuals might process or evaluate them. Like all texts, the final examination essay is socially constructed: There are teacher/grader and student roles, one of which predominates; there are certain types of prompts, most of which are quite open-ended (see the students' comments on the practice essay); and there is a preference among graders, whatever they might claim, for a five-paragraph essay form. Because of the pressures on the students to pass the final, the class and I studied features of the final graded writing, emphasizing the particular values of the audiences who would be grading the texts,[13] the constraints of the context, and the possible topics. We also talked about their writing: the ways in which to make arguments, writing strategies, and other factors that influence success. And we practiced timed writing with typical prompts—frequently.

However, my principal mission was to prepare students for writing for a number of occasions beyond the final, particularly for analyzing writing situations that they might confront in the university and in their professional lives. In addition to buying a grammar reference textbook, the students were

---

[12] On campus, students are forbidden to take certain classes until they have met the lower division writing requirement.

[13] Most, of course, are middle-aged, liberal, U.S.-born, monolingual women. The students have difficulty writing for this audience, particularly because the graders do not represent a discipline with which they can identify (see Johns, 1991).

asked to subscribe to *Newsweek*[14] because it provided a number of current topics and a variety of genres to study and emulate.[15] Students used the magazine readings to construct texts of a variety of types for a number of audiences. They also drew from *Newsweek* sources as data for their argumentation, a very important skill in academic writing (see Carson, Chase, Gibson, & Hargrove, 1992). At one point, the students decided to write a letter to the *Newsweek* editor because they were displeased with the particular construction of Asian culture within one of the articles. After this decision was made, we spent considerable time studying various letters to the editors for their organization, argumentation, and use of language. Students reflected on the nature of these letters with each other and in writing. Then, we talked at some length about audience: how they might write a letter that would appeal to both the general audience of the magazine and the editors who made publishing decisions. It became very clear to the class that their letters to the editor might take a position that was unusual or adversarial. Thus, they would have to assume very different roles from those they were required to take, as students, in the final examination. The letter to the editor was one of their favorite assignments. When I asked the students at the end of the semester to discuss the assignments that they liked the best, a Vietnamese American responded in this way:

> One of the assignments I like the best is to write a letter to the editors of *Newsweek* magazine. That was the first time I've ever wrote to magazine editors. If felt so interested.... By writing to them, I can judge the information from the article as well as telling my opinion about it.

Sometimes, the students experimented with roles and purposes of writers that were very different from those in their own lives. When the Hale-Bopp suicides occurred near us in San Diego and the articles about this event appeared in *Newsweek*, I gave students the opportunity to imagine that they were one of the cult members and explain to their parents why they had joined. This was an interesting assignment for the students, for most would never consider joining this cult. In fact, like many language minority students, they were very close to their parents and felt that they should do nothing that might offend them or lose their face in the community. Nonetheless, when asked about his favorite assignment, a Vietnamese American student said the following:

> My favorite was writing to explain to my parents why I joined the cult. I had fun in writing this informal letter because I had to play a role of a person who believe in their causes and purposes. On the other hand, I was not at all interested in joining because I think that the people were making a desperate attempt to belong to something. I had to put aside my beliefs in order to write and to read the [*Newsweek*] article for important beliefs and pretend to believe in them.

---

[14]The total cost for 10 weeks was $12, which was cheaper than most textbooks.

[15]The students also studied the genres of their own preferred magazines, as noted earlier.

However, the absolute class favorite and best-written assignment during the semester was a serendipitous one. The new president of the university was planning to visit our department, Rhetoric and Writing Studies, and the students and I viewed this occasion as an opportunity for writing something that might have a direct impact on their lives. Thus, we decided together on a memo. The students began by researching the new president's public speeches and comments, principally because they wanted to understand his values and interests so that they could make the best impression. I provided information about the conversations he was having with various stakeholders in the college community in which I was taking part. Throughout, the student interest in understanding the president as audience, and what he knew and valued, remained high.

In addition to exploring the issue of audience, the students felt that it was important to examine their roles and purposes as writers, particularly how their memos could have the most impact. We talked about the fact that when writing the president, it is very important that they make themselves understood. As a result, this was the best paper for most of the students in the class, although they had very little time to revise.[16]

After considerable discussion of their audience and writer roles, purposes, and responsibilities, the students began to consider how the memo should be structured. Although they knew the basic conventions of the memo form, they were concerned with what topics they might include and in what order. Together, we negotiated this move structure: first, to introduce themselves and talk briefly about their backgrounds, because the president is very interested in maintaining diversity on the campus.[17] Second, the students would write about their personal goals, and, third, they would make some suggestions for improvements to the campus. The students agreed that the final, short paragraph should say something positive so that the president would finish reading the memo "with a good feeling."

In the paragraph on "improvements," many of the students discussed the examinations, suggesting that the they not be tested in formal, timed situations, and arguing that they were much better writers when they had real audiences and purposes and time to plan their texts.[18] Here is a text portion from a Vietnamese American student:

> My name is ... and I am a junior at SDSU after I transfer from El Camino College in Los Angeles. My major is pre-nursing and I am a bilingual student who just came here for about five years. I am attending in SDSU because I want to complete my education in order to have a better job to take care of my family.

---

[16]In two cases, I used this paper in the appeals process for those students who failed the final examination. And it was successful!

[17]Currently, the San Diego State campus is 50% non-White. Of this group, about 35% of the students are language minority. However, because the campus is popular, its leadership has decided to raise its entrance requirements and phase out remedial classes, including ESL. These moves will undoubtedly have considerable impact on language minority students, who often need a bridging literacy class to assist them in succeeding in university classes.

[18]As the results of this memo demonstrated.

Right now, I am a full-time students and a full-time worker which is very stressful time for me.

Dr. Johns asked us to tell you what we think SDSU's future goals should be. Here are my suggestions:

• Making[19] a lower-division writing competency test more fairly by giving students more time. We cannot write a complete formal essay in a short time.

• Let students take major courses before passing the test. By doing that way, the students do not feel bored and have more opportunity to move up.

• SDSU should have a writing center so students can come up when they need help.

Thank you for taking your time to read this memo. I hope that SDSU will be much better in the next 10 years.

But other students had different agendas. Here is the text of a memo from a Spanish speaker in the class:

I would like to introduce myself, I am an ESL student, Spanish being my first language. This is my second semester in SDSU, at this moment I am a junior Electrical Engineering student. I transferred from Southwestern College which is located in Chula Vista. I decided to come to SDSU because it is close to my home, it is affordable, and it has a good reputation.

The reason of seeking a higher education is because I want to be of help to my community. I want to have my own business in the community and to develop electronic equipment.

SDSU can make my goal and the goal of all engineering students easier by improving the engineering facilities. The major problem at this time is the computer lab in the engineering building.[20] It has computers that are very old and slow. They are of GGMKZ, also the computers are in terrible shape. If you just go and use them for five minutes, you will find out what I really mean.

Other than this little problem, SDSU is a great university.

These memos were given to the president when he visited our department. A few weeks later, he wrote a memo to my class, thanking them for their comments. A second memo was to me, asking for a two-page position paper on the testing requirements at SDSU and discussing whether our testing discourages language minority students from applying.

---

[19]This student was also taking a business writing class and he knew that important points in memos to busy people need to be highlighted in some way.

[20]Although many students on campus have their own computers, some language minority students, who tend to come from lower income families, do not. If we are going to attract and keep these students, we need good computers on campus.

CONCLUSION

No doubt the composition of many classes for language minority students is similar to the one described here: The students are Americans and they have been educated in the public school and college system.[21] Yet they are considered remedial in that the students have not mastered the grammar of standard academic English. The curriculum for these classes is fairly open, but the final examination is a timed composition class essay.

What I argued here is that these language minority students need a class that takes an outward-looking, Socioliterate Approach. First, students need to be encouraged to discuss what they already know about the social construction of texts and the interactions of readers and writers. When they prepared the memo to the president, for example, they were very wise about his role and what would be most appealing to him. Second, students need to discuss at some length how many features of texts influence readers: language, careful editing, text layout, and other factors. Because I have attempted to learn several languages (Spanish, Swahili, Chinese, and Arabic) after passing the Critical Period, I am very sympathetic with the fact that our language minority students may never attain perfect grammar in their writing. And, in my view, that is all right. However, they need to know what kinds of texts should be error-free and work with a proficient monolingual English speaker to correct any minor errors they may have.

If we take the attitude that students may go elsewhere to have small errors corrected, then we can concentrate on other issues: reader and writer roles and purposes, the ways language can be used to achieve ends with particular readers, and contexts for reading and writing. On the other hand, if we become fixated on making our students discover their personal identities, or feel good, then other goals, much more important to their future lives, will be neglected. A socioliterate classroom attempts to focus first on the big picture: the context of the text to be processed and the social forces influencing it. However, it does not neglect the student as a social being, one who understands and processes texts within a variety of social contexts.

REFERENCES

Berkenkotter, C., & Huckin, T. N. (1995). *Genre knowledge in disciplinary communication: Cognition/culture/power.* Hillsdale, NJ: Lawrence Erlbaum Associates.

Browning, G., Brinton, D., Ching, R., Dees, R., Dunlap, S., Erickson, M., Garlow, K., Manson, M., Poole, D., & Sasser, L. (1997). *California pathways: The second language student in public high schools, colleges, and universities.* Glendale, CA: California Teachers of English to Speakers of Other Languages.

---

[21]A very good publication discussing the complexity of the language minority student population in California, and their English skills, is *California Pathways: The Second Language Student in Public High Schools, Colleges and Universities.* Browning, Brinton, Ching, Dees, Dunlap, et al. (1997), published by CATESOL.

Carson, J. G., Chase, N., Gibson, S., & Hargrove, M. (1992). Literacy demands of the undergraduate curriculum. *Reading Research and Instruction, 31,* 25–50.

Carson, J. G., & Leki, I. (Eds.). (1993). *Reading in the composition classroom: Second language perspectives.* Boston: Heinle & Heinle.

Christie, F. (1993). The "received tradition" of literacy teaching: The decline of rhetoric and the corruption of grammar. In B. Green (Ed.) *The insistence of the letter: Literacy studies and curriculum theorizing* (pp. 75–106) London: Falmer Press.

Davies, F. (1995). *Introducing reading.* London: Penguin.

Feathers, K. M. (1993). *Infotext: Reading and learning.* Markham, Ontario: Pippin.

Grellet, F. (1981). *Developing reading skills: A practical guide to reading comprehension exercises.* Cambridge, England: Cambridge University Press.

Horowitz, D. M. (1986). Essay examination prompts and the teaching of academic writing. *English for Specific Purposes, 5,* 107–120.

Huckin, T. (1997, March). *Discourse analysis and literacy education.* Presentation at the Conference on College Composition and Communication, Phoenix, AZ.

Johns, A. M. (1991). Interpreting an English competency examination: The frustrations of an ESL science student. *Written Communication, 8,* 379–401.

Johns, A. M. (1997). *Text, role and context: Developing academic literacies.* New York: Cambridge University Press.

Leki, I. (1995). Coping strategies of ESL students in writing tasks across the curriculum. *TESOL Quarterly, 29,* 235–260.

Martin, J. (1985). *Factual writing: Exploring and challenging social reality.* Oxford, England: Oxford University Press.

MacDonald, S. P. (1998, April). *Critiquing the critiques of epistemic voice.* Presentation at the Conference College Composition and Communication, Chicago, IL.

Murray, D. E. (Ed.). (1992). *Diversity as resource: Redefining cultural literacy.* Alexandria, VA: Teachers of English to Speakers of Other Languages.

Prior, P. (1995). Redefining the task: An ethnographic examination of writing and response in graduate seminars. In D. Belcher & G. Braine (Eds.), *Academic writing in a second language: Essays on research and pedagogy* (pp. 47–82). Norwood, NJ: Ablex.

Ramanathan, V., & Kaplan, R. B. (1996). Audience and voice in current L1 composition textbooks: Some implications for L2 writers. *Journal of Second Language Writing, 5,* 21–33.

Ratteray, O. M. T. (1985). Expanding roles for summarized information. *Written Communication, 2,* 257–272.

III

The Programs

10 Connections: High School to College

Nancy Duke S. Lay
Gladys Carro
City College of New York
Shiang Tien
John Jay College
T. C. Niemann
Sophia Leong
Lower East Side Preparatory High School

The City University of New York (CUNY) is the nation's leading public urban university. It is composed of 10 senior colleges, 6 community colleges, a technical college, a graduate school, a law school, a medical school, and an affiliated medical school and has an operating budget of more than $1 billion. In 1993, CUNY enrolled nearly 208,000 students in degree-credit programs (Access to Excellence: The Faculty of the City University of New York, 1994–1995). From its start, the Free Academy, one of the colleges of CUNY, has guaranteed free access to all college aspirants. Townsend Harris, who founded the Free Academy in 1847, had served on the New York City Board of Education. It was during his tenure on the Board that he led the campaign to establish the Free Academy, the institution that was to become City College of New York (CCNY). Harris founded CCNY to offer an opportunity for higher education to the children of the burgeoning working class and immigrants. At that time, New York City, with a population of more than 500,000, had only two colleges with fewer than 300 students. Higher education was available only to the wealthy and privileged. Against this background of inequality, Harris proposed what amounted to an egalitarian ideal: "Open the doors to all—let the children of the rich and poor take seats together and know no distinction save that of industry, good conduct, and intellect" (City College of New York, Office of Public Relations, Press Release, 1997).

CUNY has always valued the pluralism and diversity of our students. Its population has always reflected the population of New York City, including its immigrants. Of the 898,213 documented immigrants into the city between 1982 and 1991, 28% came from countries in the anglophone and francophone Caribbean (Jamaica, Guyana, Haiti, Trinidad, Tobago, and Barbados); 25.9%

175

came from Spanish-speaking countries in the Caribbean, Mexico, and South and Central America (the Dominican Republic, Colombia, Ecuador, Honduras, Peru, and El Salvador); and 20.2% came from Asian countries (China, India, Korea, the Philippines, Hong Kong, Pakistan, and Bangladesh).

In 1992, the racial and ethnic composition of CUNY first-time freshmen was 26.9% White, non-Hispanic; 40.9% transfer students; 34.2% Black, non-Hispanic; 27% transfer students; 27.3% Hispanic; 16.8% transfer students; 11.5% Asian; and 15.2% transfer students. To meet the aspirations of all the students, and to provide a preliminary assessment of their educational needs, CUNY undertook a study in 1995 that analyzed the effect of recent trends in immigration from foreign countries and migration from Puerto Rico. The study estimated that by the year 2000, more than 50% of CUNY first-time freshmen will have been born outside of the United States or in Puerto Rico (Immigration/Migration, 1995).

The result of a 1991 study indicated that CUNY's students at that time were similar in most respect to those of the previous 20 years, and that CUNY's low-cost, high quality education represented their principal avenue of access to New York's economic mainstream. About 50% had a low family income—under $22,000 in 1990. Most were "on their own": 53% were over 22-years-old, 56% were not living with their parents, and 23% were helping to support their children. These students needed to work: 66% were employed. Fifty-eight percent said in a survey that it is a financial strain to attend even low-tuition CUNY, and 66% said they needed to attend a college near home (CUNY Office of University Relations, PSC-CUNY, 1991). The majority of CUNY students at the time of the survey were female. Often, their parents had not completed high school. Immigrant students tended to have difficulty with English, and thus with passing the two language basic skills tests at CUNY—reading and writing.

For many of these students, CUNY was the only access to higher education. Eighty percent of CUNY students came from the New York City public schools. The predominance of New York City high school graduates in CUNY's population made articulation between CUNY and the city schools an extremely important thread. Studies such as Richardson and Skinner (1991) showed that when a high school graduate is well prepared, he or she has a better chance of succeeding in college. The 16 years that youngsters spend becoming educated is surely enough time that, with cooperative effort, high schools and colleges can transform them into useful, well-rounded, educated citizens of New York City and the world.

The students moving from high schools to college need strong English language skills. It is known that the more comprehensible input the students have, the better they are in terms of their success in college. Literacy development needs to start early with special emphasis on integrative skills, active engagement in the process of learning the language, and asking questions about learning. Many CUNY students have good literacy skills in their native languages. However, they need to learn how to formulate and test hypotheses about what they are learning, take risks, and read a lot (Hudelson, 1989;

Krashen, 1989; McLaughlin, 1984). With intensive reading and writing activities, coupled with structured exposure to English, such as interaction in groups, collaborative learning, and parental involvement, these students can be successful.

Because Chinese students are one of the three major groups of second language (L2) students in CUNY, we focus here on the voices of Chinese students as they travel from the learning halls in high schools to higher institutions of learning. These students come from the People's Republic of China, Hong Kong, Taiwan, Singapore, Malaysia, and some from Central America. In this chapter, we also include experiences and philosophies of two writing teachers from high schools describing how they perceive their work with Chinese students. Writing teachers need to understand some of the linguistic, academic, sociocultural, and political issues that face Chinese students while trying to improve their English language proficiency and hoping to belong to the larger U.S. society. Effective academic writing instruction depends on a broad awareness of all the factors that enter into these students' experience. And finally, we describe some of the CUNY initiatives that connect New York City high schools and CUNY, and those that have assisted ESL programs and their students in achieving the goals to a successful college career.

In the next section, we present interviews with high school and college Asian students to find out what they have to say about their education and needs, and their hopes that CUNY can do a better job of preparing them for the workforce. The questions were predetermined, but the interviews remain flexible pending on the flow of the conversation and responses.

VOICES OF CHINESE STUDENTS

Zhu, Hua, and Ping are all Chinese students from the Peoples' Republic of China. All of them were in Lay's intermediate ESL reading class in spring of 1997. They came directly to New York and were admitted to the New York City public schools, and later were accepted into City College of New York (CCNY). Lay interviewed each of them separately for approximately 1 hour. They also wrote some of their responses. The questions Lay asked were predetermined and general, asking students to relate their experiences in learning English, especially writing, in high school and in college.

Zhu

When Zhu was 16 years old, he entered U.S. high school in the 10th grade. At that time, he could not speak one whole English sentence. He said,

> I could only say yes and no. The school put me in an ESL class. My counselor told me that I need foundation of English. I was in the ESL class for two years and it helped my English a lot. However, I still have problems. When I see other native American students speak with the teacher very nature and they would laugh together. Sometimes I tried to speak with the American teacher;

everytime I failed not because of poor English. I did not know why. I tried to speak with native students. They always look at me like I am strange, then I felt embarrassed and my face turned red. However, one of the things that cheer me up was my grade was excellent, especially in Math. The American students always asked me about Math, and I was patient and kind to teach them. After that, I had a few American friends. Another good thing is that my family loved me so much. They supported me everytime, even when I got bad attitude. They were not angry at me. I think it is very difficult for Chinese student to be an American student in my high school. During lunch time, the Chinese students sat with the Chinese, the Spanish students with the Spanish students, and the American students with Americans. They never mix together. One time, I had an opportunity to have an American friend. The American student asked me, "Do you want to hang out with me on the street; we can protect you." And another one said that he was going to give me a lot of free things. I really wanted to say "OK" but in my mind I thought that they are going to give me drugs and I have to give money to them. So I said "No, thank you." I do not know what I am afraid of. After I got into college, I became more daring. I speak with other race people very naturally. I tried to make friends with them, and I was successful. However, the other Chinese students in my class think that I was stupid, but I am not; I just want to make friends. I would say that the biggest problem for Chinese students is to become Americanize because they are shy.

Zhu's story highlights several important factors in Chinese students' experiences in U.S. high schools and their linguistic and academic preparation for college writing. When students like Zhu feel awkward about interacting with their teachers, they are unlikely to speak up in class. Because participation in class discussions is an important skill in many college classrooms in its own right as well as instrumental in developing academic literacy, students' lack of confidence ultimately has an impact on their writing skills. Zhu's story also underscores the social isolation that these students may feel in classrooms where they feel reluctant to interact with native English-speaking peers or are rejected by them. However, these students find that their academic strengths, such as math skills, can be a tool to help them in developing a peer network. Finally, Zhu suggested the importance of family support in helping students through the sometimes frustrating and discouraging experience of negotiating U.S. academics.

Hua

At the time of the interview, Hua had lived in the United States for 2 years and 8 months. Before she went to college, she had studied in a high school in Brooklyn and graduated from that high school. During her 2 years in U.S. high school, she said that,

> my English did not have big improvement. I just came to college this semester, and I feel my English has improved very fast. I believe I am getting more knowledge in college than in high school. Why? I think the methods in college are

better than in high school and the teachers' teaching attitude is an important factor. In high school, students have little chance to practice English. In the reading class that I attended, the teacher asked the students to read the text, and gave some words to make sentences for homework. Students did not discuss the contents of the texts. In the writing class, the teachers taught us some grammar; they seldom asked students to write essays. So, many of the students could not write a good essay. But now, there is a big difference in college. I can acquire some knowledge everyday, and I have a chance to practice English in class. Now I know how to write essays because I wrote many essays this semester. I believe that skills come from practice.

I think learning English to need long time, and must persevere in practicing English, including reading, writing, speaking, and I hope teachers in school give students more chances to practice English and use English. I want to repeat the phrase "skills come from practice."

In Hua's experience, high school literacy preparation was inadequate for college in at least two ways. She noted that the nature of high school tasks tended toward discrete skills development—grammar, vocabulary—at the expense of more open-ended, extensive reading, writing, and discussion. Furthermore, she said that literacy experiences in classrooms should be constant and copious in order to prepare for college.

Ping

Ping had just finished his first semester in college at the time of the interview. Like Hua, he felt that the experiences with writing between college and high school were very different. In high school, he said that the teacher required them to write "short and easy" essays. He felt that many of the students were not concerned about their ESL classes because almost all of the students "would pass the class without any pressure." He reported that most instruction consisted of reading novels and answering some questions on the board. All they had to do was find the answers in the novel. Every semester, Ping's teacher would assign an essay. However, Ping felt that it did not matter how many words or whether the sentences are correct or clear. Unlike Hua's high school instruction, Ping said that very little "grammar" or language lessons were done in class. Ping felt that perhaps he had some problems with the language, but he never knew which sentences in his essays were correct and which ones were wrong. So, he ended up writing one-paragraph essays.

Like Hua, Ping felt that high school experiences did not prepare him for the more rigorous expectations of college level reading and writing. Since attending college, he had realized that the essay is very important in writing classes. During midterms and finals, his writing teacher required him to write a 300- to 500-word essay. He felt that the requirement was "hard" and "strict." "Everyday we need to write an essay and at the end of the term, a research paper of 24 pages." In his mind, high school was more fun and light, but he regretted that he did not work hard enough because he needed the training for his future.

Regarding the Chinese culture, Ping said that parents teach their children to be obedient and respect their teachers. However, in U.S. high schools, Ping observed that unlike Chinese students, the U.S. students always quarrel with their teachers. Sometimes they even hit the teacher from the back. Like Zhu, Ping also said that he really wanted to make friends with American students, but it was not easy for him because of the language and culture: "if you ask me to forget my country's culture, and learn American culture, that is impossible. So most of my friends are Chinese," said Ping. He added, "humor is characteristic of the American culture, but I don't know how to learn it... I cannot accept it. Maybe I need a long time to adapt." Thus, although they are in English-medium high school classrooms, students like Ping may not be able to engage in the sorts of interactions with native speakers that might facilitate the development of spoken and written English for college.

In speaking about Chinese culture, Ping also noted the interdependence of families. For example, he reported that many of his Chinese classmates had had part-time jobs because they wanted to help their parents. He also believed that Chinese immigrant parents tend to be overprotective. For example, his own parents did not want him to speak to strangers or go to a "strange" place.

In summary, all three of these students did not seem to feel that they received many chances to practice extended writing before college. They noted that class size in general is large and writing assignments are not given regularly. Many find U.S. classroom behavior hard to understand and feel uncomfortable participating in discussions. They are used to formal style of the classroom and they do not speak immediately for fear of making mistakes and "loss of face." They also encounter some U.S. teachers and students who are not very patient or understanding, or carry negative stereotypes of Chinese newcomers. Whatever the cause, if immigrant students do not feel comfortable in joining class discussions, their grades in college writing classes may be lower, because most teachers' evaluations of students include class participation. Instructors need to understand that when these students do not speak, it does not mean that they have nothing to say. They just need the right comfort zone at the right time. Writing teachers can use small collaborative groups, but, they need to make sure that the students understand the rationale for these activities. Moreover, we should prepare college academics on how to deal with the discomfort of L2 students. Constant dialogue and faculty development workshops are just a few of the ways that all teachers, writing as well as content teachers, can work together. Language takes time to learn, and from our experiences at CCNY, we have found that a good support system can help these students to succeed. For example, we have utilized modified supplemental instruction in linked courses. Supplemental instruction is a form of tutoring. Tutors are selected from among students who have previously taken the content course and performed well in it. The tutors' main focus is to help students learn the process of learning in the context of a particular course and a particular instructor.

VOICES OF HIGH SCHOOL WRITING TEACHERS

To understand L2 teaching and learning of writing and academic skills to immigrants in U.S. high schools, it is helpful to look at both sides of the classroom—the students' and the teachers'. Shiang Tien, then a counselor at Lower East Side Preparatory High School (LESP) in the New York City public school system, interviewed two exemplary teachers at his school to talk about their experiences.

T. C. Niemann is an English teacher at the school, which is an alternative high school that serves a large population of new immigrant students. Often, students do not have strong speaking, listening, and writing skills when they enter this school. Compared to other majority high school students, who begin their high school career in the middle teens, these students are older. Most are in their late teens or early 20s. Despite their language difficulty, Niemann sees this population as often possessing strong cognitive and academic ability, especially in subjects like math and science. Before he came to LESP, Niemann taught Hispanic adults in another neighborhood. After teaching these two culturally distinct groups, he has learned to adapt his manifold teaching approaches to serve the varying needs of his students.

Niemann's major emphasis is in teaching ESL students how to write. He observed that their most frequent difficulties in writing are in formulating ideas and organization. He emphasized how to formulate an idea before students can write about it. At this point, he tells them not to worry about the rules of English grammar; content of an article always comes first. He also teaches students how to organize ideas, leading to a process of the thought from Point A to Point B to Point C. He noted that his students often engage in a process of transference from the first language (Chinese) to the second language (English). When students describe their writing to him, he acknowledges that their thoughts are complicated. He sees his job as supplying language because they lack the capability to express equivalent English words. The limited vocabulary that his students have enables them to speak or write in a very simple form of English. He sees students struggling to convey their thoughts using the basic words and phrases at their command. The largest feeling of frustration among his Chinese students, he believes, is not being able to have enough English vocabulary to use. For novice language learners, he has had success with a strategy in which students copy words, phrases, and sentences from others or use other people's ideas that match their thoughts. Lacking language competence, students believe others' words are better or more suitable to express their related topics. As students gain in proficiency, Niemann designs activities to encourage originality.

To build up his students' confidence Niemann gives them abstract prompts and asks them to write simple phrases and then to add additional elements gradually. Word-processing programs facilitate the accomplishment of this objective. Students are told to print assignments only after they have made multiple revisions. Niemann tells students to choose one project that will be printed and collected into a small book at the end of the term. Their essays and reports are desktop published. Students' original artwork is scanned into their project. This project enables students to apply organizational skills. By doing a long-term project, students work on one section at a time. During the operation, they acquire many kinds of practical skills such as learning word processing, creating tables, incorporating graphics, and finally desktop publishing. Through the writing process, they learn to organize different parts of the project. They see their progress as they revise their work. Individual work and teamwork efforts are interwoven into the project.

Niemann strives to make learning mutual. Although students learn about U.S. customs, he sensitizes himself to Chinese cultural norms and their implications for instruction. For example, when in a group setting, Niemann observes that Chinese students often are reluctant to be distinguished from others while Americans strive to appear different from their peers. Whereas Americans emphasize individual importance, he believes that Chinese students look for agreement first, not for difference among themselves. As a result, Niemann suggested that Chinese students may be more likely to work together. They can get work done faster because they arrive at a consensus more quickly.

Niemann is also sensitive to Chinese students' reticence to speak individually. He observed that they do not want to be viewed as stupid or foolish among classmates if they respond incorrectly. In this sense, Niemann said that they need encouragement to speak out on their ideas and not feel embarrassed. Nevertheless, if asked to project their voices, sing, or cheer within the safety of a chorus, Niemann finds that they will take greater risks. He encourages his Chinese students to take risks in order to learn from mistakes, assuring students that the learning process includes making mistakes, and that it is perfectly normal to make mistakes and learn from them while in school. In general, Niemann finds that Chinese students' greatest strengths are in their persistence, focus, and determination. To remedy the lack of exposure to an English environment, he works with them after school, and tries to maximize the relevance of in-school assignments to their lives.

Another exemplary secondary school teacher interviewed by Shiang Tien at LESP is Sophia Leong, an English and Math teacher. Like Niemann, most of her students at LESP are recent immigrants. On average, she finds that her students have strong math skills but their English skills are poor. She sees herself as strict and demanding, expecting them to function in an English-speaking environment. She expects students to try to communicate in English from the first day of her classes. For example, she gives those students who need it an English-Chinese, Chinese-English mathematics dictionary and asks them to memorize the necessary English math terms within 1 month. They have to answer the entire math problems or questions in English. Geometry proofs are done in English and students are penalized for misspellings and statements lacking in precision or accuracy.

Her students are under pressure to make a fast transition. In her English and math classes, she does not speak a single Chinese word to students. Her teaching philosophy is to help students to hear, to think, and to speak English on all occasions. She urges them to make their transition while with her at LESP before they go on to college. She only speaks Chinese to new students in her homeroom if they have been in the United States for a few weeks or months. She uses Chinese only to convey information related to school policy, holidays, regulations and up-to-date events. If this information were not communicated in Chinese, her homeroom students would not be well informed.

In her College Now class, an upper level English class, she teaches her seniors vital information about college application procedures, SATs, writing personal statements, requirements for different colleges, and techniques for interviewing. In addition, she teaches students how to do a research paper and how to do research in a modern library, including Internet searches. In this class, students learn research paper writing skills, which they will need in college.

Leong believes that the greatest obstacles for all her students are the lack of English-speaking environment and opportunity to use English. Leong observed that New York City is unique in a way that students are not living in an English immersion environment in their first few years. They do not read English newspapers, nor do they have time for television. Family members, friends, and classmates are mostly nonnative English speakers. In addition, the working sites where they usually get their jobs—garment factories and restaurants—require very few English skills. Therefore, students may spend only 5 hours a day 5 days a week at school learning English. Most of the time they are using their own native languages. This has been the greatest difficulty for them to improve their handle on English. Despite hard work, they often do not make substantial progress in reading or understanding.

Leong asserted that teaching English to L2 learners is different from teaching native speakers. Because her students are adults, not children and because they already know their native language, their native language skills may either help or confuse them in learning English. Leong said that in many cases, her students may have learned some English before they came to the United States. They can speak very simple English words but they are not fluent. Writing is a major issue for Leong's students; they have to learn to write in English that is different from their native language in many ways. In her class, Leong does not give formal lectures on English grammar. Instead, she helps students by pointing out their mistakes and by modeling for them. She asks her students to think and try to find out whether a subject, or a verb and an object are needed to have a complete thought in one sentence. She tells her students that people will not comprehend fully with an incomplete sentence. She forces her students to express the completeness of their thought in a sentence. Short answers are not permitted in writing. When students translate their thoughts from Chinese to English, Leong believes often times they lose track of the logic of their thought. Their sentences become fragmented and the basic elements of a sentence are missing. To help them to find out the missing link, she always asks them whether their responses made sense in Chinese. In this effort, she helps them to realize the missing parts of their sentences.

She would like all of her students to have more time practicing English in English-speaking settings, to do less work after school, and spend more time on English to get more reinforcement and support either from school or their families. Because of all the obstacles and their diligence, she is very proud of her students' achievements. She notes that many of them have gone on to CUNY and The State University of New York (SUNY). In 1996–1997, she reported that 16 students won scholarships to private universities and colleges. The students who have gone on to the private colleges and SUNY from her point of view, are doing better than their counterparts in CUNY because they live in English-speaking surroundings on a daily basis and are totally immersed in it. Of course, those students have to struggle in a different way from their CUNY friends because they have fewer Chinese students on which to rely. They have to be strong psychologically and emotionally to succeed.

CUNY INITIATIVES

As a result of the CUNY study conducted in winter 1995 that indicated an increase in students whose first language is not English in CUNY by the year 2000 (Immigration/Migration, 1995), the university decided to strengthen ESL programs on each of its campuses. At this time, the university was also experiencing heavy budget cuts from the state and the trend of downsizing was becoming a national phenomenon. There was a paradox: on one hand, immigration trends said that we were getting more students, on the other hand, the lowest ESL levels in senior colleges were eliminated. Students were restricted in the courses for which they could register and could only take certain introductory and core courses until they passed the CUNY freshmen skills assessment tests in writing, reading, and math. Students were not allowed to repeat a skills course more than once. How should CUNY assist ESL students under these difficult conditions and at the same time, help them make the transition into mainstream courses as soon as possible?

The Language Immersion Programs

The CUNY Language Immersion Program, now under the aegis of Adult and Continuing Education, was created to provide an intensive and extended language learning opportunity, tuition-free or low cost, to CUNY's increasing numbers of immigrant students at the beginning level of English proficiency (25 hours per week) in reading, writing, speaking, and listening. Although these students have been already admitted to the university, attendance at the institute is voluntary and defers formal enrollment at a particular campus until such time as students are ready to participate successfully in the regular college curriculum (*Language Immersion Institute Report*, 1995). After two periods/sessions of intensive work, students are allowed to return to the initial college they have chosen. The CUNY ESL task force has opposed the establishment of immersion programs outside the campus (CUNY ESL Task Force Position Statement; Minutes of the CUNY ESL Council) and has promoted the establishment of on-campus programs. Since 1995, several on-campus language immersion programs have been created. However, there are still some unanswered questions regarding the off-campus immersion program that remains: Is there an allocation from each campus to the off-campus immersion program? What happens when students return to campus still deficient in English language skills? Do campuses have the obligation to accept these students?

College Preparatory Initiative (CPI)

Many New York City high school students enter into CUNY with deficiencies for different reasons—insufficient high school preparation, previous educational experiences abroad, and lack of English language exposure and practice. For example, some students received a General Education Diploma (GED) in their native language instead of a regular high school diploma, and depending on the high school abroad, there is an imbalance of educational preparation especially with English language instruction. Many of these students are strong in their math skills, yet English skills require tremendous and intensive work in order to cope with the U.S. classroom. Students often find that expectations in college are considerably different from high school. Many of the students enter college thinking that they are still in high school. To improve the situation, CUNY Board of Trustees implemented the CPI in 1992 in collaboration with the New York City Board of Education. The CPI is "a set of prescribed educational competencies designed to prepare students effectively for college and the world of work" (CPI, 1993). CUNY research shows that when high school students come in with "a strong foundation of college preparatory courses," they are more likely to succeed in college work (CPI, 1993). The New York City Public Schools and CUNY established joint faculty discipline committees to develop the academic competencies. The committees are comprised of more than 180 faculty from almost every public high school and every CUNY college. They represent the academic areas of English, ESL, mathematics, science, social studies, foreign languages, and the visual and performing arts.

Representatives both from CUNY and the New York City high schools met in several conferences to map out the agreed-on competencies required in specific disciplines (Report on the Recommendation of the Third CUNY/NYC Public Schools Faculty Conference on School System Collaboration: Forum on Implementation, 1992). For example, several ESL faculty members from CUNY joined forces with New York City high schools administrators and teachers in developing language competencies that both groups deemed necessary skills to survive in college. In summer 1995, with funding from CUNY, CUNY instructors and 45 high school ESL instructors from different boroughs met for several days of workshops in which they shared information by presenting different syllabi, materials, texts, and exams. Reading, writing, listening, and speaking skills were identified based on different language levels. There was a workshop on the CUNY assessment skills in writing, another one on state-of-the-art approaches used in colleges, and another one on the incorporation of content into ESL classes. How does one look at a piece of writing? What kinds of feedback should one give? How much writing and reading is necessary? What exit criteria are recommended to make sure that the expectations required in college are followed in high schools? The group also distinguished between academic skills in ESL classes and survival skills classes.

Until recently, high schools have given newcomer students considerable latitude in choosing courses to take. Often times, immigrants end up taking many nonacademic courses, and shy away from math, English, and science. The heart of CPI is the phase-in of more stringent academic course distribution requirements in high schools (before entering CUNY) by the year 2000 that will culminate with the expectation of sixteen units (English, 4 units; social studies, 4; math, 3; foreign language, 2; lab science, 2; visual performing arts, 1; CUNY Matters, July 1994). International students (I-20 status, who come directly from abroad and do not attend U.S. high schools) with foreign credentials will also be expected to meet the same CPI units. Non-CUNY transfer students who graduate from high school after June 1993 must submit their high school transcripts for CPI evaluation.

There have been some positive signs already as a result of the CPI. Data collected by the Office of Academic Affairs, CUNY Central Office, have been very encouraging and with the support of the New York City Schools chancellor, some of the initiatives and new proposed requirements have been followed through and continued. For example, beginning with fall 1995 entering ninth grade, high school students are required to take Regents-level math and science courses for graduation. The chancellor hoped that this change will result in higher percentage of students entering the highly regarded Regents diploma. In addition, the units of math and science requirements have been increased from two to three units. The Office of Academic Affairs continues to monitor the impact of CPI on students coming to CUNY.

CUNY ESL Task Force

In 1994, the university, sensing that ESL was a university-wide cross-disciplinary issue, put together a task force that looked into the needs of ESL programs and students. It was a 20-member task force (which included ESL instructors, coordinators, chairs from senior and community colleges, representatives from the Bilingual Council, high schools, English, and consulted a wide range of faculty and administrators) that met for 1 year thrashing out different issues that affect ESL students. The major issues were program structure, admissions, assessment of ESL students, low-level ESL students, instruction and advising, mainstreaming, instruction across the curriculum, and faculty. As a result, in spring 1994, a report of the CUNY ESL Task Force (CUNY, Spring 1994) was published that outlined several recommendations to the chancellor. One of the major recommendations was the "main-streaming of ESL students into other college courses." At the same time, the data collected showed that the 1990 cohorts (even before they passed the reading and writing assessment tests), had median cumulative GPAs that compared favorably to those of native students. A provisional report conducted in 1996 (Carro & Watts, 1997) also supported this finding. This recommendation to mainstream ESL students into other college courses was a strong force that prompted CUNY to empower ESL programs either to allow ESL students the opportunity to take regular courses while taking ESL, or develop linked courses with other disciplines.

Another factor that has come into play is that strict limits are being imposed on the number of noncredit hours students can take before their financial aid is exhausted. At CCNY, for example, our ESL courses were credit-bearing courses until 1996. There were three levels, consisting of seven courses and one for graduate students. Most students needed the three-level sequence to qualify for freshmen composition. While taking ESL, they were allowed to take other mainstream courses depending on their math levels and skills assessment test scores. Now the situation is worse. Since 1996, the lowest level of ESL has been eliminated. Furthermore, credits were abruptly eliminated because the school of engineering, a professional school, was not willing to accept the ESL credits for their students. The impact on the students has been tremendous because they could not become full-time students without having some real credits. Thus, we have developed linked courses with other disciplines (core [required courses of every CCNY student] and electives). By linking with a regular college course, ESL students can at least receive three college credits from the linked course (as most ESL courses now have lost their credits), which qualifies them for financial aid as a full-time student. We are also in the process of getting credit back for ESL by developing separate English courses for engineering students. The road is not going to be easy; it is an ongoing process, and one that is multifaceted with no simple solutions.

Request for Proposals (RFP) and Campus-Based ESL Innovative Programs

One of the recommendations of the ESL Task Force Report (1994) was to mainstream ESL students into regular courses as soon as possible. ESL students were spending too much time at the college before they could take credit-bearing courses. In many cases, they used up all their financial aid before they started their regular courses. Our goal was to mainstream them as soon as possible without sacrificing their development of English academic skills. Different models were presented and examined. To support the recommendation of the ESL Task Force, the university started an initiative for spring 1997 to fund a new set of innovative ESL programs on the different campuses. The emphasis of these projects would be on assisting ESL students acquire the necessary academic skills to handle regular courses. Faculty development projects including content-area faculty were also encouraged. As a result, 15 campuses submitted different innovative proposals amounting to $350,000, and the university made several awards ranging from $30,000 to $50,000.

It was also an effort of the university to bring campuses together, to share and exchange ideas and information. For example, two proposals might call for similar kinds of consultants for faculty training programs. Instead of duplicating these efforts, the two campuses could be trained at the same time by the same consultants. Moreover, the RFP exercise allowed each ESL program in CUNY to do a little soulsearching of what it was doing: How effective are the programs in helping ESL students progress and how can we make our program more credible and strong? The progress of these programs and courses was monitored carefully by the Office of Academic Affairs in such a way that a positive report could be demonstrated to the state for future funding.

Linking With Content/Core Courses

Most ESL programs have developed linkages between ESL courses and credit-bearing courses to give ESL students an edge. This linkage serves as a motivation because the ESL students are now taking college courses although they are still in ESL programs. The financial aid problem is also partially solved because students need certain number of credits to get financial help. With the stringent cuts on graduation credits, and most ESL courses not carrying credits, ESL students were doomed to suffer from a lack of financial aid as a result of not having sufficient credits to be considered full time. Research also shows that many ESL students are able to handle regular courses even while taking ESL—they received good grades sometimes while failing ESL classes (Patkowski, Fox, & Smodlaka, 1995). Since 1986, the ESL department at CCNY has offered writing, reading, and oral communication skills as stand-alone courses. Pressured by the administration in 1996, the ESL Department at CCNY was asked to link all ESL courses with numerous humanities courses without much planning and research. The mandate raised many questions, including: Which courses employ writing, reading, and speaking skills that are appropriate for ESL students? What kinds of assignments as well as language activities do these courses have? What teaching mode is being used by the instructor? Is the instructor flexible? Is the course making meaningful connections with what the student will take the following semester? How do we accommodate students whose outside work and family obligations do not mesh with the inflexible scheduling of linked courses? Which courses are necessary for students majoring in different disciplines? Are we trying to please administration and provide enrollment for courses with insufficient students? In spring 1997, student enrollment in ESL courses dropped tremendously and the department reexamined its linked courses, its curriculum, and different possible reasons for the change. We have stopped the across-the-board linking and focus only on a few core and elective courses. The most stable linked package is the one that includes an ESL writing and reading course and a world civilization core course. "This linked course began during the Fall of 1994 with only one section and did not blossom into several sections until Fall 1996" (Carro & Watts, 1997, p. 8).

The most important benefit for ESL students is that they are taking core courses that are required for graduation, so that time is not wasted on taking just any courses. "Evaluations indicated that students in the lecture section of World Civilization became proficient at taking notes. Their general listening skills increased dramatically" (Carro & Watts, 1997). World civilization is a required course at CCNY, and to link this course with the upper-ESL writing/reading courses help students in those core courses. Coupled with this, ESL instructors linking with the core courses have revised their own teaching strategies and are more demanding of ESL students in terms of reading and writing. They have not become tutors to the core courses; actually, the students see them as language teachers who are able to guide them in the realities of college work. Higher level of linguistic skills, such as critical thinking skills, analysis, and synthesis have been an important component of the writing and reading classes. There have been very positive exchanges among faculty members working together in the world civilization panel.

Combined ESL Courses, Focusing on Science and Technology

Another experiment in progress at CCNY is to offer an accelerated course for students in the sciences. Its principal goals are to (a) accelerate the mainstreaming of qualified students, (b) prepare students for the reading and writing that is required of them in their majors, and (c) acquaint students with the social issues raised by scientific advances (Gloria Silberstein and Michael Golder, personal communication, September, 1997). Participating students are able to complete two semesters of study in one semester, with an additional 3 weeks of study following the regular term.

Students are selected in terms of their reading scores and writing placement, math scores, and most important of all, their availability. The students must not be working. If they are continuing students, they must be recommended by the instructor. Since CCNY is the only CUNY college with a school of engineering, many of our international students major in engineering and the sciences. They are highly motivated and they complete twice the amount of work required in a regular course during the regular term. The results have been very positive and promising. Most of the students registered in the course were motivated to do the intense work and they did successfully at the end of the term. More concrete data needs to be gathered to see the long-term effects on their college career. In the summer of 1998, we encountered problems where many of these qualified students had to work because of the tuition increase. Thus, the number of students has decreased in this accelerated/combined course.

CONCLUSION

In summary, the communication started between CUNY with the New York City Board of Education has proved to be crucial for a new generation of immigrant students to do well and to become productive citizens of New York

City. More work has to be done. It is hoped that as high school students move from one institution to another, we, the writing and language teachers, will be there to support them, and make sure that they are receiving the best education we can give them. CUNY can then keep its promise of providing access to and excellence in education to the future citizens of the world.

REFERENCES

Access to Excellence: The Faculty of the City University of New York (1994–1995). New York: The City University of New York.

Carro, G., & Watts, J. (1997). *Provisional Report: PSC-CUNY Grant 1996–98, A Study on ESL Students Linked with CORE World Civilization.* New York: The City University of New York.

City College of New York, Press Release. (1997, September), Office of Public Relations, New York: The City College of New York.

College Preparatory Initiative: Questions and Answers. (1993, February). Office of Student Services, New York: The City University of New York.

CUNY Matters, (1997, July). Office of University Relations. New York: The City University of New York.

CUNY ESL Task Force Position Statement. (1993). New York: The City University of New York.

CUNY ESL Task Force Report, (1994). CUNY, Office of Academic Affairs. New York: The City University of New York.

CUNY Office of University Relations, PSC-CUNY. (1991). New York: The City University of New York.

Hudelson, S. (1989). *Write on: Children writing in ESL.* Englewood Cliffs, NJ: Prentice-Hall.

"Immigration/Migration and the CUNY Student of the Future." (1995). New York: The City University of New York, Winter 1995.

Krashen, S. D. (1989). We acquire vocabulary and spelling by reading: Additional evidence for the input hypotheses, *The Modern Language Journal, 73,* 440–464.

Language Immersion Institute Report. (1995, February). New York: The City University of New York.

McLaughlin, B. (1984). Second-language acquisition in childhood: Preschool children. Hillsdale, NJ: Lawrence Erlbaum Associates.

Patkowski, M., Fox, L., & Smodlaka, I. (1995). *A Comparison of the Grades of ESL and Non-ESL Students in Selected Courses at Ten CUNY Colleges.* Joint project of the CUNY Language Forum and the CUNY ESL Council, unpublished manuscript, New York: The City University of New York.

Report on the Recommendation of the Third CUNY/NYC Public Schools Faculty Conference on School System Collaboration: Forum on Implementation. (1992, September 12). New York: Kingsborough Community College.

Richardson, R. C., Jr., & Skinner, E. F. (1991). Achieving quality and diversity: Universities in a multicultural society. New York: Macmillan.

11 University Support for Second-Language Writers Across the Curriculum

Kate Wolfe-Quintero
Gabriela Segade
University of Hawai'i at Manoa

This chapter reports on instructor and student perceptions of the academic writing support available to second-language (L2) students at the University of Hawai'i at Manoa (UHM). In the course of their educational experience, all undergraduate students at UHM are required to take a freshman writing course followed by five academic courses that are designated as writing intensive (WI). Two WI courses must be at the upper division level, although not necessarily in the student's major. This curricular requirement gives students experience writing both within particular disciplines and across the academic curriculum. The WI courses are not writing courses that are offered within a particular disciplinary area (such as technical writing for science majors), but regular academic content courses designated as WI because they require several pieces and kinds of student writing within the context of the course. The WI courses at UHM have a maximum of 20 students in each course to allow individualized attention to the students' writing. Because of this exposure to intensive writing in a variety of disciplinary contexts, students at UHM have had the opportunity to develop as writers in the process of earning their undergraduate degree (Hilgers, Bayer, Stitt-Bergh, & Taniguchi, 1995).

Our report is based on data that were collected from L2 students and instructors in WI courses.[1] Twenty-nine L2 students from 16 different majors were interviewed several times over the course of a semester while they were taking at least one WI course. In addition, 16 instructors from 10 different departments were interviewed while they were teaching a WI course. The students and instructors interviewed included all those who responded to an

---

[1]We thank all of those who worked on this research project, in particular Al Lehner, who led the project and interviewed the instructors, as well as Lara Mui, Misook Kim, Fumiko Ikeshiro, and Grace Pae. More details can be found in Lehner, Segade, Wolfe-Quintero, and Hilgers (in press). We have also used data from four other L2 students who were interviewed by Segade (1997) for a different project.

e-mail message sent to all of the potential candidates. The interviews were conducted using a protocol with open-ended questions about the experiences, needs, and resources available to students and instructors in WI courses. In addition, some of the students kept journals documenting their experiences in their WI course, and the instructors and students provided copies of their assignments and papers.

At UHM, approximately 10% of the undergraduate population of 13,000 students are L2 students. Of these, 59% are immigrant students who have had some Kindergarten through Grade 12 education in the United States. Here, we highlight what these students as well as international student English learners and their instructors said about the kinds of support available to aid L2 students in their academic writing development. The salient issues in educating L2 learners in a program of this sort were how well students had been prepared by their English and English as a Second Language (ESL) department first-year writing courses, what resources were available to students within the context of their WI courses, and what kinds of support could be found in an English department writing center. The instructors and students participating in this study reveal how these various components of the university can better aid English language learners writing development throughout the undergraduate experience.

ENGLISH AND ESL FIRST-YEAR WRITING COURSES

Undergraduate students are generally required to take at least one writing course in the first year of college. At UHM, these courses are offered by both the English department and the ESL department, depending on the students' background. L2 students who have immigrated to the United States at an early age and do not have strong L2 features in their writing take the English course. L2 students including immigrant students with persistent L2 features in their writing take the ESL course. Extensive writing samples for all L2 students are collected by the Manoa Writing Program (MWP), which is a unit of the university devoted to freshman writing concerns. Judgments about L2 students' placement are made by the ESL department in conjunction with MWP. Whether placed in an English or ESL course, students may be required to take a prerequisite writing course before they are considered ready for the 100-level course. English 100 and ESL 100 are considered equivalent by the university in fulfilling graduation requirements.

Although all sections of English 100 and ESL 100 adhere to the same set of general guidelines, ESL and English are very different disciplines with different academic cultures and priorities. Atkinson and Ramanathan (1995) compared ESL and English composition programs at a large university and found that the programs had different and even conflicting standards for what constitutes good academic writing. Braine (1996) discovered that ESL students preferred to be in the ESL rather than the English first-year writing course when given the choice. Those who chose the ESL course performed at a higher level on a holistically scored exit examination than those who chose the English course, perhaps because the English composition program assumed cultural and rhetorical knowledge about discourse conventions that could alienate ESL students (Atkinson & Ramanathan, 1995). Irrespective of these potential differences, it is assumed by the faculty as a whole that the first-year undergraduate course, regardless of the department or instructor, prepares the student to write at the university.

However, when we talked to the faculty and L2 students in the WI courses at UHM, we found that many of them felt that the English or ESL course that students had taken did not prepare them for writing at the university in several ways. The perception was that students did not gain adequate general writing skills from these courses, that their language skills were consistently a problem, that the writing they were expected to do in first-year courses was formulaic and did not work in other courses, and that they were not prepared to write the type of discourse required by disciplines other than English.

Several instructors commented on the students' general writing skills, or the lack of those skills. A computer science instructor suggested that there was a problem not with technical writing but with basic writing, "It's just plain old ability to compose grammatically correct sentences." An electrical engineering instructor felt that this was due to inadequate L2 training, observing "Somehow they're just not pickin' up those skills in whatever training that they're getting in second language."

Some instructors thought the lack of general writing skills was a problem L2 students shared with local students, whose first language may be a variety of Hawai'i Creole English (Sato, 1985, 1989). In Hawai'i, there are multiple varieties of standard English and Hawai'i Creole English that are spoken by residents and that serve as targets of acquisition for immigrant students. Because immigrant students arrive at different ages and live in different places, they also differ in which variety they have selected as a target and in how like or unlike local students they are in their language use. Many immigrant students consider themselves local if they have graduated from a local high school.

Some of the L2 students also felt that they did not have adequate general writing skills. One student commented, "If we have to write a thesis paper, I probably need help. How to write it 'cause I never wrote one before." Another student said that he had not received any training in writing prior to the WI course he was taking.

If L2 students do not have sufficient writing skills for writing academic papers in their WI courses, what could be the reason? One possibility is that knowledge of a L2 for academic purposes is difficult to achieve for anyone; it takes many years of exposure to academic contexts at an early age for a learner to perform like native speakers on standardized tests (Collier, 1987), and in Hawai'i, the spoken target language may be a nonstandard variety of English. Furthermore, studies of L2 writing processes have shown that although L2 and first language (L1) writers compose in similar ways (Raimes, 1987; Silva, 1993), L2 writing tends to be more laborious and time consuming and to present more difficulty (Hall, 1990; Silva, 1993). Tense, article, lexical, and complex syntax problems persist for many of those who have mastered the language for communication and who may know the grammar backward and forward on grammar tests. L2 writers will almost always, although to varying degrees, need help polishing their written language.

L2 students in the UHM program overwhelmingly expressed how difficult it is for them to see their own mistakes. For example, one said, "Sometimes when you write something, you don't make a mistake. But other people, 'Ahh, why you make this stupid mistake?' But you don't know it when you writing."

Students are aware of their sentence-level problems, but as we saw earlier, they are also aware that these are not their only difficulties. A possible reason for these difficulties is that the type of formulaic training that they have received in English or ESL does not apply to the writing they are expected to do in other courses. Some of the students identified aspects of this formula:

> [In the English program], they teach us how to write, "Oh, that's topic sentence. Yeah." That's simple, you know. I just bring up all my new idea to the first sentence of the paragraph or the end, that's it, right? And the introduction, my main idea, and the conclusion. That's simple, that's the format.

Several L2 students not only identified the formula, but pointed out that it did not always apply. One student observed that, "Usually main sentences are in the beginning or last sentence. That's just regular rule, and it's not always like that." Another student identified how she found her own way to approach academic writing despite what she had been told:

> Two semesters ago, I took [an ESL course]. One day have a guest come over and she talk 'how to be a good writer.' And she show us all the step and after that I try all the step to other subjects. It doesn't work. Because in my mind I have to remember, "Oh what's the first one, what's the second step." So, I had to force myself to remember. So it doesn't work ... So it's not which way is a good way, it's which way is more comfortable.

Some instructors also recognize that, aside from general writing skills, courses in English or ESL have not adequately prepared L2 students for the type of technical writing that will be done within their disciplines. Several instructors expressed that the discourse conventions students are taught in English composition courses are not relevant to their course, including this instructor in biomedicine:

> Often times they've been through language classes, they've been through expository writing type classes. Their writing style is very much like something you'd pick up on a novel off of a department store shelf. We've got to refine that writing style into something that lends itself to scientific jargon. It's very concise. It's very to-the-point. It uses a different vernacular.

On the other hand, an instructor in sociology felt that the writing training in English had been too focused on academic writing rather than on the narrative required in field research:

There's essentially a sense that field research especially encourages a lot of introspection. One of the biggest problems is this self-revelation. Even using the first singular personal is difficult for a student to do. The most difficult part for [a particular student] was shifting over from a more descriptive, academic mode, to a more narrative.

Some of these instructors suggest that the solution is to have the students do writing in courses in a specific discipline rather than in English or ESL; for example, an electrical engineering instructor said "I think it's better to have them writing in their field than writing essays in English class." In fact, the purpose for instituting WI courses at the university was precisely to encourage the development of discipline-specific writing.

When instructors say that students have not adequately learned how to write in their English or ESL preparatory courses, they are both justified and not justified. When it comes to students' language use, instructors are pointing a finger in the wrong direction. L2 students will need help with language use throughout their academic career, and a single preparatory course will not change this. However, when it comes to the methodology used in English and ESL department courses, including formulas and approaches to writing that do not apply to other disciplines, instructors may be pointing their finger in the right direction. For example, ESL faculty may tend to focus exclusively on language use (Zamel, 1985) or formulaic rhetorical forms (Atkinson & Ramanathan, 1995) to the detriment of disciplinary content, whereas English faculty may tend to focus on cultural and stylistic issues that are exclusive to the discipline of English (Atkinson & Ramanathan, 1995; Elbow, 1991). ESL and English departments need to examine what they teach about writing and how it applies to writing at the university as a whole. ESL and English are disciplines with their own conventions, conventions that do not necessarily translate across departments.

This does not mean that English and ESL courses have to become all things to all disciplines. Given the diversity of writing conventions across the disciplines, it is not possible for composition teachers to be experts in all the kinds of writing their students need to master (Elbow, 1991; Leki, 1995a; Spack, 1988). However, ESL and English teachers need to develop a more conscious awareness in themselves and their students of their own discourse conventions, as well as an awareness that they do not speak for the university as a whole or have a lock on determining what constitutes "good writing" (Leki, 1995b). To address this, Kutz et al. (1993) recommended using ethnographic techniques in first-year courses to help students discover discourse differences for themselves, which is a skill that they can transfer to their other courses. This was done in two sections of an ESL 100 course at UHM (Segade & Wooldrik, 1997; Wooldrik, 1996), in which the instructors asked students to become coresearchers of their own academic writing. The students interviewed professors from different disciplines, collected documents, and kept journals about their discoveries. Through the process of carrying out this research, the students developed an awareness of different conventions across disciplines and of the need to shift their writing style as they move across courses. Other techniques include encouraging students to critically evaluate important texts in their own field (Belcher, 1995), or integrating the study of academic genres into first-year courses (Jacoby, Leech, & Holten, 1995; Johns, 1995).

The solution is not more ESL or English courses before L2 students are considered ready to write at the university, but better ones, as well as a recognition that writing ability is developed throughout an entire undergraduate education through a variety of means of university support, and that L2 students have unique language needs that require assistance throughout their undergraduate career.

WRITING-INTENSIVE COURSES ACROSS THE CURRICULUM

Writing-intensive courses became part of the curriculum at UHM in 1988 because of the recognition that writing needs to be taught within the context of each discipline, a recognition that developed out of the writing across the curriculum (WAC) movement in education. It is now widely recognized that there are differences in the ways that each academic discipline uses written language (Elbow, 1991; Geertz, 1983; Spack, 1988), and that these different written discourses can only be learned when a student becomes an apprentice to the discipline through interaction with insiders (Elbow, 1991; Gee, 1990). To give students the opportunity to learn the written discourse conventions of a variety of disciplines, students at UHM are required to take five WI courses as undergraduates. The goal is for students to use writing as a means for learning a discipline, and to use the discipline as a means to learn situated, contextual writing. As one botany instructor said:

> I think it's pretty obvious that writing skills are not so hot in a lot of our students. And in the sciences they haven't had much practice in writing scientific papers and scientific writing, so I think that's certainly one reason for doing [a WI course].

However, not all instructors necessarily see WI courses this way. When we talked to the instructors and L2 students in WI courses, we found that many of them felt that students were expected to know how to write academic papers before taking the course, and that it was a disappointment for instructors to find out that many students do not meet their expectations. The assumption on the part of some instructors seems to be that students should not be in WI courses if they do not already know how to write. The biomedicine instructor expressed frustration over the lack of general writing skills in students: "They hadn't done the assignment properly. And, when they turned them in, they were unreadable. I mean, they were just horrible!... It was like these kids did not know how to write a term paper!" This coincides with one L2 student's point of view: "I think she assume that we should have this kind of training in high school, that's why she didn't do too much about the explanation in class." According to this student, his instructor expected him to know how to write before he enrolled in a WI course. One reason why instructors expect their students to already have general writing skills is that they want to spend their class time covering the content of the course, "Cause I just couldn't possibly cover writing skills and at the same time cover the subject matter" (computer science instructor).

Although the goal of covering a specific amount of content may be in conflict with the goal of teaching writing in the discipline, in fact the conflict is between general writing skills and discipline-specific writing skills. The very same computer science instructor did want to spend time on certain aspects of discipline-specific writing, saying that "It is a writing-intensive course, where I can talk about how you structure technical documents." The instructors' emphasis on learning to write within their discipline is not shared by most of the students. Only one student identified learning discipline-related discourse as a goal.

The majority of students were concerned with how willing their instructors were to help them with their general writing skills. One student said, "actually, she did not really talk about the writing, yeah? That's a fact." Another student compared instructors' attitudes:

> For the research paper for the English class they are in for getting your writing skill better, so they will be more patient. But for the computer class, no. They expect you to know everything, to have good writing skills. If you do not that's not their problem, right? You should go back to the ELI [English Language Institute], maybe. They don't care.

Some of the students seemed almost bitter about this, suggesting that WI courses should specifically help them learn how to write.

There are clearly conflicting assumptions here. WI instructors expect the students to come into their courses ready and able to write so that they will not have to spend time on general writing skills, but L2 students in WI courses expect that it is in this very context that they will receive help with their writing. When they do not, it is a big disappointment:

> Actually, one of my classmates, he just lean over and whisper to me. He say, "This doesn't seem like an English class. He doesn't teach us how to write, yeah? He just lecture mainly." And I thought I was the only one feeling like that.

Another remarked, "Just to have the student working alone and write as much essays as he can will not be sufficient."

In fact, L2 students in WI courses want close, personal attention to their writing. For example, one student commented, "If I have someone to let me know what's wrong with my paper and the writing style and my grammatical error and so forth, then I think that will help a lot." One instructor discovered that meeting this need made his WI course more popular, "Certain students, having learned from the grapevine that I give them a lot of feedback on their writing, will take my course."

Instructors who do work on writing adopt a variety of strategies for developing their students' writing skills. These range from breaking down the assignment into manageable parts: "These kids did not know how to write a term paper! So now, what I do is we break it down" (biomedicine instructor), to providing models: "I say, 'Take these *U.S. News & World Report* articles on science. They're written to capture your imagination. But they're authentic. They're good science.' And I say, 'Emulate that kind of thing with your own stuff'" (zoology instructor), to giving feedback on drafts: "We write sorta general suggestions, things like if the paper's disorganized, we have a kind of 'Here's how to organize your paper' paragraph. If it's lacking examples, we have a 'Here's what you need to do to get examples in' paragraph" (linguistics instructor).

One important way that instructors can support students' writing development is by giving feedback on multiple drafts of their papers. Instructors also follow different strategies when giving feedback on papers to their students. Some instructors respond mainly to content and discipline-related issues. One said, for example, "You've got to go through and basically dissect every work like you're reviewing it." Many of the instructors said that they respond to everything that they find: "Whatever I read, I edit. And that entails correcting grammar, telling them to use topic sentences, subheadings, an introduction, and a conclusion. I tell them if they've missed major sources. I try to lay it out for them." Other instructors send the students to the English department writing center to get help with their grammar. One reported, for example, "I don't do all the corrections of grammatical errors. I tell them, if they've got grammatical problems, to go and see the English program."

It seems clear from these comments that instructors view feedback as a one-shot deal, and they differ in what they choose to respond to within a single draft. Writing pedagogy suggests there should be multiple stages of feedback, with the initial stages of feedback limited to difficulties with content or discipline-related issues, because as students develop the content more fully, the language will necessarily get modified (Zamel, 1985). There is no point in fixing the grammar of a paragraph that needs to be reworked for larger reasons. Unfortunately, because of the salience of L2 students' mistakes, instructors may tend to overemphasize grammar in their initial response to a paper and not comment on the information the student set out to communicate. One instructor even refuses to read a paper that has language problems: "If I get to a paper that has mechanical difficulties … I won't read those at all. I'll give those directly back to the student and tell them that I want those papers proofread." This instructor appears to assume that the writing center exists to fix these types of language problems, which may be justified when students are overly careless in crafting a paper. But if the instructor routinely demands near perfection in language use on an early draft of a paper before being willing to give feedback on content, this attitude is problematic. Grammar should not be an issue until the final editing stage of producing a paper (Elbow, 1998).

Instructor feedback can also address problems that several or all students in the class share. That is the case with a computer science instructor who compiles a list of general problems, as well as particular problems a group had in producing a joint document, and then gives a copy to each group. Another instructor distributes a list of particular sentences from student papers and uses this for class discussion. Although many of these instructors are willing to respond to language problems, unless they allow students a chance to revise the paper, the students with nonnative language problems are often penalized in the grade that they receive. One student reported, for example, that his instructor "is very strict on grammar. You see, there is no exception for foreign students ... And the grade is not as good as we think." Another said, "I think it's hard for me. 'Cause my instructor said, 'Oh, that's a good article, good analysis, but your level of writing, it will drag you down.' So my grade become B minus."

Some instructors do meet personally with students to discuss their writing, particularly those with serious problems. One student reported, "After she grade my paper she set appointment with you and just give me suggestion like, how can I do to make my paper better." Although these students are receiving personal attention, they may nevertheless be paying a penalty in the form of a lower grade.

Many L2 students are afraid to see their instructors for help, because they feel intimidated by how the instructor might view them. For example, one expressed the fear that "If I asked them in a wrong way, they might think I care about only my grade." Other students also discussed their fear of consulting their instructors when they had difficulty understanding class materials or the nature of an assignment. One observed, "For some reason I felt it's awkward or something." Another said, "I'm really scared I guess .... Just the fact that we are only student and they are like professor." The crucial issue seems to be whether the instructor initiated the meeting in order to provide feedback, or whether the student had to initiate the meeting in order to ask for help, which is far less comfortable (Segade, 1997).

One L2 student pointed out that the feedback that the students receive can vary greatly in how useful they find it:

> This class [East-Asian Literature] is pretty good. I like the teacher, I like his attitude. He corrects grammar mistakes for me. He points out what's wrong, what's good. But for [Travel Industry Management], he doesn't [provide] any marks that tell me what's good, and he makes some mark like awkward or cross out thing, but especially for the awkward, I don't really know how to fix it.

One of the most promising feedback strategies was volunteered by an instructor in English, who has a very open, positive, yet questioning approach to elicit better writing:

> My main response is to write them back a response paper on their essay, which has no grade on it. I'll tell them what things that I wished they had written more about, parts that weren't clear to me, and parts that excited me. I look to see if there is a topic or thesis for the essay. Is there some focus? Then I would work on how the separate parts relate to the thesis. I may go through the whole

paper and say, again and again "show me how in the text you can support this claim."

This instructor encourages the students to revisit their writing in order to address his concerns, without a penalty.

The difficulties that L2 students have with surface aspects of writing does not mean that these students should not be allowed to study in an English-speaking university. It means that there should be an awareness that L2 students will need help with language. Language use is not the same as knowledge of a subject matter, and should not be viewed as indicative of how well a student knows the subject. Rusikoff (1994) found that although most faculty see content as the most important criterion for evaluation, a great majority of them believe L2 students have difficulty in their courses because of language problems. We found that is the case at UHM where some students receive lower grades in their courses because of their difficulties in writing. As Zamel (1995) pointed out, content-area faculty reactions to L2 students are varied: Some of them emphasize the resources that these students bring to the class, whereas others focus on their language problems and see them as unprepared for content-area courses.

What some instructors seem to lack is an awareness of the students' difficulty in solving writing problems. These instructors need to become aware that students need help with writing skills as well as the discourse of the discipline, and that this need is not an indication of lack of competence. They need to learn how to structure their writing assignments to maximize their influence on writing, helping with formulating writing topics, and allowing time for drafting, feedback, and revision. They need to be aware of L2 students' particular difficulties with language, and help them strategize ways of dealing with it. They need to recognize that problems with language are not a sign of incompetence or inability to master the content of the course, and they need to grapple with how they are going to evaluate language use, if at all. They need help in identifying what it means to write in their discipline in order to convey that to their students more explicitly (Chiseri-Strater, 1991; Walvoord & McCarthy, 1990; Wooldrik, 1996), including models of the type of writing that will be required of them (Leki, 1995a), and explicit rather than implicit feedback (Colleen, 1995). They need to understand why students might be afraid to come and see them, and what they can do to alter students' perceptions (Segade, 1997).

These types of issues have been addressed by the MWP in a series of technical reports, newsletters, and workshops for WI instructors, on topics such as identifying various purposes for writing, designing effective assignments, responding to students' papers, and encouraging student self-assessment. The MWP has also asked a variety of WI instructors to discuss their teaching practices explicitly in collections such as Tsutsui and Wallace (1991) and Chinn and Hussey (1993), in which the instructors describe the strategies they have used in teaching WI courses within their discipline. However, at a research university such as UHM, it is difficult to reach other instructors whose primary concern is their research, who may have little time or interest in pedagogical self-development, and who may not be philosophically committed to the benefits of WI courses (Fulwiler, 1986).

WRITING FEEDBACK CENTERS

At UHM, the only universally available writing assistance is located within the English department, which is part of the College of Languages, Linguistics, and Literature. This particular center is called the Writing Workshop, and it is sponsored by the English Department in the form of release time for faculty, graduate assistantships, and undergraduate student volunteer tutors who take a practicum course for credit. Although the Writing Workshop may not be large enough to be viewed as a full-fledged writing center, it is the only source of general writing support for undergraduate L2 students. In the past, only professors with release time offered assistance through the Writing Workshop, with only a few appointments available each week. More recently, graduate and undergraduate students have participated as peer tutors, allowing for more opportunities to provide feedback to students. The Writing Workshop has also changed in another way. In the past, there was a policy against providing feedback on grammar or editing (although some staff members would provide such help; see O'Mealy & Register, 1984), and there was a perception that L2 students should be going to ESL, not the English Department, for help with their language problems. However, there is now a more cooperative relationship between English and ESL in staffing the Writing Workshop, with ESL graduate students working as both paid and volunteer tutors, along with a more open attitude toward dealing with language issues.

Writing centers are an important type of support that universities can provide to help L2 students meet the writing demands of an undergraduate education. The purpose of a writing center is to offer a place where students can take multiple drafts of their academic papers for feedback prior to giving the paper to an instructor. Writing centers should not be seen as remedial, or places for "fixing" writing (Healy & Bosher, 1992), but as places that can aid all writers at many stages of the writing process (Broder, 1990; Clark, 1993; Cooper, 1994; North, 1984). In fact, there is a need for writing centers to develop connections to individual instructors' goals and assignments (Smith, 1986; Wallace, 1988), including having tutors who are affiliated with particular courses that students can work with throughout the course (Healy & Bosher, 1992; Rehberger, 1994; Smith, 1986). Tutors should be trained to help ESL students with language issues (Harris & Silva, 1993; Smith, 1986) and differences in cultural expectations (Powers, 1993; Thonus, 1993), and they should be made aware of the differences between international and immigrant L2 students (Leki, 1992; Thonus, 1993). Writing centers are an ideal place to support the writing of L2 students, provided that there are peer tutors trained specifically to help them.

When we talked to the instructors and L2 students in WI courses, many of their impressions of the usefulness of a writing center were related to their experiences with the Writing Workshop in its former conception. Although some of the issues may no longer apply, it is still instructive to see what they experienced, in order to evaluate how well the changes may be meeting students' needs. One major concern was the whole issue of language, and whether L2 students should obtain help with grammar from the Writing Workshop, or whether there should be a separate source of writing assistance in ESL. Another major concern was whether a writing center in English is even capable of providing help with the writing required by other disciplines, or whether there should be separate writing centers within various disciplines. Other concerns were the need for peer tutors and the difficulties students had getting appointments at the center.

All students, whether native English speakers or L2 students, need feedback on their writing, just as instructors and researchers need feedback on their writing. However, L2 students (and L2 instructors) need proportionately more help with their language use, whether that help is in making lexical choices or in editing morphological or syntactic errors. For L2 students in particular, there is a need for external proofreading when the student does not have the necessary language intuitions, although some centers are willing only to teach strategies, not do actual proofreading (Harris & Silva, 1993; Powers, 1993).

L2 students want to learn more about how to write well and they perceive the Writing Workshop as a resource. One commented, for example:

> After I write the first draft, you can let them see it. And they will tell you what is wrong, but they won't correct it. They just tell you what is wrong, and you should write a second draft and let them see it. And mostly [you get] better grades after writing and they check your paper.

Another remarked, "Since I receive the services provided by the Writing Workshop, my writing skill and grammar knowledge have been improved a lot."

However, not everyone's experiences have been helpful. One student found herself rejected because of her writing:

> I went there [the Writing Workshop] because I knew my English was not good enough, and my grammar was weak. That's why I went there to seek some help. But his attitude was like, "I don't mind looking at your paper, but the level of yours is too low, it's not good, I can't look at thing like this." I was really shocked at that. He was like "It's just not worth looking through."

Other students have not had such a negative experience, but they found that they could not get help with grammar. One said, for example, "It help, of course, yeah, it help, but not on grammar." Another observed, "They don't really give you grammar correction." This position was confirmed by an English instructor: "[The Writing Workshop faculty] will talk through content, argument, structural things, but they won't edit. It's not an editing service." It should be stressed that this was an older policy that has been changed.

The earlier policy that denied editing and grammar correction for L2 students originally stemmed from a desire among the English faculty that L2 students have their own feedback center. Nonnative speakers have different and specific writing problems that, English faculty feel, do not fall within their area of expertise:

> We have the Writing Workshop here in the English department. But our faculty doesn't feel that they should be used as a service to second language learners in its entirety. In other words, ESL needs to have a writing lab. The people who should be working with these L2 learners are not English professors who haven't studied L2 problems.

An L2 student and a WI instructor echoed this view: "I think they got lot of bilingual students here. And I think they should have some [center] for bilingual students" (student). "Given the way I use the Writing Workshop, it would be interesting if there was a more explicit Writing Workshop for second language students that had the same sort of things" (sociology instructor).

In fact, in the past, the ESL department provided a small writing center as an adjunct to the Writing Workshop, but due to problems in the working relationship of those involved, this was discontinued. Recent changes in policy have been an attempt to rectify this, with an L2 writing specialist being employed as a graduate assistant in the Writing Workshop, and volunteers from the department of ESL being encouraged to become peer tutors and take a practicum course offered in English that trains them in tutoring in the center.

L2 students can find themselves in a catch-22 situation. Many do not have the internal system that would allow them to recognize their own errors, computerized grammar checkers only help if students have the appropriate intuitions to judge the advice, instructors either refuse to look at grammar or will reduce the student's grade commensurate with how much feedback they have to provide, and writing centers may not be willing to help them with editing. As one student put it: "What I need right now is not offered, yeah? That grammar check." Another student said: "I just want to say that this kind of service is very important to students, especially for foreign students. 'Cause a lot of my friends have problems in writing. We just feel helpless. We don't know where to go."

However, we need to point out that even if students are able to find a source for grammar editing, that does not necessarily eliminate the second language students' problems, because they may then be accused of plagiarizing. In a recent case at UHM, the instructor compared an early draft of a paper with the final draft and concluded based on the language that the student did not write the final paper. The student acknowledged getting help with the language from tutors, who have written letters verifying their involvement throughout the process. The student is now being accused of a student conduct code violation (plagiarism), not based on stealing from a source, but based on receiving help with language use. Although this is an isolated case that depended on an individual instructor's interpretation of plagiarism, we find even one example chilling.

Another major area of concern is whether a writing center can provide appropriate feedback for writing done across the curriculum. WI instructors do not feel that the staff at the Writing Workshop can provide help with writing related to their particular disciplines. One math instructor contended, "If they go there, the people who would assist them would have no understanding of what they were reading." Another math instructor commented: "It's hard to see how a mathematics course or another technical course can have a big contribution to how to teach the technical language."

L2 students also feel that the workshop can not provide help with someone who is not teaching writing in disciplines other than English:

> The lady, she doesn't, I think, often see science thing. So she can only correct my grammar, but not my ideas. [For Biology], it's not helpful. And one thing is like I'm afraid that if I go to workshop, sometimes they don't know what I'm talking about right? Like let's say about Japanese Literature in Translation. So like sometimes I wonder if they understand my paper.

WI instructors expressed their desire for writing centers that would more specifically meet the writing needs of their discipline:

> It would be interesting if there was a more explicit Writing Workshop by substance for social science students. Because the way it is now, I assume that they just join 'em with the engineers and the artists (sociology instructor).

> I think it would be neat if I taught this class in conjunction with a technical writer, and had a writing lab every week where they'd bring in their documents and get focused attention (computer science instructor).

At UHM, the math department does offer a discipline-related service specifically for students who are in math courses. This service provides help with both conceptual and writing problems for students who are in math courses, and also provides two of the things that students say they want the most: peer tutors and easy availability of appointments.

In fact, L2 students described their experiences at writing centers on other campuses in terms of the value of peer tutors and availability:

> There is a place called Learning Center. And you can bring your English paper there and just sign up the time and day you want to have a tutor. And after you sign up, you go there, and the guy would read the paper, or make you read it. And then he would correct your grammar, and tell "If I were you I would write like this." Why I want to have something like that is I feel safe to sign. The people there are really nice, they're like friends. We just talk and discuss. Maybe the atmosphere.

The difficulty of obtaining any assistance was one of the chief criticisms of the Writing Workshop at UHM. Students commented on the difficulty of obtaining an appointment. Appointments must be made far in advance, and sessions are only 30 minutes long, which, students felt, was not enough time for going over an entire paper.

Another concern of the L2 students was to have peer tutors rather than faculty members reading their papers:

> I just think [TAs] know how to be a student. So when I ask a question "Oh, I had that problem when I was undergraduate." So then we kind of feel that common thing and then she try to teach me as, you know, the way she understand or the way it's more clear to her. So that helps me a lot.

One instructor understood why peer help was far less intimidating than talking to a faculty member:

> I would think probably peer help would be the easiest. I would think that part of the reason that they don't come see me, and that they don't go to the Writing Workshop, is you have to go expose yourself to an authority, and show them your inadequacy, and be judged and evaluated. If you had a friend who could help you, that would be comfortable.

Clearly, peer tutors have been part of the success of many writing centers (Bell, 1983; Wallace, 1988).

The L2 students and instructors have expressed a need for writing feedback from knowledgeable peer tutors that goes beyond what instructors are able to give, that is targeted toward the needs of various disciplines as well as language use. How this need could best be met depends on the university's resources. One possibility would be to expand the current Writing Workshop with interdisciplinary peer tutors funded by the university. In the case of UHM, the English Department has had to struggle to support the writing needs of students with very little financial support, but that could change. Another possibility would be for individual colleges to develop their own writing assistance centers, much as UHM's Math Department has done, but on a broader scale. A third possibility would be to create a centralized, interdisciplinary writing center staffed by undergraduate and graduate students from a wide variety of disciplines.

In a centralized writing center, there could be discipline specialists who help with choosing a topic, finding and working with sources, and using the discourse of the discipline, who could also be affiliated with certain courses. There could be composition specialists who help with clarity, organization, and style. There could be language specialists who are aware of the particular needs of L2 students and can help with syntactic, lexical, and morphological choices. Students would be able to make appointments with particular tutors or to drop by for the next available tutor. The advantage of a centralized center would be the increased availability to students because the resources would be consolidated. However, the disadvantage is that a centralized center can assume far too much institutional authority (Riley, 1994; Smith, 1986). Regardless of the best solution, we would not want any type of writing assistance center to supplant the current emphasis on learning discipline-specific writing in the context of very small WI courses, but to support L2 students throughout their undergraduate experience as one way among several.

CONCLUSION

The faculty throughout the UHM system are in the process of working out new systemwide goals for undergraduate education, including goals for the development of writing. In a recent draft, the introductory statement in the area of writing reads: "Written communication will be an integral part of the total student collegiate educational experience from entry to completion" (General Education Project, 1996). Writing in the academy is developmental; it begins in the first semester and continues until graduation and beyond. Writing in the academy can not be taught in one or two courses; it develops out of the whole experience of broad exposure to writing in different disciplines, as well as being apprenticed to a particular discipline as a major. The WI courses required by UHM are part of that continuing development, as one WI instructor noted: "I just look at them as here's 21 people, and 22 including myself, who could all learn a lot more about writing." On the other hand, it is incumbent on the university to provide the support that L2 students need to develop their academic writing skills further, as one student noted: "Since the university is requiring students take writing courses, I want the university to be sensitive to students' need and improve their system."

This chapter suggests that first-year writing courses in English or ESL need to be situated within the context of other disciplines at the university, by offering the opportunity to explore those contexts through ethnographic investigative techniques. Instructors, particularly at research universities like UHM, need more awareness that writing is a developmental process for all students, but especially so for L2 students because the development of academic language skills requires prolonged exposure to the academic target. Instructors need to reflect on and clarify the purposes for which they use writing in their courses and be better informed about the availability—or unavailability—of resources for L2 students. That would allow them to determine when it is worth requiring perfect grammar and mechanics, and when, instead, students should focus on the presentation and clarification of ideas that will help them develop their knowledge of course content. Instructors need to address strategies for learning how to write within their discipline, recognizing that WI courses offer a unique opportunity for them to provide personal attention to students' writing within the context of their discipline. This should become a more explicitly stated goal of WI courses. Finally, a more interdisciplinary writing center (or centers) might be able to meet L2 students' needs that otherwise go unmet, through offering peer feedback within disciplines, as well as language feedback for those who need it in a context that is nonevaluative.

Although the need for help with academic writing is a particularly difficult problem for L2 students, it is not exclusive to them. Learning how to write within a particular discipline can be difficult for all undergraduate students, even the most gifted writers (Chiseri-Strater, 1991). Some may argue that universities should not admit students who can not already write, but we argue that there are no undergraduate students who come to the university already knowing what they need to know and will learn about writing within the academy. Academic writing is learned through apprenticeship to academic disciplines. L2 students come with diverse backgrounds and diverse experiences, and that is nowhere more true than in a multilingual society like Hawai'i. There is an opportunity for each of these students to grow as academic writers, if the university is willing to support them with multiple opportunities to write and receive feedback within the contexts of different disciplines.

REFERENCES

Atkinson, D., & Ramanathan, V. (1995). Cultures of writing: An ethnographic comparison of L1 and L2 university writing/language programs. *TESOL Quarterly, 29*, 539–565.

Belcher, D. (1995). Writing critically across the curriculum. In D. Belcher & G. Braine, *Academic writing in a L2: Essays on research and pedagogy* (pp. 135–154). Norwood, NJ: Ablex.

Bell, E. (1983). The peer tutor: The writing center's most valuable resource. *Teaching English in the Two-Year College*, Winter, 141–144.

Braine, G. (1996). ESL students in first-year writing courses: ESL versus mainstream classes. *Journal of Second Language Writing, 5*, 91–107.

Broder, P. F. (1990). Writing centers and teacher training. *Writing Program Administration, 13*, 37–45.

Chinn, P., & Hussey, E. (1993). *Perspectives on writing and learning. Manoa Writing Program* (Vol. 2). Hawai'i: University of Hawai'i at Manoa.

Chiseri-Strater, E. (1991). *Academic literacies: The public and private discourse of university students*. Portsmouth, NH: Boynton/Cook.

Clark, I. L. (1993). Portfolio evaluation, collaboration, and writing centers. *College Composition and Communication, 44*, 515–524.

Colleen, B. (1995). *ESL writers' reactions to teacher commentary: A case study*. ERIC Document Reproduction Service ED 394 312.

Collier, V. P. (1987). Age and rate of acquisition of L2 for academic purposes. *TESOL Quarterly, 21*, 617–641.

Cooper, M. M. (1994). Really useful knowledge: A cultural studies agenda for writing centers. *The Writing Center Journal, 14*, 97–111.

Elbow, P. (1991). Reflections on academic discourse: How it relates to freshmen and colleagues. *College English, 53*, 135–155.

Elbow, P. (1998, March). *Plenary talk given at the Languages, Linguistics, and Literature*. Student Conference held at the University of Hawai'i at Manoa.

Fulwiler, T. (1986). Reflections: How well does writing across the curriculum work? In A. Young & T. Fulwiler (Eds.), *Writing across the disciplines: Research into practice* (pp. 235–246). Portsmouth, NH: Boynton/Cook.

Gee, J. (1990). *Social linguistics & literacy: Ideology in discourses*. New York: Falmer Press.

Geertz, C. (1983). *Local knowledge: Further essays in interpretive anthropology*. New York: Basic Books.

General education project report. (1996). Hawai'i: University of Hawai'i at Manoa.

Hall, C. (1990). Managing the complexity of revising across languages. *TESOL Quarterly, 24*, 43–60.

Harris, M., & Silva, T. (1993). Tutoring ESL students: Issues and options. *College Composition and Communication, 44*, 525–537.

Healy, D., & Bosher, S. (1992). ESL tutoring: Bridging the gap between curriculum-based and writing center models of peer tutoring. *College ESL, 2*, 25–32.

Hilgers, T., Bayer, A., Stitt-Bergh, M., & Taniguchi, M. (1995). Doing more than "thinning out the herd": How eighty-two college seniors perceived writing-intensive classes. *Research in the Teaching of English, 29*, 59–87.

Jacoby, S., Leech, D., & Holten, C. (1995). A genre-based developmental writing course for undergraduate ESL science majors. In D. Belcher & G. Braine, (Eds.), *Academic writing in a second language: Essays on research and pedagogy* (pp. 351–373). Norwood, NJ: Ablex.

Johns, A. M. (1995). Teaching classroom and authentic genres: Initiating students into academic cultures and discourses. In D. Belcher & G. Braine, (Eds.), *Academic writing in a second language: Essays on research and pedagogy* (pp. 277–291). Norwood, NJ: Ablex.

Kutz, E., Groden, S., & Zamel, V. (1993). *The Discovery of competence*. Portsmouth, NH: Boynton/Cook Heinemann.

Lehner, A., Segade, G., Wolfe-Quintero, K., & Hilgers, T. (in press). *The experiences and needs of bilingual students and instructors in writing-intensive courses across the curriculum*. Manoa Writing Program Technical Report #18, University of Hawai'i at Manoa.

Leki, I. (1992). *Understanding ESL writers: A guide for teachers*. Portsmouth, NH: Boynton/Cook.

Leki, I. (1995a). Coping strategies of ESL students in writing tasks across the curriculum. *TESOL Quarterly, 29*, 235–260.

Leki, I. (1995b). Good writing: I know it when I see it. In D. Belcher & G. Braine,(Eds.), *Academic writing in a second language: Essays on research and pedagogy* (pp. 23–46). Norwood, NJ: Ablex.

North, S. M. (1984). The idea of a writing center. *College English, 46*, 433–446.

O'Mealy, J., & Register, J. (1984). Editing/drilling/draft-guiding: A threefold approach to the services of a Writing Workshop. College *Composition and Communication, 35*, 230–233.

Powers, J. K. (1993). Rethinking writing center conferencing strategies for the ESL writer. *The Writing Center Journal, 13*, 39–47.

Raimes, A. (1987). Language proficiency, writing ability, and composing strategies: A study of ESL college student writers. *Language Learning, 37*, 439–468.

Rehberger, D. (1994). Negotiating authority among writing centers, writing programs, peer tutors and students. *English in Texas*, 50–54.

Riley, T. (1994). The unpromising future of writing centers. *The Writing Center Journal, 15*, 20–34.

Rusikoff, K. (1994). *Hidden expectations: Faculty perceptions of SLA and ESL writing competence*. ERIC Document Reproduction Service ED 370 376.

Sato, C. (1985). Linguistic inequality in Hawai'i: The post-creole dilemma. In N. Wolfson, and J. Manes (Eds.), *Language of inequality* (255–272). Berlin: Mouton.

Sato, C. (1989). A nonstandard approach to standard English. *TESOL Quarterly, 23*, 259–282.

Segade, G. (1997). *The freshman paradox: Faculty-student interaction and the socialization of ESL students at the University of Hawai'i*. Scholarly paper, Department of English as a Second Language, University of Hawai'i at Manoa.

Segade, G., & Wooldrik, S. (1997, March). *Students and teachers learning together: Collaborative research on the conventions of academic writing at the university*. Paper presented at the Language, Linguistics, and Literature College-Wide Conference, University of Hawai'i at Manoa.

Silva, T. (1993). Toward an understanding of the distinct nature of L2 writing: The ESL research and its implications. *TESOL Quarterly, 27*, 657–677.

Smith, L. Z. (1986). Independence and collaboration: Why we should decentralize writing centers. *The Writing Center Journal, 7*, 3–10.

Spack, R. (1988). Initiating ESL students into the academic discourse community: How far should we go? *TESOL Quarterly, 22*, 29–47.

Thonus, T. (1993). Tutors as teachers: Assisting ESL/EFL students in the writing center. *The Writing Center Journal, 13*, 13–26.

Tsutsui, J., & Wallace, A. (1991). *Writing-intensive activities in classes across the curriculum*. Manoa Writing Program, Volume One, University of Hawai'i at Manoa.

Wallace, R. (1988). The writing center's role in the writing across the curriculum program: Theory and practice. *The Writing Center Journal, 8*, 43–48.

Walvoord, B. E., & McCarthy, L. P. (1990). *Thinking and writing in college: A naturalistic study of students in four disciplines*. Urbana, IL: National Council of Teachers of English.

Wooldrik, S. (1996). *Academic writing exploration*. Scholarly paper, Department of English as a L2, University of Hawai'i at Manoa.

Zamel, V. (1985). Responding to student writing. *TESOL Quarterly, 19*, 79–101.

Zamel, V. (1995). Strangers in academia: The experiences of faculty and ESL students across the curriculum. *College Composition and Communication, 46*, 506–521.

12 Immigrant Student Performance in an Academic Intensive English Program

Dennis Muchisky
Nancy Tangren
University of Nebraska–Lincoln

The Programs in English as a Second Language (PIESL) at the University of Nebraska–Lincoln (UNL) is housed in the English Department and consists of an Intensive English Program (the IEP) and a Credit English as a Second Language (CESL) program that offers undergraduate and graduate writing courses. The IEP was started in the mid-1970s on a small scale as a support service to UNL's international students, and it has remained a small program up to the present time. During the five 8-week sessions of 1995–1996, the IEP enrolled 185 students. The programs' mandate comes from a 1975 report from the vice chancellor for Academic Affairs Admissions and Advising Committee, which read in part,

> If ... English study is needed, you will be required to enroll in a special English class as part of your academic program. Enrollment in special English classes during the following semesters will be required until you attain a level of language proficiency that enables you to make normal and satisfactory academic progress.

The IEP is an academic English program designed to serve "typical" international students who are, as described by Bosher and Rowenkamp (1992), "well-educated in their native countries, from urban areas, and from middle-to upper-middle class socio-economic backgrounds"(p. 3). As is the case for most university affiliated academic IEPs, international students traditionally have made up the majority of the enrollment in the program. The international student population at UNL has been fairly stable recently with the yearly enrollment ranging from 1,400 to 1,600 students. Presently, the largest numbers of students are, as is the case nationally, from the Pacific Rim with China, Korea, Japan, Malaysia, and Indonesia being the countries with the highest numbers of students in attendance.

UNL consists of two campuses within the city of Lincoln. The city campus houses the main university and the east campus houses agricultural programs. Students on both campuses are included in the ESL population. Also, traditionally, the international student population at UNL has been made up of a majority of graduate students, with 736 graduate students enrolled at UNL during the spring semester of 1997 along with 524 undergraduates. Because of credit transfer agreements with two Malaysian junior colleges, the single largest group of undergraduate students is from that country, and this has also been the largest group in the IEP.

IEP

The IEP is a noncredit-bearing program designed for students whose TOEFL scores are below 500, which at the time of this study was the score required to enter academic studies at UNL. Students in the IEP are in classes for 25 hours a week for 8-week sessions. During the time period of this study, the IEP offered three levels of instruction—beginning, intermediate, and advanced. Initial placement into the IEP, and subsequent movement through the levels is based on student performance on the program's English Placement Examination (EPE) battery, which consists of the Michigan Test of English Language Proficiency (MTELP), the Michigan Test of Aural Comprehension (MTAC), and a 30-minute composition test that is scored holistically. The scores are averaged, with the composition test being counted double, and the student is given a placement test score based on 100 points. The test is used to place students into the various levels of the IEP as well as into the CESL writing courses. At the time of this study, a score of 75 allowed a student to enter academic studies. All non-IEP applicants who entered UNL needed to present a TOEFL score of 500 at the undergraduate level.

The majority of students entering the IEP are admitted after having been conditionally accepted to UNL. They apply to the Foreign Admissions Office, are accepted for academic study, and, if their TOEFL scores are below the required minimum, are referred to the ESL program. After completing the IEP, students move into academic studies and the CESL courses by passing either the EPE or the TOEFL.

CESL

CESL courses at both the graduate and undergraduate levels are credit bearing (3 credits per course), although with one exception, they do not count toward degrees. At the undergraduate level there are three required courses (English 186, 187, and 188) and at the graduate level there are two required courses (English 886 and English 887). At the undergraduate level, English 188 fulfills the freshman English requirement. Placement into these courses is made on the basis of both TOEFL and EPE results, with particular attention being paid to the results of the composition portion of the EPE. Presently, students who receive an EPE score of 83 are waived from CESL classes, and students who enter UNL with a TOEFL score of 600 or higher are required to take only the composition part of the EPE.

IMMIGRANT STUDENTS

In the late 1980s, large numbers of immigrants began to come to Lincoln through the sponsorship of Catholic Social Services, Church World Services and the Khmer Association Refugee Center. The people who arrived in Lincoln during this period had been in refugee camps in the Philippine Islands. Because of time spent in the camps, many students suffered breaks in their education with some of the older students missing up to 5 years of education prior to their arrival in Lincoln.

As a result of the efforts of these agencies, the ESL population in the Lincoln Public Schools (LPS) increased dramatically in a short time. In the 1988–1989 school year there were 74 ESL students enrolled in secondary schools in Lincoln. By the 1992–1993 school year this number had risen to 312. The greatest increase occurred between the 1989–90 and 1990–1991 school years when ESL enrollments rose by 95%. Since that time enrollments have varied, dropping to 190 during the 1992–1993 school year and rising again to 420 for the 1996–1997 school year.

By far the single largest group of students has been from Vietnam: In January, 1992, 70% of the ESL enrollment in the public schools was made up of Vietnamese students. This percentage has decreased over time, but Vietnamese students still comprise the majority of ESL students in the public school system. The increase in secondary level ESL students in the Lincoln schools had a rather dramatic impact on the IEP.

As the students who arrived in 1989 began to graduate from high schools in Lincoln, many chose to apply to UNL. These students were required to take the EPE, a requirement implemented by the Office of Undergraduate Admission as an alternative path of to entry into UNL for students whose ACT scores would have otherwise disqualified them from admission. In fact, the cause of the low ACT scores was language proficiency—particularly for this early group of students who sought entry into the university after completing 1, 2, or 3 years of high school locally. Graduation from high school was made possible at this point only because all of the ESL classes that the students took were accepted for admission to UNL.

ADMINISTRATIVE ISSUES

The increased ESL enrollments in the public schools did not affect the IEP directly until the 1992–1993/1993–1994 school years. However, prior to that time contact was made with LPS ESL teachers and counselors to discuss UNL's English language proficiency requirements and the application procedure for both academic studies and the IEP. During the 1991–1992 school year, the coordinator of the PIESL and the university's undergraduate foreign admissions officer met with secondary school ESL program teachers and administrators to discuss admissions requirements and application procedures to both UNL and the IEP. The meeting was initiated by the undergraduate foreign admissions officer who was receiving a significant number of applications from local public school students. Although the number of immigrant students heavily impacted the admissions office and the IEP, their effect on other administrative units was less noticeable, and it was only the coordinator of the PIESL and undergraduate foreign admissions officer who were involved in working with the public schools.

This meeting produced an agreement to allow resident alien students to use the EPE results in lieu of a TOEFL score. Both UNL and LPS officials were seeking ways to encourage immigrant students to enter UNL. It was the view of the coordinator that the Programs in English as a Second Language as a part of the state university system, had a responsibility to this group of students. This was particularly the case because the local community college offered only conversation and writing courses that met 1 or 2 hours per week. The level and duration of these courses did not permit the students the opportunity to raise their overall English proficiency to the level required by the UNL.

In the mid-1980s, the PIESL staff had begun on-site testing of ESL students at the high school which was the primary secondary level ESL site. The test instrument used was the program's EPE battery. After the upsurge in public school ESL enrollments, their program expanded, and likewise the PIESL testing program expanded. The EPE came to be offered twice a year to students in the two high schools with ESL programs, and the test was also available at regularly scheduled test dates at UNL. An 8-week wait is required between tests.

IEP Funding

The IEP is a self-supporting unit, and student tuitions drive the program. The tuition costs for the IEP are comparable to UNL's out-of-state undergraduate tuition. However, an IEP student receives 25 hours of classroom instruction: more than double that received in credit classes. At a very early date in the history of the program, the in-state tuition for the IEP was set at 60% of the out-of-state tuition. Nevertheless, the cost remains considerably above that of regular full-time in-state enrollment at UNL. At the same time, the program itself faces a considerable dilemma serving these students. Clearly, a tuition-driven program like the IEP could easily find itself insolvent if its tuition were reduced by 40%. When the resident tuition plan was instituted, it was done so as a service to a community that had a very small resident ESL population. At the time, it was not expected that the population would ever be a sizable one.

All of the immigrant students discussed here received financial aid in the form of Pell Grants. As the application procedure is quite complex, students required a great deal of assistance in obtaining funds, placing additional demands on the program staff. The office secretary became a financial aid counselor, spending far more time working on immigrant student applications than on international student applications. She has also acted as a liaison between the admissions office, the financial aid office, and the student. Current UNL policy calls for the student to be academically admitted to the university, and then carry the admission letter to the financial aid office. Once the student's eligibility for aid is determined and the funding letter is issued, the student is then admitted to the IEP.

Before leaving the issue of funding, it should be noted that the amount of the Pell Grant is not sufficient to pay for more than one 8-week session of full-time studies per semester, even with the in-state tuition plan. The Pell Grant provides $1,150 per semester, which falls short of the $1,600 needed for two sessions of full-time study. What frequently happens is that a student studies fulltime for one session and then requests to drop down into part-time study. This results in stagnation—some students remain in the program on a part-time basis over the course of four sessions with little improvement. Students are advised against this, but it is difficult to turn away students who are determined to study. Although it is possible for students at the advanced level of IEP to enroll in a credit course, the immigrant students in this study who moved to part-time status had not achieved the required level of language proficiency to enroll in a credit class.

LANGUAGE PROFICIENCY SCORES

During the 1992/1993 and 1993/1994 academic years, which are the focus of this study, 22 refugee students from Vietnam entered the IEP. These students had been declared academically eligible for study at UNL based on a review of their high school transcripts but had not met the language proficiency requirement. And they were clearly not "typical" international students. Thirteen of the 22 were part of what Rumbaut and Ima (1988) referred to as the "1.5 generation"—"those who are born in Southeast Asia but educated in the United States." Rumbaut and Ima argued

> that the key difference [marking members of the 1.5 generation] involves those youths whose age at arrival was pre-puberty versus those who arrived post-puberty (or roughly younger than 11 or older than 15 at arrival in the United States). The older students (post-puberty at arrival) are more handicapped by language deficiencies, and they have had less time to 'learn the ropes' of the new system.... (p.103)

Rumbaut and Ima suggested that the 1.5 generation faces "two salient issues: (1) adolescence and the task of managing the transition from childhood to adulthood, and (2) acculturation and the task of managing the transition from one culture to another"(p.102). They go on to say that the "'1.5 generation' of refugee youth form a distinctive cohort in that in many ways they are marginal to both the old and the new worlds, and are fully part of neither of the them"(p. 103).

The Vietnamese students discussed here were all permanent residents of the United States and all had attended high school in Lincoln, even those who had previously graduated from high school in Vietnam. The students had lived in Lincoln for at least 1 year prior to entering UNL. In contrast, the international students in this study were attending the university on F–1 visas and at the time of the study had been in the United States for a semester or less.

The first concern related to the Vietnamese students was that not only were their scores on the language proficiency section of the EPE lower than those of the international students in the program but also that the score pattern was very different, with the MTAC scores being significantly higher than the MTELP scores (see Table 12.1).

Thirteen of these students were fully part of the 1.5 generation and had all graduated from local high schools. Six of the students in this group of 13, after having studied in IEP over a period of time, failed to achieve the necessary placement exam score to enter UNL. Students are tested at the end of each IEP session, and the six students who failed averaged three IEP sessions before withdrawing from the program. Three of the students spent one session in part-time status. These six students averaged 1.1 years of residency in the United States prior to entering the IEP. The seven students who successfully completed the IEP averaged 2.4 years of residency in the United States prior to entering the program.

The other nine Vietnamese students, who had graduated from high school in Vietnam, averaged 1.4 years of prior residency in the U.S. Eight of the nine successfully completed the IEP and entered academic studies. Clearly, the students who graduated from Vietnamese high schools performed better in the IEP than those who graduated from local high schools.

Although the group of students who are studying in the intensive language program is small, these outcomes parallel results reported by Bosher

TABLE 12.1
Score Comparisons

	MTELP	MTAC	T-Value	P
Local School Graduates *(n = 13)*				
Entry	51.8	67.4	3.87	.01*
Exit	63.5	77.7	4.24	.001*
International Students *(n = 10)*				
Entry	59.5	58.9	0.09*	NS
Exit	79.8	80.6	0.30*	NS

*$p < .05$

and Rowenkamp (1992, p. 1). They examined the university class performance of 53 students (both international students and refugee and immigrant students) at the University of Minnesota. They reported "a negative correlation between years of education completed in the United States, length of residency in the United States and academic success." They also reported a strong correlation between MTELP and MTAC scores for international students but found that refugee and immigrant students in their study tended to have higher scores on the MTAC and lower scores on the MTELP. And they found that those students who graduated high school in their home country scored significantly higher on the objective part of the Michigan English Language Assessment Battery (MELAB) while U.S. high school graduates scored significantly higher on the listening portion of the MELAB. The student performance in mainstream university classes seems to parallel the performance of the IEP students at UNL.

In comparing the test scores of Vietnamese home country (HC) high school graduates to those of the Lincoln high school (LS) graduates, it was found that at entry into the IEP, the HC graduates scored significantly higher on the MTELP than did the LS graduates. The LS graduates scored higher, but not significantly so, on the MTAC. (see Table 12.2).

TABLE 12.2
Entry Scores

	LS Graduates (n = 13)	HC Graduates (n = 9)	T-Value	P
MTELP	46.2	58.6	2.68	.05*
MTAC	69.8	64.5	.86	NS

*p < .05

On exit from the program, the HC graduates still scored significantly higher than the LS graduates on the MTELP, and also higher, but not significantly so on the MTAC (see Table 12.3).

TABLE 12.3
Exit Scores

	LS Graduates (n = 13)	HC Graduates (n = 9)	T-Value	P
MTELP	69.2	77.7	2.43	.05*
MTAC	76.6	79.2	.59	NS

*p < .05

STUDENT OUTCOMES

High scores on the MTELP consistently serve to distinguish between those students who ultimately succeeded in completing the IEP and entering academic studies and those who did not. This outcome also suggests that the students might face some difficulties once they enter academic studies as well. Bosher and Rowenkamp (1992, p. 1), who studied the performance of immigrant students in academic classes, found that "the most important predictor of academic success [as evidenced by GPA] was the number of years of schooling in the native country, followed by the student's objective score on the MELAB."

Because MTELP scores do seem to be an predictor of academic success, a major concern related to placement is that the students in this study generally score higher on the MTAC; significantly so for the LS graduates, and that these high scores on the MTAC often carry the students into academic studies. As was noted earlier, the overall EPE score is an average of the MTELP, the MTAC and twice the composition score. The exit test scores for the seven local high school graduates who successfully completed IEP were as shown in Table 12.4.

For all but one of the students, the score on the MTAC was higher than the score on the MTELP, and for the group as a whole, there was a significant difference between the scores. All seven of the students passed the placement exam as a result of their MTAC score. Of the eight Vietnamese HC graduates, three passed as a result of higher MTAC scores; however, for the whole group, the test score differences were not significant. In discussing their results, Bosher and Rowenkamp (1992, p. 8) stated that:

TABLE 12.4
Exit Scores

MTELP	MTAC	COMP	EPE
68	88	73	75*
84	78	68	75
70	84	76	76*
69	87	75	77*
66	81	76	75*
66	79	77	75*
70	84	75	76*

* passing score on EPE due to MTAC Score

while it has been suggested that performance on a standardized test of discrete items which focuses on the formal properties of language does not accurately reflect a person's ability to use the language in real situations.... there is also evidence that suggests the lower the language proficiency, as measured by scores on standardized tests, the greater the role it plays in academic success.... In other words, while language proficiency does not guarantee academic success, without it academic success is less likely.

If we examine the test results within Cummins' (1984, 1986) language proficiency framework of context-embedded versus context-reduced communication and cognitively undemanding versus cognitively demanding tasks, it would seem that the MTAC is more a test that would fall into the context-embedded and cognitively undemanding quadrant of that framework and that the MTELP is more a measure of the context-reduced cognitively demanding academic language proficiency skills. It may be then that we are placing students at risk by allowing them entry into academic studies on the basis of these test results, which for the refugee students are skewed by the MTAC results. That is to say, that the students whose tests scores show more balance between the MTAC and MTELP sections of the test would seem to have the capability to operate in the context-reduced cognitively demanding quadrant of Cummins' framework, while the students with significant difference in the two test scores might have less facility in this area.

This is not, however an impossible situation because, as Cummins (1986) pointed out, "cognitive involvement, in the sense of amount of information processing, can be just as intense in context-embedded as in context-reduced activities" (p.154). In other words, could the students' listening abilities (as reflected in the high MTAC scores) allow them to get enough information from context-embedded situations such as class lectures to make up for what they might miss because of their low level abilities (as reflected in the low MTELP scores) in context reduced situations such as reading academic texts?

Given the failure rate of the LS graduates and the discrepancies existing between the MTELP and MTAC scores, it seemed that the explanation offered by Collier and Cummins accounted for the performance levels of this group of students in the IEP. Collier (1989) in discussing the situation of a group of immigrant students that she had studied pointed out that:

Adolescents with good cognitive development in the first language ... reach high levels of proficiency in basic L2 skills in 2 to 3 years, with the possible exception of native like pronunciation. However, during this period of acquisition of the second language, these students received no assistance with continuing content area achievement, except for sitting in mainstream classes in which they could not understand the language of instruction. As a result, their academic achievement lagged behind that of the native English speaking peers. It appears that secondary students cannot afford the loss of 2 to 3 years of academic instruction while they are mastering basic L2 skills, if their expectations are to compete successfully with native speakers who plan to pursue a university degree. (p. 520)

The implicit solution would seem to be to provide content instruction, and this is done in the Lincoln ESL program. So why do students continue to show these results?

Cummins (1978) explains that older students' better performance in academic settings is strongly related to the development of L1 school skills. His interdependence hypothesis predicts that the development of L2 school language is partially dependent upon prior level of development of L1 school language. (Collier, 1989, p. 516)

The higher success rate for the HC graduates offers support to the interdependence hypothesis. So does the general pattern of years of schooling for the ESL population in the LPS system. The following figures taken from LPS enrollment data illustrates the problem. The data for 15- and 16-year-olds who were enrolled in LPS during the 1995–1996 school year show that of the twenty-nine 15-year-olds (who should have 10 years of schooling); six had full schooling, eight had missed 1 year, six 2 years, three 3 years, five more than 3 years, and one had had no schooling prior to entering LPS. Similarly, of the twenty-five 16-year-olds (who should have 11 years of schooling), none had had full schooling, four had missed 1 year, four missed 2 years, three missed 3 years, and 14 had missed more than 3 years. Although this type of data was not collected from the students in our study, we would expect a similar pattern.

The exit scores recorded by the local high school graduates highlight the dichotomy that exists for program directors. We are at the same time educators and admissions officers. We are responsible for developing and overseeing the program of instruction and also for enforcing the standards that the students must meet in order to enter into academic studies. Having to tell a student that he or she has failed is always difficult; however, for our international students failure was often just a temporary setback. For our immigrant students, it was frequently a terminal setback. Demands outside of class no doubt contributed to student failure. Although it is true that the Vietnamese students in our study received financial aid, it is also true that many of the students worked while attempting to study. Several students had full-time jobs and were attempting to attend 5 hours of class in addition to working for 8 hours.

As a whole, the students were hard working and very determined to enter the university. Their frustration at being unable to achieve their goals was equaled by the frustration among the faculty at seeing the students make little or no progress over a long period of time. As was mentioned earlier, given the score pattern of those local high school graduates, we were unsure that the students would be successful in the university. Nonetheless, we were all pleased when students did make the required proficiency level as they then at least would have the opportunity for academic study.

CLASSROOM ASPECTS

Student Characteristics

Lincoln has not been a major center of immigration. Other locales have likely had more experience with the challenges of the immigrant student, but the faculty in this relatively small program in a rather homogeneous city found themselves in a situation that seemed to develop overnight, and therefore were challenged to respond more directly than may have been the case at other schools where immigration increased at a slower rate or where the town's population has historically been more diverse.

Addressing any classroom situation is, of course, primarily the responsibility of the faculty, and in the PIESL most pedagogical decisions are made by the teachers themselves. There are too many contributing factors to ensure that one can ever teach the same curriculum in the same way to all classes each term and expect the same results; therefore, teachers have learned to be flexible. When distinct groups of students suddenly appear in the classroom, it is necessary to give consideration to pedagogical decisions demanded by their presence. When this new group of immigrant students began appearing in our IEP classes at UNL, we responded to the challenges raised by these students by first describing the characteristics that distinguished them from the international students in the program. The description offered here is based on a survey of qualitative observations of the seven teachers directly involved with the students in the program during the period of the study.

One of the first things teachers noticed when the number of immigrant students suddenly increased was how their students' skills varied from those of our international students. The immigrant students brought to the classroom a greater facility with the spoken language and a higher level of listening comprehension compared to the international students lower level of oral proficiency and greater facilities in reading and writing. Of course, students within a particular class always vary in individual language experience, but this variance gains special pedagogical significance when it distinguishes one group of students from another. In an attempt to adequately describe this characteristic, it is important to refer briefly to the type of language proficiency needed for academic purposes.

Because of the work of Cummins in the 1970s and 1980s, educators, especially those who address the special needs of both bilingual and second language students, have made a distinction between context-embedded and context-reduced language. Context-embedded language is used in interpersonal social contexts where there are both paralinguistic and situational clues and where the participants can negotiate meaning. Context-reduced language, "relies primarily (or at the extreme of the continuum, exclusively) on linguistic clues to meaning" (Cummins, 1986, p. 152). It is the con-text-embedded language that is used in much of the immigrant students' public school experience.

Context-reduced language is more used in university classrooms as, for example, in discussions of the unseen atom or in relating a piece of fiction to personal experience, and this type of language requires that a greater amount of information be processed relying on linguistic rather than extralinguistic clues. Content classes, even those at the high school level, presume that students have, or are developing, this type of language proficiency. Cochran (1985), in a paper on strategies for teaching limited English proficient students, pointed out that because the immigrant students have often either taken a predominance of ESL classes or have been enrolled in ESL content courses in high school, they have largely missed the opportunity to develop this level of language, whether in their first (L1) or second language (L2). On the other hand, the international students in our classes (those who have come to the United States to attend the UNL after graduating from high school in their HC) have already acquired at least some of these language skills in their L1 and are now learning to manipulate English in the same way.

In Cummins' (1979) words, "the level of L2 competence attained is partially a function of the type of competence that has been developed in L1 at the time when intensive exposure to L2 begins" (p. 236). Simply stated, the international students have academic language experience in their L1, whereas the immigrant students who did not graduate high school in their HC, have not had as much experience with academic language, sometimes none at all. The immigrant students did however come to the classroom with much better abilities in listening, a greater facility with spoken English, and a much better knowledge of the cultural aspects of U.S. life.

The IEP faculty immediately observed these differences between the two groups. Their insights are revealed in such comments as, "I sometimes have to explain concepts [to immigrant students] that are familiar to the rest of the students, for example, what I mean by a word like 'narrator.'" Note that it is the *concept* that had to be explained, not just the definition of a new English vocabulary word. Another teacher commented that the immigrant group seemed less involved in activities more demanding than the "'fun' or 'social' parts of the class." And another teacher summed up the general view noting that this group seemed to be lacking in "mature academic experience."

The focus of the IEP is not just teaching English as a language, but as a critical means to another important end—academic success. In a 1989 study of achievement scores of L2 students, Collier found that students who arrive in a new country as adolescents with little or no prior L2 language instruction, and who must then continue academic work in the L2, are least likely of all L2 students to achieve national norms in content areas. Those who are able to gain academic success require more time. Many of the immigrant students in our program arrived as adolescents with little prior L2 instruction.

Another distinguishing characteristic of these immigrant students is that they bring with them some common language characteristics. ESL teachers will, of course recognize that all language groups do this to some extent. Among the Vietnamese students this is at least partly explained by the strong ethnic community of which these students are a part. For example, the LS immigrant students (interestingly, often joined in this characteristic by Vietnamese HC graduates), although they know the correct form of a particular verb, have a difficult time pronouncing verb endings, and, in the words of one teacher, "never seem to speak any clearer."

This particular feature of spoken language can be seen in the students' writing as is evidenced in the following examples:

The teacher is the one who <u>teach</u> us every thing.
The dressing from Asia culture is really strange when <u>compare</u> with the way American dressed.

Furthermore, although teachers and other students outside their own group will indicate that they do not understand what is being said, the immigrant students in our program seem to understand each other easily, even offering assistance when one of the group is asked to repeat an oral response. They seem to have become comfortable with their language and are not motivated to fix something they do not see as broken. A revealing example of just how adequate this common language is was reported by one of our teachers. One day as class was beginning, two Vietnamese students were arguing about a point that was to be discussed in the class. The teacher glanced over and said, "If you're going to argue in class, at least do it in English." The students looked at her in surprise and said, simultaneously, "We are!"

Although there are other large groups of students from a single country on the UNL campus (Malaysian, Korean, Chinese), the Vietnamese group is different in terms of number and longevity. The Vietnamese population in Lincoln is approximately 3,000 and it has been for more than 10 years. It is a permanent community in a way that the student communities are not. In Lincoln, there are Vietnamese neighborhoods, churches, restaurants, and stores. The community is cohesive, and it uses English internally. These factors contribute to a pidginized variety of oral English that is reflected in the language patterns the Vietnamese students use in the classroom.

The third characteristic cited by the teachers in the IEP is actually behavioral, notable because it seemed to separate the immigrant students from the international students we had become accustomed to in the program. There was considerable concern that this group of students sometimes seemed less involved in classroom activities. Such comments as, "I must try extra hard to give them a sense of academic motivation," and, "It is sometimes difficult to get them to submit written assignments," seemed representative. It was further noted that many of these students appeared to be comparatively "lacking in self-motivation," and "mellowed toward academics." It was also frequently noted that these students are culturally savvy, displaying little of the cultural naiveté seen among international students. Within any group there are, of course, exceptions to all of these behaviors; teacher responses were directed at describing the group of students as a whole. Nevertheless, it is clear that this profile is very different from one that would describe the behavior of the international students entering the university directly from their native countries to which we had become accustomed.

The final distinguishing characteristic of the immigrant students in the program is the varying levels of ability among the different language skills: speaking, listening, reading, and writing. As discussed in the context of the test results cited earlier, it was quickly noted by teachers that these students display a higher level of aural skills than writing skills. Additionally, it was observed that as a group they seem to be very fluent orally, especially in social situations, but to have severe pronunciation problems, including, especially, a very "unacademic vocabulary."

In summary, then, we found ourselves in a classroom divided; we were going to attempt to improve the L2 skills of our typical international students (a challenge we had become comfortable with), and our unfamiliar and quite distinct group of immigrant students (a new challenge we were not at all comfortable with). All of these students still faced the restrictions of time and impending placement tests.

Particularly relevant to our concerns with immigrant students, Adamson (1993) proposed that academic competency in a language "includes possessing a critical mass of general language proficiency, background knowledge of particular content material, and strategies for enhancing and utilizing this knowledge to complete academic tasks" (p. ix). He further suggested that students must be able to vary their strategies, adapting to specific academic challenges in their study of either language or content-course material. Adamson's ideas of academic competence proved especially salient in the IEP situation, as we too are concerned with the students' general ability to speak English, and also, to accomplish specific academic tasks in an L2. Additionally, we now found ourselves with more diversity within the same class than had previously been the case. Adamson offered insightful suggestions as to how all of these students, the international students and the immigrant students, could be successful by building language proficiency, learning academic strategies, and developing the skills to vary these strategies. We found that although we are obviously limited in our ability to offer these students background knowledge in specific content material, what we could do was focus on language proficiency in an academic context.

A brief review of Adamson's model of how ESL students accomplish academic tasks is helpful to this discussion. Adamson divided his model into two parts: first, the knowledge and abilities that students draw on to achieve a basic understanding of material and, second, the academic strategies that students can use to increase basic understanding and eventually complete tasks. For Adamson, basic understanding is reached by accessing three kinds of knowledge and abilities. The first of these is universal pragmatic knowledge, which includes basic-level concepts and image schemata (knowledge constructed by human concept-making capacity). As Adamson explained, drawing on the studies of Saville-Troike and Kleifgen (1986), this is the kind of knowledge that children use to communicate when they do not speak the same language. The second kind of knowledge relates to skills in an L2, or language proficiency as described in Spolsky's (1989) preference model. Adamson found some features of Spolsky's model, which allows for different profiles of proficiency among learners who will exhibit different typical features at varying degrees of strength, to be very important to academic success and relates them directly to his own notion of academic competence. The third kind of knowledge includes school language or scripts for school and subject-specific language. Adamson emphasized the importance of subject-specific background knowledge, noting that it often compensates for low proficiency in the target language. School scripts refers to that knowledge that allows the students to make inferences and predictions about the meaning of events that occur at school.

The second part of the model discusses the academic strategies that are used in the accomplishment of academic tasks by a L2 learner. Study strategies, such as note taking, enable students to move from basic understanding to enhanced understanding of content material they did not understand well at first encounter. Production strategies, such as obtaining reactions to drafts, enable students to complete assignments with less than a full understanding of the materials. If understanding, however, falls below a certain point, students resort to the use of coping strategies that bypass understanding altogether. Examples of such coping strategies that we have seen include general approaches such as studying only for test results, and more specific tactics such as copying homework. Students sometimes find success through such coping strategies, but this success is often limited, short term, and at the high cost of missed understanding. Our goal is to avoid these altogether and our hope is that the success we see in all of our students is not gained this way.

Writing Issues

Significant among distinguishing language features of these immigrant students were notable differences in writing characteristics. In order to more accurately assess specific writing issues, we assigned the students in our study into four groups: international students (IS), Vietnamese home country graduates (HCG), Lincoln high school graduates who completed the IEP (LS1), and Lincoln high school graduates who did not complete the IEP (LS2).

In order to quantify the writing scores we used the Composition Correctness Score procedure (Brodkey & Young, 1981). In this procedure, (1.) the first 250 words of the essay are counted, and then for each essay, the raters:

2. Go through the essay up to the 250th word underlining every mistake—from spelling and mechanics through verb tenses, morphology, vocabulary, and logical connectives between sentences.

3. Assign a weighted score to each error, from 3 to 1. A score of 3 is a severe distortion of readability or flow of ideas which throws the reader off the sense of the message through the intrusion of an erroneous linguistic element; 2 is a

moderate distortion; 1 is a minor error that does not affect readability in any significant way.

4. Calculate the essay Correctness Score by using 250 words as the numerator of a fraction, and the sum of the errors as the denominator (p.160).

Student essays from each of the four groups were blind-graded in accordance with the criteria: a word count was taken, and a score of 1, 2, or 3 assigned to each error. A score was then calculated for each of the essays. A sample paragraph from one of the essays with error scores indicated is shown here:

"Living away from family, young people have more self

-confident and they can organize their live better when they

    2   2

get married. because they used to living alone, they know some

            1   2

difficulties their life."

    3

The mean scores for the four groups of students on their entry and exit compositions are listed in Table 12.5.

Both on entering and exiting the IEP, international students have the highest composition scores, and t-test results showed that the difference between the entry and exit scores for this group of students is significant at the $p< .005$ level. On entry into the program, the LS1s who succeeded in the IEP have the second highest scores, followed by the HCGs, and then the LS2s who did not succeed in the IEP. On exit from the IEP, the HCGs move ahead of the both local school groups. The difference between their entry and exit scores is also significant at the $p< .005$ level. The LS2 group obtained the lowest scores on entry and exit and also showed the least improvement over time.

It is interesting to note that the local high school students wrote the longest essays on entry into the program (see Table 12.6).

The fact that the local students produced longer essays but received lower composition scores may be explained by turning once again to Cummins' distinctions between context-reduced and context-embedded language. The local students have achieved a degree of oral fluency that allows them to pro-

TABLE 12.5
Composition Scores

	IS (n = 10)	HCG (n = 8)	LS1 (n = 7)	LS2 (n = 6)
Entry Score	4.51	3.70	4.44	2.54
Exit Score	6.72	5.83	5.13	3.79

TABLE 12.6
Words Per Composition

	Entry Words	Exit Words
IS (n = 10)	200	277
HCG (n = 8)	195	314
LS1 (n = 7)	295	264
LS2 (n = 6)	282	312

duce a significant amount of language. However, because of the lack of academic language the essays become speech written down rather than written language. Chafe (1982), in discussing the differences between spoken and written language, said that "written language tends to have an 'integrated' quality which contrasts with the fragmented quality of the spoken language" (p. 380). Among the characteristics of spoken language, Chafe cited the stringing together of idea units without connectives, frequent use of coordinating conjunctions, and use of first-person reference. The following essay from one of the local high school graduates who did not complete the IEP demonstrates these qualities:

Yes, I believe in distinctions between men's and women's jobs

Because betwen men and women are different, some place they give men jobs harder, heavier. And women they have better jobs than men.

Sometime they have jobs just only for men can do it, or just only for women. many jobs for different people, some of them can not do this job with the best but with different job they can do best. Before in my country they thought women can do anythings outside—I means like to be a engineer, mathmatics, science, build the house, go into the war—the women just only stay do things in the house like take care children, cook, clean house—But now the women can do anything from outside to inside, women can get equal with men, sometimes before have jobs never had women but now women can do it to.

The analysis of this essay as speech written down is further supported, we believe, by the fact that the LS1 group—the group that succeeded in the IEP, and whose essay scores improved significantly over the period of their enrollment—decreased their essay length. The LS2 group—the group that failed in the IEP and whose essay scores showed the least improvement—increased the length of their essays over the course of their study.

Although they continued to evidence some problems with grammatical structures, for example the use of prepositions and some verb tense problems, the students who successfully improved their writing scores generally demonstrated improved ability in incorporating useful and effective organizational features into their essays. To varying levels, they were able to present clear and controlled theses. These papers had more suitable focus so that students were more successful in adequately supporting a main point. The students also kept focus and were less likely to drift to other unrelated ideas.

Additionally, the successful students demonstrated an increased level of ability to include introductions and conclusions in their writing. Transitional expressions were added and used more appropriately in the papers of the successful students. Again, many of these transitions occur infrequently in spoken language, so it is not surprising that they are less frequently used in the papers of those students who persisted in writing down spoken language.

The final writing feature that the students who passed the IEP demonstrated was the use of varied and complex sentence structures. Compared to the students who failed to improve, this group of students used longer sentences with appropriate subordination. The following excerpt is from the essay of one of the Vietnamese high school graduates who successfully completed the IEP:

> Some people think that it is good for young people to live with their family because the parent can support and gives a good idea for young people. But in my opinion young people should move away from home as soon as they are able to support themselves because it is important for them to be independent and self-sufficient before considering marriage.

> Although young people have some difficulties when they live away from their family, they have freedom, they can decide problems in their life. For example, When I was 20 years old I lived away from my family. The first time I have some troubles about cooking, money—little by little I got used to it

> Further more young people have more experience about society when they communicate with people because they can decide every things. They know how to spend their money, their time. When they get married they have had experiences about life.

> In conclusion living away from family is very important for young people before they get married because they will get more experience about life, society, and they will be independent and self-sufficient before considering marriage.

In discussing the integrated nature of writing, Chafe noted the use of participles, relative clauses and series, devices that appear in the previous essay in contrast to the earlier cited essay. Generally speaking, these most pronounced qualitative distinctions showed the writing teachers that our successful students were able to move quickly to gain the conscious control that is necessary to improve writing. They were able to build on this concept of academic language to a notably higher degree in a short period of time. This observation brings us back to the conclusion drawn earlier that part of what we had to build into a curriculum to best benefit this diverse group was material designed to develop academic language skills.

Pedagogical Adaptations

Faced with planned curriculum and methods that were not working as effectively as had been anticipated, the faculty adjusted and adapted quickly. Focusing on the learner, we found a need to look again at our classroom practices. Our instructional goal was to build a curriculum that would aid in the advancement of academic language. Intensive language programs have always worked to do this in short periods of time with students from a variety of cultural and educational experiences. Now with the addition of immigrant students a new element was in the mix and, when the mix is new the curriculum demands a new look.

The faculty became deeply involved in the process of reflection, research, discussion, and planning that led individual teachers to some permanent pedagogical changes in curriculum and methodology. An interesting note is that many of the initial, almost instinctive adjustments that the teachers made were very successful and have been incorporated at the program level. The next step in the process was to consolidate individual successes and mutually benefit from our combined experience. It was found that focusing on the abilities needed by all of students, and working within the classroom on teaching methods that allow for more varied combinations of knowledge, abilities, and strategies resulted in a more effective curriculum for all of the students.

Following are some examples of representative classroom activities and methods that were found to be effective. The method mentioned most frequently centers on interactive grouping. Teachers found that using learning groups in this mixed classroom provided a forum in which students were able to contribute to the group the knowledge, abilities, and strategies that they were strong in and benefit from the contributions of the other students, thereby gaining in basic understanding, increasing that level of understanding, and observing and practicing useful study and production strategies. Suggestions regarding the size of groups, the type of activities assigned, and the specific role of each participant in such groups varied, even more than in previous semesters. Faculty reported that they were especially thoughtful in determining which individuals should be in which groups and how tasks were to be assigned within the groups.

A brief review of Slavin's (1981) cooperative learning strategies reveals a specific methodology that is clearly suitable in a situation such as ours. Slavin summarized the critical elements of cooperative learning as lessons structured for positive interdependence, heterogeneous grouping, identification and practice of specific social and academic behaviors, and evaluation through whole-class wrap-up, individual testing, or group recognition. Teachers found activities such as news and interview teams (complete with video cameras), library research projects, sentence structure contests, and even brainstorming for essay topics successful uses of learning teams.

Another example of a cooperative learning strategy reported as especially effective in this varied group is signaling answers instead of speaking them, for example having students answer questions simultaneously with simple gestures, such as thumbs up or thumbs down. Nonverbal responses and whole-class responses help to equalize student participation, and take the focus off of one individual. This strategy was found to be an effective solution to problems of domineering personalities and lack of confidence among students as new linguistic manipulations are tried out, both of which were of more concern in our program now. This was so because the immigrant students, many of whom possessed greater fluency in English than the international students, were nonetheless reluctant to enter into classroom discussions.

Yet another method that reflects the principles of cooperative learning is jigsaw activities. Different students are given different pieces of information and must work together to solve a problem or complete a task. Any activity that requires a student to make a choice from among alternatives can be used as a nonverbal or signaling activity designed to increase language proficiency. Additionally, activities such as these allow students to vary production strategies and try out strategies that are new to them. Teachers reported that activities that equalize speaking time were also effective in these classes. Use of a "talking pen," where a pen is passed from student to student (in a random or set way) to designate a speaker, is an example of a method that proved adaptable to numerous language lessons.

These suggested activities are offered as examples of ways to address the needs of both the immigrant students and the international students in mixed classes. Learning activities such as these involve to varying degrees the use of social and academic language, allow for the development of different skills (reading, writing, listening, speaking), and effectively control the behavior of the group, allowing for participation while controlling dominant personalities and encouraging even the most reluctant individuals in the class. They are clearly useful in increasing basic understanding of English and practicing a variety of study and production strategies that will lead to enhanced understanding and completion of academic tasks.

Another type of effective learning activity was to utilize the special experiences of immigrant students. Allowing for positive contributions from the members of the class is a strategy that is familiar to teachers, and with minimal consideration can be easily and effectively accomplished here. Many teachers noted that the immigrant students' years in this country and, specifically, their high school experiences have prepared them to be "experts" on aspects of U.S. culture unfamiliar to the international students. Their experience has also given them insights into idiomatic and slang language used by young people in this country. Additionally, one teacher reported success using the immigrant students to lead discussions on problems all students face when trying to adjust to a new culture. Trivia games about U.S. culture and life in Lincoln were effectively created and led by the immigrant group and participated in by all the students.

These last suggestions, however, clearly must be utilized only in the social aspects of the class. Writing teachers found that the immigrant students benefited from writing topics and prewriting discussions and reading that led toward essays that were less personal and self focused. These students were accustomed to writing and speaking in very social ways about personal ideas and experiences. The ESL writing classes offered at the local high schools focused on personal writing. As a result, the immigrant students were accustomed to writing about themselves and their personal situations. They needed practice in academic language. We found that offering topics that focused away from their personal lives helped the students to begin to understand and practice the required differences between writing and speaking.

The last examples of strategies described here are those we used to address the problem of lack of academic experience among the immigrant students, as compared to the international students. It has been noted that this lack of experience with academic language often resulted in less motivation to become productively involved in classroom activities or to attempt academic tasks. It was noticed that the immigrant students responded very well to any activity that centered on autobiographical information, especially when spoken. This was found to be an effective starting point. Teachers of speech classes, for example, would have students present their personal life stories. They sometimes used getting-to-know-you games that called on students to guess identities from small amounts of personal data. Involvement in activities where students were confident that they had necessary knowledge seemed to spur involvement. In effect, what these teachers found was that beginning with strategies that the students felt comfortable, or familiar with could lead to newer experiences later.

Initial participation is only the first step toward developing academic language skills in students. It was necessary to continuously reinforce and encourage immigrant students. One teacher said that she often comments in class on the challenges these students face, recognizing how far they have already progressed and building their confidence to continue. Once the immigrant students were participating in the class activities it was, of course, necessary to encourage them toward more advanced knowledge and skills. Faculty found it helpful to give very detailed assignments, describing exactly what the students were expected to do. One teacher gave the students actual checklists so they could make sure that their work was complete. Student–teacher conferencing was also suggested. These are not new ideas. The point here is that the immigrant students, who are very aware of their test scores, seem to rely heavily on the knowledge, skills, and strategies they recognized as their strongest, becoming more hesitant and obviously less confident with assignments that required venturing into areas of proficiency, or language skills about which they were less confident. This of course, is not surprising, but the difference here is in the variety of levels within one classroom and the fact that the immigrant students seemingly have been able to rely on a mixture of their strengths and coping skills as they have progressed through the public school system.

Another, very insightful, suggestion for effectively managing the special challenges of a class composed of immigrant students and international students was made by one teacher who noted the dividing effect that the apparent differences in these two groups can have on a class, and suggested that the students participate together in setting class goals. The setting of goals, she reported, can serve to unite the class and insure feelings of involvement and personal responsibility. She found this to be a motivational tool also. This is a first-day activity that gives positive results throughout the term.

The student is a principal factor in pedagogical decisions made by teachers. But it is essential that we not get so involved in issues of motivation or behavior that we lose sight of our main purpose: providing opportunities for our students to increase their English language ability. Students must have the necessary language proficiency and strategies to read an economics textbook and fill a blue book in a history exam.

ACADEMIC PROGRESS

The First Year

We also tracked student performance once out of PIESL. Perhaps not surprisingly in light of the research, the HCGs who began academic studies during the 1993 academic year were performing in a manner consistent with the performance of typical international students. In fact, after one semester of university study, their mean GPA of 3.36 on a 4.0 scale was higher than the mean GPA of 3.08 for a group of 10 randomly selected international students who went through the IEP at the same time.

The performance of the LS1 graduates who began their studies during the 1994 academic year was better than anticipated. One of the students was on academic probation; however, the mean GPA of the seven students at the end of their first semester was 3.09. During their first semester, the LS1 students averaged only 11 credits, and among those credits were remedial courses which do not meet degree requirements. However, the picture changed during the second semester. The GPA for HCGs dropped slightly from 3.65 to 3.34, whereas the LS1 and LS2 graduates showed an increase in mean GPA to 3.22. The local graduates were still taking remedial courses during this period. After the first year, this group of refugee students was coping well.

After the First Year

A review of transcripts for the two groups, LS1 and HCG, shows a somewhat different picture at the end of their second school year. The LS1 group was having a difficult time. They were averaging 8.7 credits per semester with a GPA of 2.68. As a group, they had collected 18 withdrawals and had received six failing grades. Four of the seven students had been on probation and one of them had been placed on probation for a second time. The HCG group was faring better, averaging 11.1 credits per semester with a GPA of 3.27. None had been placed on probation. As a group they had received seven withdrawals and received one failing grade.

Although the LS1 group was moving along slowly, they were still in school after 2 years. Unlike Bosher and Rowenkamp (1992), we found that the longer students were in the school system, the more likely were their chances for success. It may be that the background knowledge—the school scripts—that the students develop during this time contribute to their success. And although Adamson (1993) discouraged the use of coping strategies, we suggest that the students are coping by being selective in their course choice and credit loads. It may be successful only as a short-term strategy, but it may also buy them some time to develop the skills they need as they progress.

POSTSCRIPT

Since the initial influx of immigrant students into the IEP, immigrant enrollment has declined since 1997. The single most significant factor in the decline is a new set of university admissions standards for entering freshmen. The new requirements include 4 years of high school English. ESL classes do not fulfill this requirement. Therefore, students entering high school in the 10th grade are unable to meet the 4 year requirement without spending extra time in school. The LPS permits students to attend classes until they are 21. Nonetheless, as a result of these new standards, more of the ESL students are applying to the local community college, which has no language proficiency requirement, to begin their academic studies. As a result, the number of immigrant students in the IEP has declined. During the 1996–1997 academic year, only four immigrant students entered the IEP. Given the new entrance requirement, this trend is likely to continue.

REFERENCES

Adamson, H. D. (1993). *Academic competence theory and classroom practice: Preparing ESL students for content courses.* New York: Longman.

Brodkey, D., & Young, R. (1981). Composition correctness scores. *TESOL Quarterly, 15,* 159–167.

Bosher, S., & Rowenkamp, J. (1992). *Language proficiency and academic success: The refugee/immigrant in higher education.* Eric Document ED 353914.

Chafe, W. (1982). Integration and involvement in speaking, writing, and oral literature. In D. Tannen (Ed.), *Spoken and written language: Exploring orality and literacy* (pp. 35–53). Norwood, NJ: Ablex.

Cochran, C. E. (1985). *Effective practices for bilingual/ESL teachers: classroom strategies for limited English proficient students.* Trenton: New Jersey State Department of Education, Trenton, Division of Compensatory/Bilingual Education.

Collier, V. (1989). How long? A synthesis of research on academic achievement in a second language. *TESOL Quarterly, 20,* 509–531.

Cummins, J. (1979). Linguistic interdependence and the education development of bilingual students. *Review of Educational Research, 49*(2), 222–251.

Cummins, J. (1984). *Bilingualism and special education: Issues in assessment and pedagogy.* Clevedon, England: Multilingual Matters.

Cummins, J. (1986). Language proficiency and academic achievement. In J. Cummins & M. Swain (Eds.), *Bilingualism in education* (pp. 138–161). New York: Longman.

Rumbaut, R., & Ima, K. (1988). *The adaptation of southeast Asian refugee youth: A comparative study.* ERIC Document ED 299372.

Saville-Troike, M., & Kleifgen, J. (1986). Scripts for school: Cross cultural communication without a common language. *Linguistics, 25,* 81–106.

Slavin, R. E. (1981). Synthesis of research on cooperative learning. *Educational Leadership, 38,* 655–660.

Spolsky, B. (1989). *Conditions for second language learning.* Oxford, England: Oxford University Press.

Contributors

Linda Lonon Blanton is professor and former head of English at the University of New Orleans, where she teaches English as a second language, linguistics, ESL methodology, and rhetorical theory. Dr. Blanton has published on academic writing in *College ESL, English Language Teaching Journal, TESOL Journal, ESP Journal*, and *Journal of Second Language Writing*. She also sits on the editorial advisory board of JSLW. Dr. Blanton's latest series of composition textbooks, entitled *Multicultural Workshop: Books 1–3*, and coauthored with Linda Lee, has recently come out from Heinle & Heinle (Boston). She is the author of *Varied Voices*, an ethnography of children's language and literacy learning in a Moroccan school (Heinle & Heinle, 1998).

Gladys Carro-Kowalcyk teaches in the ESL department in the City College of New York.

Yuet-Sim D. Chiang teaches courses in reading and composition, and composition theory and practice at the University of California–Berkeley. Her research focuses on the impact of English literacy on the linguistic and cultural identities of language minorities, and the processes with which these (sometimes contradictory) identities are articulated both by students and by composition theorists and practitioners. You can direct your comments to her at chiang@uclink4.berkeley.edu. Originally from Singapore, Dr. Chiang's research is closely related to and influenced by her own literacy journey.

Dana Ferris is an associate professor of English at California State University, Sacramento. She has published articles on ESL writing in *TESOL Quarterly, Journal of Second Language Writing, Research in the Teaching of English*, and *TESOL Journal*. She is coauthor (with John Hedgcock) of *Teaching ESL Composition: Purpose, Process, and Practice* (Lawrence Erlbaum Associates).

Jan Frodesen directs the ESL Program at UC–Santa Barbara. She has taught ESL and basic writing in the UC system for 12 years. She is coauthor of three ESL textbooks and has contributed chapters of ESL writing for *Teaching English as a Second or Foreign Language* and *Academic Writing in a Second Language*.

Linda Harklau is assistant professor in Language Education at the University of Georgia, where she teaches courses in teaching additional languages, nonnative language literacy, and research methodology. Her work has appeared in *TESOL Quarterly, Anthropology and Education Quarterly,* and *Educational Policy*. She was the recipient of the 1995 TESOL/Newbury House Distinguished Research Award. Her research focuses on English language and literacy learning in secondary and post-secondary classroom settings.

Beth Hartman earned her MA in English as a Second Language at the University of Minnesota in 1994. She teaches ESL in western Wisconsin.

Ann M. Johns is a professor of Linguistics and Writing Studies at San Diego State University (CA). She is also codirector of her university's Freshman Success Programs, which include linked (adjunct) composition and general education courses. She has published widely on issues of academic reading and writing, and she recently completed a volume for Cambridge University Press entitled *Text, Role and Context: Exploring and Developing Academic Literacies.*

Nancy Duke S. Lay is a professor and chair of the ESL Department, City College of New York. She has been teaching ESL and conducting teacher training workshops here and abroad for 20 years. She has been a member of the ESL Sub-committee of CPI (College Preparatory Initiative) in CUNY.

Sophia Leong is an English and math teacher at Stuyvesant High School in New York.

Ilona Leki is professor of English, director of ESL at the University of Tennessee, author of *Understanding ESL writers: A guide for teachers*, coeditor of *Journal of Second Language Writing,* and winner of 1996 TESOL/Newbury House Distinguished Research Award.

Kay M. Losey is associate professor of English and director of the Writing Program at the State University of New York at Stony Brook. She has taught basic writing to nonnative speakers of English in California, North Carolina, and New York. She was awarded the 1992 Richard Braddock Award for the outstanding article in *College Composition and Communication*. She has also published in *TESOL Quarterly* and *Review of Educational Research*. Her book, *Listen to the Silences: Mexican American In-*

teraction in the Composition Classroom and the Community was published by Ablex in 1997.

Dennis Muchisky is assistant professor of English/TESL at Central Missouri State University. He has over 20 years of ESL teaching experience in both the United States and abroad.

T. C. Niemann is an English and computer teacher at Lower East Side Preparatory High School in the New York City school system.

Judith Rodby is associate professor of English and Composition Coordinator at California State University, Chico. She is the author of *Appropriating Literacy* and numerous articles about ESL composition. Her current research is in mainstreaming "basic writers" and the context-bound nature of what we call literacy "skill."

Mary Schmida is a doctoral student in Education in Language, Literacy, and Culture at the University of California–Berkeley. She has taught in the College Writing Programs for three years, and is currently working on her dissertation, which focuses on issues of language loss, creolization, and linguistic and cultural identity.

Gabriela Segade is an ESL instructor at the Hawai'i English Language Program, University of Hawai'i at Manoa. She is interested in second language writing pedagogy and in the social dimensions of teaching and learning ESL at the college level.

Meryl Siegal is associate professor of Applied Linguistics and director of the TESL Certificate Program at Holy Names College in Oakland, California. She is currently in Senegal on a Fulbright Scholar Grant. Her research deals with language acquisition in multilingual societies and issues of learner agency and subjectivity. She was the recipient of the 1995 Outstanding Dissertation of the Year Award from AERA, Second Language Special Interest Group, and a 1996 Wenner-Gren Foundation grant for work on Japanese second language acquisition and ideology.

Norinne Starna teaches in UC–Santa Barbara's Program of Intensive English for underrepresented students. As a graduate fellow at the University of Pittsburgh, she taught basic reading and writing. She has contributed a chapter on issues of education for the composition textbook *Writing Off Center* (Harcourt Brace).

Nancy Tangren is a lecturer in the Programs in English as a Second Language at the University of Nebraska–Lincoln. She has taught ESL for 14 years, focusing on composition at all levels.

Elaine Tarone is a professor and director of the Center for Advanced Research in Language Acquisition (a National Language Resource Center) at the University of Minnesota.

Shang Tien is a counselor in the Educational Talent Search program at John Jay College, City University of New York, and a college advisor at Lower East Side Preparatory High School in the New York City school system.

Kate Wolfe-Quintero is an associate professor in the Department of English as a Second Language at the University of Hawai'i at Manoa. She is the Director of the English Language Institute and the Hawai'i English Language Program, two intensive-English language programs at UH. Her research has focused on lexical and grammatical development in the writing of second language students.

Author Index

Subject Index